P9-DEV-134

DOUBLEDAY
CELEBRATES
100 YEARS OF
EXCELLENCE

BOOKS BY PHILLIP LOPATE

Essays and Non-Fiction

Portrait of My Body

The Art of the Personal Essay (editor)

Against Joie de Vivre

Bachelorhood: Tales of the Metropolis

Being with Children

Novels

The Rug Merchant

Confessions of Summer

Poetry

The Eyes Don't Always Want to Stay Open

The Daily Round

PORTRAIT

of MY

BODY

Photograph by Rudy Burckhardt

PHILLIP LOPATE

Anchor Books/Doubleday

New York London Toronto Sydney Auckland

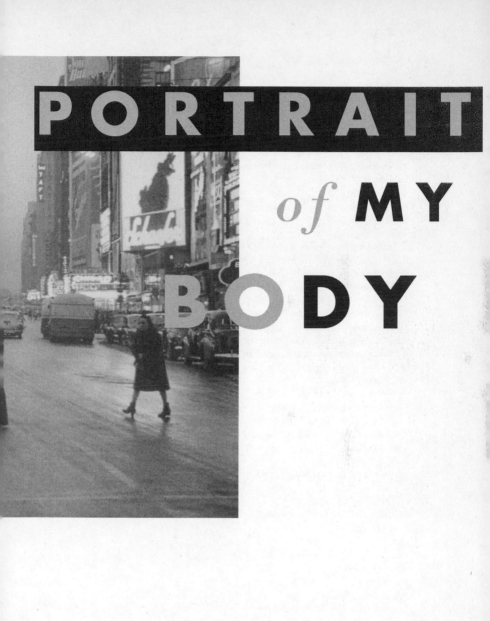

PORTRAIT

of MY

BODY

An Anchor Book
PUBLISHED BY DOUBLEDAY
a division of Bantam Doubleday Dell Publishing Group, Inc.
1540 Broadway, New York, New York 10036

ANCHOR BOOKS, DOUBLEDAY, and the portrayal of an anchor
are trademarks of Doubleday, a division of Bantam Doubleday Dell
Publishing Group, Inc.

Portrait of My Body was originally published in hardcover by Anchor Books in
September 1996.

"The Moody Traveler" first appeared in *The New York Times*. "Portrait of My
Body" first appeared in *Michigan Quarterly Review*. "The Dead Father: A
Remembrance of Donald Barthelme" and "The Invisible Woman" first appeared
in *Threepenny Review*. "The Movies and Spiritual Life" first appeared in *The
Movie That Changed My Life*, edited by David Rosenberg, Viking, 1991.
"Resistance to the Holocaust" first appeared in *Testimony: Contemporary Writers
Make the Holocaust Personal*, edited by David Rosenberg, Times Books, 1989.
"On Leaving Bachelorhood" first appeared in *The Forward* and *New York
Woman*. "Detachment and Passion" first appeared in *Southwest Review*. "Terror
of Mentors" first appeared in *The Ohio Review*. "Delivering Lily" first appeared
in *Creative Nonfiction*.

Book design by Cheryl L. Cipriani

The Library of Congress has cataloged the Anchor hardcover edition of this
work as follows:
Lopate, Phillip, 1943–
Portrait of my body / Phillip Lopate.
p.   cm.
I. Title.
PS3562.O66P67   1996   95–26607
814'.54—dc20
CIP

ISBN 0-385-48377-5
Copyright © 1996 by Phillip Lopate
All Rights Reserved
Printed in the United States of America
First Anchor Books Trade Paperback Edition: October 1997

10 9 8 7 6 5 4 3 2 1

CONTENTS

INTRODUCTION

I have always admired the kind of writer who makes a saga out of his life, a Jack Kerouac, Henry Miller, Louis-Ferdinand Céline, or Blaise Cendrars, who is somehow able to spin book after book out of autobiographical experiences. These writers have no doubts about the value of their past and their right to tell you about it. With minimal fictionalizing (sometimes not even that), they take you aside and tell you all that has happened to them, as juicily as they can, breaking only for philosophical asides and occasional bursts of lyrical bombast.

I have, as I say, considerable admiration for these authors, and have even decided to do the same: that is, to write directly out of the materials of my life. The only difference, the one *drawback* in my program, is that I have not had nearly as exciting a life as these gentlemen. I will never enlist in the merchant marine or become a Congo doctor or a revolutionary, or

2   go whoring in Paris, though I tell myself regularly that I should do these things if I want to be one of these world-embracing autobiographical writers. But I am not an adventurer; I refuse to become an adventurer. I persist in recording the details and encounters of my cautiously ordinary urban life, which I like well enough, in personal essays, educational memoirs, autobiographical poems and novels. With a few exceptions (such as my novel *The Rug Merchant*), it is all first-person confession.

This raises a question: What gives me the right to assume my life is worth taking so seriously? Is it arrogance? Self-centeredness? Yes . . . but not entirely. We must remember that most writers have only their own story to tell (in however disguised a form it finally emerges). In my case, I can also report better through my eyes what the world looks like than by pretending omniscience. I want to record how the world *comes at me*, because I think it is indicative of the way it comes at everyone. And to the degree that it is not, then my peculiarities should strengthen the reader's own sense of individuality. I offer my accounts of experience so that readers can take what is relevant to themselves, assuming (perhaps wrongly) that there is enough commonality in what has happened to me to touch other people. I mean it when I say I don't consider my life any more significant or exemplary than most; and I am at least as interested in other people as in myself—maybe more so. But I need this apparatus of vision, this "I," however distorted, to bring the world back to my page, because I know by now that I can depend on it.

As for Mr. "I," there are many versions of him, disguises and talking heads, like the heads that the ventriloquist Edgar Bergen used to alternate on the puppet body of Charlie McCarthy, depending on the routine. Pío Baroja, the Spanish novelist, had another way of speaking of this first-person variety:

An author always has before him a keyboard made up of a series of I's. The lyric and satiric writers play in the purely human octave; the historian in the octave of the investigator. When a writer writes of himself, perforce he plays upon his own "I," which is not exactly that contained in the octave of the sentimentalist nor yet in that of the curious investigator. Undoubtedly at times it must be a most immodest "I," an "I" which discloses a name and a surname, an "I" which is positive and self-assertive, with the imperiousness of a Captain General's edict or a Civil Governor's decree.

In first-person writing, there is a thin line between the charming and the insufferable. For a while now, I have dreamt of pushing at this line, slipping over occasionally to the other side, stretching the boundaries of acceptable first-person behavior, increasing like a dye the amount of obnoxiousness in my narrator—just for the thrill of living dangerously. At the same time, I don't want to "lie": I want to give an accurate testimony and not distort the fundamental nature of my character. Of course, as soon as a writer elects the nonfictional first person, distortions and subjectivities become unavoidable. Every personal essay, it might be said, is built around a self-deception as much as a truth. My approach is to assume a certain amount of guilt toward the truth beforehand, in order to get on with the work.

We are all ignorant when it comes to knowing ourselves. No less an authority on himself than Montaigne insisted, *"Que scay-je?"*—"What do I know?"—or, as we would now say it with a responsibility-avoiding shrug, "What do I know?" Montaigne was explaining the Pyrrhonian philosophers' defense of doubt when he made this pronouncement, and it is worth quoting his

4 actual words: "This idea is more firmly grasped in the form of interrogation: 'What do I know?'—the words I bear as a motto, inscribed over a pair of scales." What intrigues me about this passage is that Montaigne immediately connects the very attractive (to me, anyway) concept of skepticism, including self-skepticism, with the more disturbing ethical question of judgment.

For it is one thing to blow the whistle on oneself; quite another, to judge others. In the essays that comprise this book, I have often had occasion to draw the portraits of others, weighing their characters and destinies. The danger of writing about others in relation to oneself is that it is easy to fall into a self-serving model, in which (consciously or unconsciously) one is always asserting one's superiority. I can understand some readers thinking I have not entirely escaped this flaw; and indeed, I think it myself. But these others—friends, lovers, family members, colleagues—have been too important for me to forgo wrestling with the meanings of their lives in these attempts. I prefer trying to render honestly the limits of my empathy rather than exaggerating it for cosmetic purposes, or affecting more maturity than I in fact possess. Mine are (to borrow Lamb's suggestive title) "Imperfect Sympathies," for which I apologize in advance.

The dread of all publishing companies is to be caught publishing a random collection of pieces. Actually, I see nothing wrong with random collections—if I am interested enough in the mind of an essayist I will gladly follow him or her anywhere—but unless the writer is very famous, there is little chance these days of such potpourris seeing print. Not being very famous, I am obliged to insist that the book you hold in your hands isn't (shudders!) a random collection of previously published pieces, but, for better or worse, a coherent, thematically interconnected work, a chunk of which is appearing in print for the first time.

What makes it, in my eyes at least, coherent? Partly its exclusions. After I edited *The Art of the Personal Essay*, a historical anthology that argued for the viable tradition of this form, I felt a (self-imposed) pressure to have my next book represent the personal essay, and therefore eliminated all those writings—literary essays, film and architectural reviews, magazine articles about urbanism and travel, ephemeral "relationship" pieces—that might be construed more as occasional journalism or criticism. I was then left with thirteen personal essays that seemed to have more body to them. Rereading them, I discovered a remarkable consistency in their preoccupations and themes—which may say more about the limited stock of my brain than anything else. In any case, to get to the point, these patterns all converged on what I might call *the carapace of self*: that is, the resources and limitations of a self that has hardened into a recognizable shell. Whichever way I turned, I came upon an ego defending itself, even when I would have most liked to wish it away. The inescapability of ego is certainly one of the key ideas in these essays.

Another is *detachment*, as both desirable and problematic attainment. Again and again, I seem to be musing about the proper distance to locate myself in relation to the world: one that will allow for perspective without shutting off feeling. Can there be such a thing as a warm detachment? How much detachment is good to maintain toward oneself? The title essay, "Portrait of My Body," speaks to that self-conscious split.

6   In these essays, I have often used as jumping-off point an analysis of my *resistance* to something: often an idea or phenomenon that is held up as admirable. I like the way that psychoanalysts talk about analyzing their patients' resistance to the therapeutic process and to the doctors themselves; it seems to me a good model for clearing the ground in essay writing as well, so that one can begin to grapple with one's true feelings and ideas about a subject. Not that the resistance should have the final word, necessarily, but that it has to be taken into consideration before progress can be made. In the case of "Resistance to the Holocaust," I was asked to contribute an essay to a volume called *Testimony*, about Jewish writers' personal responses to the Holocaust. This piece got me into no end of trouble, partly because the subject stirs such knee-jerk passions; but I still stand by it. Another example: I was asked by a friend to write for a special *Ohio Review* issue on the subject of mentors. Since I never, properly speaking, had a mentor, I thought I would have to decline, then realized I could try to analyze the reasons for my resistance to that arrangement.

A certain skeptical resistance to "transcendence" and mystical modes of thought in general, coupled with an underground attraction to them, is another ambivalence explored in the book, particularly in the essays "The Movies and Spiritual Life" and "Detachment and Passion."

Carapace of self, detachment, resistance, wariness toward transcendence—looking at this list so far, I would be inclined to say that such a personality, were it anyone else's, revealed a panic around issues of merger and intimacy. Maybe so. It has also been more difficult for me to find concepts to express my convictions, involvements, and surrenders, though they are an important part of me as well.

It occurs to me after the fact that one reason I may have started off by looking at resistance so often was that I was partly resisting the commissioned task. Assignments can be a wonderful spur to the imagination, but they also necessitate bending your wayward thoughts to someone else's idea. Many of the essays in this book began in this way, with a request from a book or magazine editor for a specific text; and I am grateful beyond measure for these opportunities. But I have also continued the adventure of writing essays that no one asked for; and these are often the most troubling and personal in nature. Some of the longest pieces in the book—the essays about my father, Donald Barthelme, and Greenwich Village—as well as the one about my baby daughter's birth, were all written under compulsion rather than commission. In the six years during which this book was written, I seem to have been much preoccupied with fathers, father figures, and paternity.

Finally, the book is held together by a linear chronology of events. If read in sequence, these thirteen essays constitute an informal memoir of my life since the publication of my last collection, *Against Joie de Vivre*. Essayists go to immense trouble to arrange their pieces for book publication in an order that will best bring out themes and hidden narratives, knowing all the while that some smart-alecky readers will always skip ahead, jump around, and jumble the whole thing up. Not that I don't understand the impulse to slip free of the table of contents' order: I do it myself when I read other writers' collections. But if you *were* to follow the sequence prescribed herein, you might find it a less confusing experience. On the other hand, maybe not. Just forget I mentioned the whole thing.

Photograph by Rudy Burckhardt

PART ONE:

THE MOODY TRAVELER

Traveling alone has its pluses: you can go where you want when you want, and you are spared that runaway irritation which comes of suddenly spotting all the little flaws in your companion (who alone seems to be detaining you from perfect enjoyment) and the tension of having to keep that knowledge secret. However, the minus is that you will have no one to blame but yourself for the occasional rotten mood. The ecstasies and lone epiphanies of the morning museum eventually evaporate, and by late afternoon, after a mediocre, overpriced lunch has made you sluggish, you are ready to turn the big guns on yourself. To travel is to brood, and especially if you are your sole company. I would go so far as to recommend traveling alone as an excellent way of catching up with all the poor opinions of yourself that you may have had to suppress during the busy, camouflaging work year, when it is necessary to appear a self-approving, winning member of society.

I remember one such afternoon in beautiful Florence when the charm I derived from my personality was at a low point. I had mapped out my agenda for a visit to the nearby hill town of Fiesole. Though I could have taken the excursion bus near my hotel, I commanded myself to hike, ostensibly because it was good exercise, and because you see so much more on foot, but in actuality, I realize now, to punish myself.

As I slogged uphill past "rows of cypresses and sumptuous villas" (Michelin guide), my mind was so filled with worthless thoughts that broke off and told me so little—that I had the impression not of a walk through a real landscape but of one continuous spiteful déjà vu. It was a playback of all those times I had walked enviously and stupidly through the world of rich houses where I didn't belong. Nothing less than owning a villa, *any* villa, on this Italian hill would satisfy me. Yet I saw so little of the actual residences I coveted, their gardens or marble sculptures or whatever I was supposed to look at, that even in my surly mood this envy struck me as comic. Envy for a landscape I took so little trouble to observe? Perhaps we only envy that which we look at superficially; and a deeper look would take care of our urge for possession? Nah. In any case, I kept walking.

I arrived at a flat village square cut into the hill, where tourist buses were parked in the afternoon heat. Fiesole. Was it sunny? Clouded over? I wasn't interested enough to notice. I headed for a café that seemed to exist on the trade of tourists waiting for their bus driver to return from who knows where and start his engine. I sat down at the nickel-plated soda fountain, with the momentarily satisfied sense of having stumbled on a "find." Not that the stopover was attractive, but it was at least an oasis of decrepitude: there were dusty cutout doll books

and movie magazines, and a faded Italian novelization of Erich
Segal's *Love Story*. I ordered a Campari, hoping for a mindless
respite. Yet just as soon as I had drained it, a spasm of restless-
ness overcame me and I paid and walked out.

By now I was thoroughly fed up with my impatience. I was
determined to slow down and practice "the discipline of seeing." It was a sometime conviction of mine that, wherever one
found oneself, the world was rich enough to yield enjoyment if
one but paid close attention to the details. Or, as John Cage
once said, when something bores you, keep looking at it and after a while you will find it intriguing. Inside, however, I re-
belled against this notion, which struck me as forced qui-
etism—an aestheticizing trick to bring about the opposite of
what one knows to be true. The day is boring, horrible? Very
well, that's the card I've been dealt. Let's not pretend it's any
better.

I was still arguing these two positions when I sat down on
a bench overlooking what I knew most people would think a
magnificent vista. All of the Arno Valley and Florence were
stretched before us. The city fathers had wisely provided
benches. Not only was this undeniably and obviously a magnificent vista, but it was an "officially recognized" magnificent
vista, even more annoying. But then, what *had* escaped the
tourist industry's exploitative eye in Italy? Where could one
find any beauty in this country that was fresh and unframed?

This line of thinking soon struck me as foolish petulance.
The truth is, I loved Italy, so what was I whining about?

I literally forced myself to concentrate on the Italian family a few benches over. The son was leaning semidangerously
over the hilltop. That could be interesting. But then he sat
down next to his father, who was cutting an orange rind circu-

larly with a fruit knife. I wondered if this orange paring was an Old World custom. (Vapid anthropologizing to replace self-ennui.) The mother was taking thick sandwiches out of a plastic bag and handing them all around. They seemed a big, warm, friendly family—two daughters, one son, a father, a mother—speaking casually to each other, eating their picnic lunch, playing with the dog.

To fathom the secret of that Italian familial harmony, I watched them covertly for ten minutes, dividing my attention between their interactions and the landscape below, and came to the conclusion that they weren't as warm as I had originally given them credit for. They simply ate a great deal. The more I watched them, the more it dawned on me that there was absolutely nothing exceptional about them. That in itself was unusual. Most families yield up fairly rich pathologies, but this one did not interest me in any conceivable way. My hypothesis about steady attention to detail was being contradicted.

At about this time an elderly Italian man, tall, angular, bald, toothless save for one top incisor, looking in his mid-seventies—about the age of my father, in fact—came up and asked with gestures if he could sit on my bench. This seemed a little odd, as there was another bench completely unoccupied, but who was I to deny a fellowman my company if he thought he could reap some nourishment therefrom? Had I not been complaining of the burden of my solitude? Perhaps this old guy would amuse me or turn into a *vivid anecdotal experience*, the goal of all tourists at loose ends.

"What is your name?" he asked me in halting English. I told him. "And yours?" Nicola. He tried out his few English questions on me, I answered him in my limited Italian. It was the sort of conversation one has on the road often, and which

seems to exist in order to prove that the stiff dialogues of phrase
books are, in fact, the height of naturalism. The old man began
to talk about his work in a garage (I think he said he was a retired mechanic) and to complain that now he had nothing to
do. He told me about his sons, his wife, his vineyard. These
Italians, I reflected, are unquenchably sociable, they love to
chatter. True, I had my doubts that this was going to lead to a
vivid anecdotal experience, and was already feeling bored,
since I understood only one out of every three sentences, but I
congratulated myself on being such a good and patient listener.
The man is obviously lonely, I thought; he reminds me of the
aged pensioner in De Sica's *Umberto D*; perhaps I can reap from
him some necessary lesson in humility and human dignity.
Meanwhile, he was talking my ear off in Italian, and I was nod-
ding and pursuing some interior reverie about how sad it is that
society is so afraid of the old, how wrong that we back off
squeamishly from them, and he had just gotten to the part
where he told me his wife had died when he seized my hand in
an iron grip.

At first I did nothing, pretending it was a sort of international brotherhood handshake; but then I tried to pull away,
and discovered that the old man was not letting go. I stared at
his frayed white shirt, buttoned to the top, pulled taut by his
chest; he was like a wooden plank, not a scrap of fat on him. I
looked around for help to the picnicking family, but they had
apparently wandered off without my noticing. Now he grinned
in what seemed a possibly rather lecherous manner—at the
same time trying to reassure me that he was not going to hurt
me. He only wanted to hold my hand. So we sat there, my hand
sweating in his. He had very large brown fingers, liver-spotted
around the webs.

I immediately recalled a strange incident that had once happened to my sister. She had entered a subway car in New York and sat down next to a blind man. He had a braille book open in his lap. She stared without embarrassment at his face, which was lined, blotched as if from poison ivy. There was no reason to assume he felt her interest. It so happens that my sister is very pretty, but how could the blind man know that? Suddenly he took hold of her arm. She thought he wanted her to help guide him out of the train or across the platform, and began to explain that it wasn't her stop yet, but he paid no attention. She felt his hand working down her arm until it had captured her hand. He began squeezing each of her fingers separately, all the while kneading her palm. She could not take her eyes off their two hands, like starfish swimming locked together. She felt she should scream, but no sound came out; she just sat there, paralyzed, ashamed and, my sister admitted candidly, fascinated. "This man was an artist of hands," she recalled. He had supreme tactile sensitivity. Finally his grip loosened, he closed his eyes, and she looked down at his brown pants, which were stained near the fly. It outraged her that he might ride the subways daily and molest women and they would probably say nothing, just because he was blind.

Anyhow, this old toothless Italian next to me was by no stretch of the imagination an artist of hands. He simply had a very powerful grip. I began to speculate about his secret life, in and around his role as good family man and laborer, of chance pickups. I didn't even know if he was gay necessarily, or if he was so starved for human touch, the memory of young flesh, that it didn't matter which sex he accosted. How many tourists before me had he done this with? Were we all Americans? I wondered. If he did try any funny stuff, I thought I could hold

him off. But all he seemed to be doing so far was holding my
hand and smiling—every so often he would wriggle the wrist a
little in the air and grin at me, as if we were both relaxing from
a good arm-wrestle.

By this time other tourists had joined us on the hilltop (to
my relief) and were consuming the landscape. I, too, looked
down at the vista, since I had nothing better to do and was
tired of trying to figure out the old man's game. Now the shifting pattern of light over the valley—a dusky evening light that
brought out the muted pinks, the muddy browns, the raked
greens of cultivated countryside and, in the distance, Florence,
all salmon and white walls—seemed to me extremely fetching.
For the first time all day, I was able to enjoy the physical world
around me. Were I given to looking on the bright side, or religious allegories, or megalomania, I might say that the old man
was an angel sent down by God to handcuff me to one spot and
force me to attend the earth with pleasure.

I suppose part of what kept me from retrieving my hand was
the flattering knowledge that *someone* at least desired me,
needed me at that moment, in this place through which I had
taken it upon myself to travel alone. For the longest while, neither of us said anything. Then he got up, gave me a courtly
bow, muttered *"Grazie"* in a hoarse, dry voice, and strode off.
Watching his bald brown head and stiff back recede, I laughed
disbelievingly at what had just happened. The weirdness of it
had driven away my black mood, and I kept laughing all the
way home on the tourist bus. For those who do not like happy
endings, my apologies.

PORTRAIT OF MY BODY

I am a man who tilts. When I am sitting, my head slants to the right; when walking, the upper part of my body reaches forward to catch a sneak preview of the street. One way or another, I seem to be off-center—or "uncentered," to use the jargon of holism. My lousy posture, a tendency to slump or put myself into lazy, contorted misalignments, undoubtedly contributes to lower back pain. For a while I correct my bad habits, do morning exercises, sit straight, breathe deeply, but always an inner demon that insists on approaching the world askew resists perpendicularity.

I think if I had broader shoulders I would be more squarely anchored. But my shoulders are narrow, barely wider than my hips. This has always made shopping for suits an embarrassing business. (Françoise Gilot's *Life with Picasso* tells how Picasso was so touchy about his disproportionate body—in his case all shoulders, no legs—that he insisted the tailor fit him at home.)

When I was growing up in Brooklyn, my hero was Sandy Koufax, the Dodgers' Jewish pitcher. In the doldrums of Hebrew choir practice at Feigenbaum's Mansion & Catering Hall, I would fantasize striking out the side, even whiffing twenty-seven batters in a row. Lack of shoulder development put an end to this identification; I became a writer instead of a Koufax.

It occurs to me that the restless angling of my head is an attempt to distract viewers' attention from its paltry base. I want people to look at my head, partly because I live in my head most of the time. My sister, a trained masseuse, often warns me of the penalties, like neck tension, that may arise from failing to integrate body and mind. Once, about ten years ago, she and I were at the beach and she was scrutinizing my body with a sister's critical eye. "You're getting flabby," she said. "You should exercise every day. I do—look at me, not an ounce of fat." She pulled at her midriff, celebrating (as is her wont) her physical attributes with the third-person enthusiasm of a carnival barker.

"But"—she threw me a bone—"you do have a powerful head. There's an intensity . . ." A graduate student of mine (who was slightly loony) told someone that she regularly saw an aura around my head in class. One reason I like to teach is that it focuses fifteen or so dependent gazes on me with such paranoiac intensity as cannot help but generate an aura in my behalf.

I also have a commanding stare, large sad brown eyes that can be read as either gentle or severe. Once I watched several hours of myself on videotape. I discovered to my horror that my face moved at different rates: sometimes my mouth would be laughing, eyebrows circumflexed in mirth, while my eyes coolly gauged the interviewer to see what effect I was making. I am something of an actor. And, as with many performers, the mood I sense most in myself is that of energy-conserving watchfulness; but this expression is often mistaken (perhaps because of the way brown eyes are read in our culture) for sympathy. I see myself as determined to the point of stubbornness, selfish, even a bit cruel—in any case, I am all too aware of the limits of my compassion, so that it puzzles me when people report a first impression of me as gentle, kind, solicitous. In my youth I felt obliged to come across as dynamic, arrogant, intimidating, the life of the party; now, surer of myself, I hold back some energy, thereby winning time to gather information and make better judgments. This results sometimes in a misimpression of my being mildly depressed. Of course, the simple truth is that I have less energy than I once did, and that accumulated experiences have made me, almost against my will, kinder and sadder.

Sometimes I can feel my mouth arching downward in an ironic smile, which, at its best, reassures others that we need not take everything so seriously—because we are all in the same comedy together—and, at its worst, expresses a superior skepticism. This smile, which can be charming when not supercilious, has elements of the bashful that mesh with the worldly—the shyness, let us say, of a cultivated man who is often embarrassed for others by their willful shallowness or self-deception. Many times, however, my ironic smile is nothing more than a neutral stall among people who do not seem to appreciate my "contribution." I hate that pain-in-the-ass half-smile of mine; I want to jump in, participate, be loud, thoughtless, vulgar.

Often I give off a sort of psychic stench to myself, I do not like myself at all, but out of stubborn pride I act like a man who does. I appear for all the world poised, contented, sanguine when inside I may be feeling self-revulsion bordering on the suicidal. What a wonder to be so misread! Of course, if in the beginning I had thought I was coming across accurately, I never would have bothered to become a writer. And the truth is I am not misread, because another part of me is never less than fully contented with myself.

I am vain about these parts of my body: my eyes, my fingers, my legs. It is true that my legs are long and not unshapely, but my vanity about them has less to do with their comeliness than with their contribution to my height. Montaigne, a man who was himself on the short side, wrote that "the beauty of stature is the only beauty of men." But even if Montaigne had never said it, I would continue to attribute a good deal of my self-worth and benevolent liberalism to being tall. When I go out into the street, I feel well-disposed toward the (mostly shorter) swarms of humanity; crowds not only do not dismay, they enliven me; and I am tempted to think that my passion for urbanism is linked to my height. By no means am I suggesting that only tall people love cities; merely that, in my case, part of the pleasure I derive from walking in crowded streets issues from a confidence that I can see above the heads of others, and cut a fairly impressive, elevated figure as I saunter along the sidewalk.

Some of my best friends have been—short. Brilliant men, brimming with poetic and worldly ideas, they deserved all of my and the world's respect. Yet at times I have had to master an impulse to rumple their heads; and I suspect they have developed manners of a more formal, *noli me tangere* nature, largely in response to this petting impulse of taller others.

The accident of my tallness has inclined me to both a seemingly egalitarian informality and a desire to lead. Had I not been a writer, I would surely have become a politician; I was even headed in that direction in my teens. Ever since I shot up to a little over six feet, I have had at my command what feels like a natural, Gregory Peck authority when addressing an audience. Far from experiencing stage fright, I have actually sought out situations in which I could make speeches, give readings, sit on panel discussions, and generally tower over everyone else onstage. To be tall is to look down on the world and meet its eyes on your terms. But this topic, the noblesse oblige of tall men, is a dangerously provoking one, and so let us say no more about it.

The mental image of one's body changes slower than one's body. Mine was for a long while arrested in my early twenties, when I was tall and thin (165 pounds) and gobbled down whatever I felt like. I ate food that was cheap and filling, cheeseburgers, pizza, without any thought to putting on weight. But a young person's metabolism is more dietetically forgiving. To compound the problem, the older you get, the more cultivated your palate grows—and the more life's setbacks make you inclined to fill the hollowness of disappointment with the pleasures of the table.

Between the age of thirty and forty I put on ten pounds, mostly around the midsection. Since then my gut has suffered another expansion, and I tip the scales at over 180. That I took a while to notice the change may be shown by my continuing to purchase clothes at my primordial adult size (33 waist, 15½ collar), until a girlfriend started pointing out that all my clothes were too tight. I rationalized this circumstance as the result of changing fashions (thinking myself still subconsciously loyal to the sixties' penchant for skintight fits) and laundry shrinkage rather than anything to do with my own body. She began buying me larger replacements for birthdays or holidays, and I found I enjoyed this "baggier" style, which allowed me to button my trousers comfortably, or to wear a tie and, for the first time in years, close my top shirt button. But it took even longer before I was able to enter a clothing store myself and give the salesman realistically enlarged size numbers.

Clothes can disguise the defects of one's body, up to a point. I get dressed with great optimism, adding one color to another, mixing my favorite Japanese and Italian designers, matching the patterns and textures, selecting ties, then proceed to the bathroom mirror to judge the result. There is an ideal in my mind of the effect I am essaying by wearing a particular choice of garments, based, no doubt, on male models in fashion ads—and I fall so far short of this insouciant gigolo handsomeness that I cannot help but be a little disappointed when I turn up so depressingly myself, narrow-shouldered, Talmudic, that grim, set mouth, that long, narrow face, those appraising eyes, the Semitic hooked nose, all of which express both the strain of intellectual overachieving and the tabula rasa of immaturity . . . for it is still, underneath, a boy in the mirror. A boy with a rapidly receding hairline.

How is it that I've remained a boy all this time, into my late forties? I remember, at seventeen, drawing a self-portrait of myself as I looked in the mirror. I was so appalled at the weak chin and pleading eyes that I ended up focusing on the neckline of the cotton T-shirt. Ever since then I have tried to toughen myself up, but I still encounter in the glass that haunted uncertainty—shielded by a bluffing shell of cynicism, perhaps, but untouched by wisdom. So I approach the mirror warily, without lighting up as much as I would for the least of my acquaintances; I go one-on-one with that frowning schmuck.

And yet, it would be insulting to those who labor under the burden of true ugliness to palm myself off as an unattractive man. I'm at times almost handsome, if you squinted your eyes and rounded me off to the nearest *beau idéal*. I lack even a shred of cowboy virility, true, but I believe I fall into a category of adorable nerd or absentminded professor that awakens the amorous curiosity of some women. "Cute" is a word often applied to me by those I've been fortunate enough to attract. Then again, I attract only women of a certain lopsided prettiness: the head-turning, professional beauties never fall for me. They seem to look right through me, in fact. Their utter lack of interest in my appeal has always fascinated me. Can it be so simple an explanation as that beauty calls to beauty, as wealth to wealth?

I think of poor (though not in his writing gifts) Cesare Pavese, who kept chasing after starlets, models, and ballerinas—exquisite lovelies who couldn't appreciate his morose coffeehouse charm. Before he killed himself, he wrote a poem addressed to one of them, "Death Will Come Bearing Your Eyes"—thereby unfairly promoting her from rejecting lover to unwitting executioner. Perhaps he believed that only beautiful women (not literary critics, who kept awarding him prestigious prizes) saw him clearly, with twenty-twenty vision, and had the right to judge him. Had I been more headstrong, if masochistic, I might have followed his path and chased some beauty until she was forced to tell me, like an oracle, what it was about me, physically, that so failed to excite her. Then I might know something crucial about my body, before I passed into my next reincarnation.

Jung says somewhere that we pay dearly over many years to learn about ourselves what a stranger can see at a glance. This is the way I feel about my back. Fitting rooms aside, we none of us know what we look like from the back. It is the area of ourselves whose presentation we can least control, and which therefore may be the most honest part of us.

I divide backs into two kinds: my own and everyone else's. The others' backs are often mysterious, exquisite, and uncannily sympathetic. I have always loved backs. To walk behind a pretty woman in a backless dress and savor how a good pair of shoulder blades, heightened by shadow, has the same power to pierce the heart as chiseled cheekbones! . . . I wonder what it says about me that I worship a part of the body that signals a turning away. Does it mean I'm a glutton for being abandoned, or a timid voyeur who prefers a surreptitious gaze that will not be met and challenged? I only know I have often felt the deepest love at just that moment when the beloved turns her back to me to get some sleep.

I have no autoerotic feelings about my own back. I cannot even picture it; visually it is a stranger to me. I know it only as an annoyance, which came into my consciousness twenty years ago, when I started getting lower back pain. Yes, we all know that homo sapiens is constructed incorrectly; our erect posture puts too much pressure on the base of the spine; more workdays are lost because of lower back pain than any other cause. Being a writer, I sit all day, compounding the problem. My back is the enemy of my writing life: if I don't do exercises daily, I immediately ache; and if I do, I am still not spared. I could say more, but there is nothing duller than lower back pain. So common, mundane an ailment brings no credit to the sufferer. One has to dramatize it somehow, as in the phrase "I threw my back out."

Here is a gossip column about my body: My eyebrows grow quite bushy across my forehead, and whenever I get my hair cut, the barber asks me diplomatically if I want them trimmed or not. (I generally say no, associating bushy eyebrows with Balzackian virility, *élan vital*; but sometimes I acquiesce, to soothe his fastidiousness). . . . My belly button is a modest, embedded slit, not a jaunty swirl like my father's. Still, I like to sniff the odor that comes from jabbing my finger in it: a very ripe, underground smell, impossible to describe, but let us say a combination of old gym socks and stuffed derma (the Yiddish word for this oniony dish of ground intestines is, fittingly, *kishkas*). . . . I have a scar on my tongue from childhood, which I can only surmise I received by landing it on a sharp object, somehow. Or perhaps I bit it hard. I have the habit of sticking my tongue out like a dog when exerting myself physically, as though to urge my muscles on; and maybe I accidentally chomped into it at such a moment. . . . I gnash my teeth, sleeping or waking. Awake, the sensation makes me feel alert and in contact with the world when I start to drift off in a daydream. Another way of grounding myself is to pinch my cheek—drawing a pocket of flesh downward and squeezing it—as I once saw JFK do in a filmed motorcade. I do this cheek-pinching especially when I am trying to keep mentally focused during teaching or other public situations. I also scratch the nape of my neck under public stress, so much so that I raise welts or sores which then eventually grow scabs; and I take great delight in secretly picking the scabs off. . . . My nose itches whenever I think about it, and I scratch it often, especially lying in bed trying to fall asleep (maybe because I am conscious of my breathing then). I also pick my nose with formidable thoroughness when no one, I hope, is looking. . . . There is a white scar about the size of a quarter on the juicy part of my knee; I got it as a boy running into a car fender, and I can still remember staring with detached calm at the blood that gushed from it like a pretty, half-eaten peach. Otherwise, the sight of my own blood makes me awfully nervous. I used to faint dead away when a blood sample was taken, and now I can control the impulse to do so only by biting the insides of my cheeks while steadfastly looking away from the needle's action. . . . I like to clean out my ear wax as often as possible (the smell is curiously sulfurous; I associate it with the bodies of dead insects). I refuse to listen to warnings that it is dangerous to stick cleaning objects into your ears. I love Q-Tips immoderately; I buy them in huge quantities and store them the way a former refugee will stock canned foodstuffs. . . . My toes are long and apelike; I have very little fellow feeling for them; they are so far away, they may as well belong to someone else. . . . My flattish buttocks are not offensively large, but neither do they have the "dream" configuration one sees in jeans ads. Perhaps for this reason, it disturbed me puritanically when asses started to be treated by Madison Avenue, around the seventies, as crucial sexual equipment, and I began to receive compositions from teenage girl students declaring that they liked some boy because he had "a cute butt." It confused me; I had thought the action was elsewhere.

About my penis there is nothing, I think, unusual. It has a brown stem, and a pink mushroom head where the foreskin is pulled back. Like most heterosexual males, I have little comparative knowledge to go by, so that I always feel like an outsider when I am around women or gay men who talk zestfully about differences in penises. I am afraid that they might judge me harshly, ridicule me like the boys who stripped me of my bathing suit in summer camp when I was ten. But perhaps they would simply declare it an ordinary penis, which changes size with the stimulus or weather or time of day. Actually, my penis does have a peculiarity: it has two peeing holes. They are very close to each other, so that usually only one stream of urine issues, but sometimes a hair gets caught across them, or some such contretemps, and they squirt out in two directions at once.

This part of me, which is so synecdochically identified with the male body (as the term "male member" indicates), has given me both too little, and too much, information about what it means to be a man. It has a personality like a cat's. I have prayed to it to behave better, to be less frisky, or more; I have followed its nose in matters of love, ignoring good sense, and paid the price; but I have also come to appreciate that it has its own specialized form of intelligence which must be listened to, or another price will be extracted.

Even to say the word "impotence" aloud makes me nervous. I used to tremble when I saw it in print, and its close relation, "importance," if hastily scanned, had the same effect, as if they were publishing a secret about me. But why should it be *my* secret, when my penis has regularly given me erections lo these many years—except for about a dozen times, mostly when I was younger? Because, even if it has not been that big a problem for me, it has dominated my thinking as an adult male. I've no sooner to go to bed with a woman than I'm in suspense. The power of the flaccid penis's statement, "I don't want you," is so stark, so cruelly direct, that it continues to exert a fascination out of all proportion to its actual incidence. Those few times when I was unable to function were like a wall forcing me to take another path—just as, after I tried to kill myself at seventeen, I was obliged to give up pessimism for a time. Each had instructed me by its too painful manner that I could not handle the world as I had previously construed it, that my confusion and rage were being found out. I would have to get more wily or else grow up.

Yet for the very reason that I was compelled to leave them behind, these two options of my youth, impotence and suicide, continue to command an underground loyalty, as though they were more "honest" than the devious strategies of potency and survival which I adopted. Put it this way: sometimes we encounter a person who has had a nervous breakdown years before and who seems cemented over sloppily, his vulnerability ruthlessly guarded against as dangerous; we sense he left a crucial part of himself back in the chaos of breakdown, and has since grown rigidly jovial. So suicide and impotence became for me "the roads not taken," the paths I had repressed.

Whenever I hear an anecdote about impotence—a woman who successfully coaxed an ex-priest who had been celibate and unable to make love, first by lying next to him for six months without any touching, then by cuddling for six more months, then by easing him slowly into a sexual embrace—I think they are talking about me. I identify completely: this, in spite of the fact, which I promise not to repeat again, that I have generally been able to do it whenever called upon. Believe it or not, I am not boasting when I say that: a part of me is contemptuous of this virility, as though it were merely a mechanical trick that violated my true nature, that of an impotent man absolutely frightened of women, absolutely secluded, cut off.

I now see the way I have idealized impotence: I've connected it with pushing the world away, as a kind of integrity, as in Molière's *The Misanthrope*—connected it with that part of me which, gregarious socializer that I am, continues to insist that I am a recluse, too good for this life. Of course, it is not true that I am terrified of women. I exaggerate my terror of them for dramatic effect, or for the purposes of a good scare.

My final word about impotence: Once, in a period when I was going out with many women, as though purposely trying to ignore my hypersensitive side and force it to grow callous by thrusting myself into foreign situations (not only sexual) and seeing if I was able to "rise to the occasion," I dated a woman who was attractive, tall and blond, named Susan. She had something to do with the pop music business, was a follower of the visionary religious futurist Teilhard de Chardin, and considered herself a religious pacifist. In fact, she told me her telephone number in the form of the anagram, N-O-T-O-W-A-R. I thought she was joking and laughed aloud, but she gave me a solemn look. In passing, I should say that all the women with whom I was impotent or close to it had solemn natures. The sex act has always seemed to me in many ways ridiculous, and I am most comfortable when a woman who enters the sheets with me shares that sense of the comic pomposity behind such a grandiloquently rhetorical use of the flesh. It is as though the prose of the body were being drastically squeezed into metrical verse. I would not have known how to stop guffawing had I been D. H. Lawrence's lover, and I am sure he would have been pretty annoyed at me. But a smile saying "All this will pass" has an erotic effect on me like nothing else.

They claim that men who have long, long fingers also have lengthy penises. I can tell you with a surety that my fingers are long and sensitive, the most perfect, elegant, handsome part of my anatomy. They are not entirely perfect—the last knuckle of my right middle finger is twisted permanently, broken in a softball game when I was trying to block the plate   but even this slight disfigurement, harbinger of mortality, adds to the pleasure I take in my hands' rugged beauty. My penis does not excite in me nearly the same contemplative delight when I look at it as do my fingers. Pianists' hands, I have been told often; and though I do not play the piano, I derive an aesthetic satisfaction from them that is as pure and Apollonian as any I am capable of. I can stare at my fingers for hours. No wonder I have them so often in my mouth, biting my fingernails to bring them closer. When I write, I almost feel that they, and not my intellect, are the clever progenitors of the text. Whatever narcissism, fetishism, and proud sense of masculinity I possess about my body must begin and end with my fingers.

THE DEAD FATHER:

A Remembrance of Donald Barthelme

Donald Barthelme had a squarish beard that made him look somewhat Amish and patriarchal, an effect enhanced by his clean-shaven upper lip. It took me a while to register that he had a beard but no mustache; and once I did, I could not stop wondering what sort of "statement" he was trying to make. On the one hand, it connoted Lincolnesque rectitude and dignity, like that of the ex–Surgeon General, C. Everett Koop. On the other hand, it seemed a double message: bearded and shaven, severe and roguish, having it both ways. Finally I got up the nerve to ask him, in a kidding way, why he shaved his mustache. He told me that he couldn't grow one because he'd had a cancerous growth removed from his lip. This reply made me aware of all I didn't, probably would never, know about the man, and of my inclination to misjudge him.

I loved to watch Donald. In a way, I could never get enough of him (which is something one says about a person who always withholds a part of himself. I know, because it has been said about me). We worked together for the last eight years of his life, and were close colleagues, friends, almost-friends—which was it? I found Barthelme to be an immensely decent, generous, courtly, and yet finally unforthcoming man. He was difficult to approach, partly because I (and I was not alone here) didn't know what to do with his formidable sadness, partly because neither did he. Barthelme would have made a good king: he had the capacity of Shakespearian tragic monarchs to project a large, self-isolating presence.

The combination of his beard, bulk, and steel-rimmed eye-glasses gave him a stern Ahab appearance that he was perfectly happy to let intimidate on occasion—only to soften it with a warm glint in his eye, like a ship's captain putting his trembling crew at ease. Having read Barthelme's whimsical miniatures, I had expected a smaller, more mercurial, puckish man, certainly not this big-shouldered, hard-drinking, John Wayne type. I couldn't get over the discrepancy between his physical solidity and the filigreed drollness of his art. Somewhere locked inside that large cowman's frame must have been a mischievous troll; and I kept stealing glances at Donald to see if the little man would put in an appearance. As time went by, however, I learned to read his jeweled sentences in the manly baritone my ear came to identify as intrinsically Barthelmean, and the sense of contradiction all but disappeared. It became natural that our fin de siècle exhaustion and cultural despair should be enunci-ated by a tall Texan with cowboy boots.

I had been teaching in the University of Houston's cre-ative writing program for a year—the program, started by two poets, Cynthia Macdonald and Stanley Plumly, had recruited me from New York in 1980 as their first fiction writer—when the great news came down that Donald Barthelme would be joining us. Barthelme's arrival caused universal rejoicing: this would really put our program on the map, not only because Barthelme was a "name" writer but because he was one of the handful who commanded a following among graduate writing students. Indeed, probably no other short story writer was more imitated by M.F.A. students in the seventies and early eighties.

I was initially surprised that a writer of Barthelme's stature would relocate to Houston. True, he had been offered an endowed chair, a hefty salary, and regular paid sabbatical leaves, but that would not normally be enough to pry most established fiction writers from their comfortable lives. The key to the "seduction" (recruitment is the eros of academia) was that Barthelme was coming home. Though by birth a Philadelphian, he had grown up in Houston and was educated at the University of Houston, the same school that would now employ him. Barthelme was still remembered around town for his youthful cultural activities, reporting for the Houston *Post*, launching the UH literary magazine, *Forum*, directing the Contemporary Art Museum in the early sixties. Then he'd gone off to New York with regional upstart energy to make his mark (like Robert Rauschenberg, Andy Warhol, Merce Cunningham: our avant-gardists almost always seem to come from the provinces), and a few decades later was returning famous— or as famous as serious writers become in America. It was also a family move: his aging parents, his three brothers—Pete, Frederick, and Steve—and his sister Joan still lived in Houston or near enough by. Marion Knox, Donald's second wife, was

pregnant, and they both thought Houston might be an easier
place to raise a child than Lower Manhattan.

I had no idea what to expect from Barthelme as a colleague:
whether the weight of such a star might throw off-kilter the
fragile balance of our program. But Donald proved not to have
an ounce of the prima donna in him. On the contrary, he was
the ultimate team player, accepting his full share of the petty,
annoying bureaucratic tasks, sitting on boring departmental
committees, phoning our top applicants to convince them to
choose our program, lobbying university bigwigs with his good-
ole-boy communication skills. A would-be graphic artist ("the
pleasure of cutting up and pasting together pictures, a secret
vice," he once wrote), he designed all our posters and letter-
heads. Donald had one of the most pronounced civic con-
sciences I have ever come across, and was fond of exhorting us
with the Allen Ginsberg line: "Come, let us put our queer
shoulders to the wheel."

Each Tuesday noon we would have a meeting of the creative writing staff to determine policy. These lunch meetings
took place on-campus in the Galaxy Room of the School of
Hotel Management; eating there was like going to a barber
school for a haircut. Donald would be the first to arrive. He
would order a large glass of white wine, which he would ask to
have refilled several times during lunch. After we had all settled in and ordered (trial and error had convinced me that, despite poignant attempts to retool the menu, only the grilled
cheese sandwich was reliable), Cynthia Macdonald, the program's founding mother and an ex–opera singer, would, with
her operatic sense of urgency, alert us to the latest crisis: either
our graduate students were in danger of losing their teaching
stipends, or some English professor was prejudiced against our

majors, or the university was hedging on its budget commitments, or a visiting writer had just called to cancel a reading.

Barthelme, who abhorred stinginess, preferred to settle the smaller crises by dipping into the "Don Fund," as the discretionary monies attached to his academic chair came to be called. He thus made it possible to circumvent the bureaucracy, save the students' literary magazine, advertise an impromptu reading, or preserve the program's honor when a visiting literary dignitary like Carlos Fuentes came to town, by taking him out to a fancy restaurant.

Sometimes, however, the problem was stickier and had to be thrashed out by Cynthia, Donald, Stanley Plumly (who left after a few years, replaced by the poet Edward Hirsch), and myself, as well as a rotating visiting cast that included Ntozake Shange, Rosellen Brown, Richard Howard, Joy Williams, Jim Robison, Mary Robison, Meg Wolitzer. In the familial dynamic that developed over the years, Cynthia and Donald were Mommy and Daddy, with the rest of us siblings contending for their favor. During heated discussions Donald would often wait until everyone else had declared a position, and then weigh in with the final word, more like an arbiter than an interested party. He was good at manipulating consensus through democratic discussion to get his way; and we made it easy for him, since everyone wanted his love and approval. At times he would inhibit opposition by indicating that any further discussion on an issue he regarded as settled was extremely dumb and ill-advised. Still, when a vote did go against him, he bowed sportingly to majority will. He often seemed to be holding back from using his full clout; he was like those professional actors who give the impression at social gatherings of saving their energy for the real performance later on.

Sometimes in the midst of the meeting, I would raise my eyes and find Donald's gaze fixed on me. What did he *see*? I wondered. He would immediately look away, not liking to be spied in the act of exercising curiosity. At other times I would catch Donald at this funny habit: he would sniff his sleeve a few inches above the wrist, taking a whiff of his arm, either because he liked the smell of his sweat or because he needed to ground himself, establish contact with his body when his mind was drifting toward Mars.

Though we usually agreed on specifics, Donald believed more fully in the mission of writing programs than I could. There was much talk about having to maintain our position as one of the top three writing programs in the country. By what standards, aside from wishful thinking, this ranking had been determined I never could ascertain: presumably it had something to do with the faculty's repute, the number of applications we received, and the publishing fortunes of our alumni. In any case, Donald was ever on guard against anything that might "dilute the quality of the program." Sometimes I would recommend bringing in visiting writers who might be less well-known but who could give our students a broader perspective stylistically or multiculturally. "But are they any *good?*" Donald would demand, and I knew what he meant: if they were any good, why hadn't he heard of them?

Donald was a man with a great sense of loyalty to family, neighborhood, academic institution, and publisher. *The New Yorker* had published him throughout his career, and he believed in the worth of those who appeared in its pages; ditto, those authors active on the executive board of PEN, the international writers organization. The other side of the coin was that he showed a massive incuriosity toward writers outside the mainstream or his personal network. If a novelist was recommended to us for a teaching post by his brother Rick—arriving under the familial mantle, as it were—he would display serious interest. But if you mentioned a good living writer he didn't know, his response was a quick veto. There was something of the air of a Mafia don about Barthelme's protection: he treated his own circle of friends (Grace Paley, Ann Beattie, Roger Angell, Susan Sontag) as family, and he proposed their names for our reading series year after year. His refusal to consider literary figures who were not inside his particular spotlight used to drive me up the wall, partly because it seemed to leave out many worthy small press/experimental writers and partly because I had not escaped the hell of anonymity so long ago or so conclusively as not to identify with these "unknown" wretches. But from Donald's point of view, I had nothing to worry about; I was good enough to be on the writing faculty team, therefore I was one of the saved.

Ironically, Barthelme was himself an experimental, iconoclastic writer, so that there was a certain contradiction between his antitraditional literary side and his involvement in rank, the Establishment, continuity. (What else is being a teacher but an assertion of belief in continuity?)

There was always a formal side to Barthelme that I associate with the English—a Victorian dryness he used to comic effect. It crops up in his earliest stories, like the "The Big Broadcast of 1938": "Having acquired in exchange for an old house that had been theirs, his and hers, a radio or more properly radio *station*, Bloomsbury could now play 'The Star Spangled Banner,' which he had always admired immoderately, on account of its finality, as often as he liked." This qualifying, donnish quality was accompanied by an equally British terseness in social situations. "I think not," he would say in response to some proposal he considered dubious, and that would be that.

Or he would signal the conversation was at an end for him by taking your arm at the elbow and guiding you off on your rounds. I was at first astonished by this gesture, which seemed like an eruption of regal impatience. At the same time, I found something reassuring in his physical steering of me, like a father picking up his child and placing him out of harm's way.

Much of Donald Barthelme's fiction consists of witty dialogue. Yet when I think of Donald in real life, I recall few bon mots; I remember rather his underlying silence, which has now, in death, prevailed. Silence seemed his natural condition; his speech had very little flow: you never knew when it was going to dry up. Of course, Donald talked well, in the sense that he chose his words economically and with care. His listeners would often smile at the sardonic spin he gave to well-worn figures of speech. (Among others writers, I've known only John Ashbery to take as much delight in fingering clichés.) But the pearls of wit or wisdom one might have expected from him were rare; and this was because, I think, fundamentally he did not view speech as the vehicle for expressing his inner thoughts. Rather, he treated speech as a wholly social medium, to which he subscribed as a solid, dues-paying citizen, dipping into the common fount.

What one looks for in the conversation of writers is a chance to be taken back into the kitchen where they cook up their literary surprises: a sudden flash of truth or metaphor. Around Donald, what you got was not so much the lyrical, imaginative Barthelme as the one who re-created social inter-

40 course like a game, a tennis match, with parrying one-liners keeping the interlocutor off-balance. His remarks tended to stop rather than advance conversation.

When you waxed serious around Donald, you would expect to have your wings clipped, since he regarded getting worked up about anything in public as inappropriate. "Down, boy," he frequently mocked if I started to expatiate on a subject. These interventions felt more like a fond head-pat than anything malicious. But I never could figure out if he consistently played the referee in order to keep everyone around him at a temperature suitable for his own comfort, or out of some larger sense of group responsibility, which, in his eyes, conflicted with solo flights of enthusiasm.

Barthelme clearly considered it bad form to talk about books or the writing process in public. Perhaps he thought it too pedantic a topic to bring before intellectually mixed company. It also appeared that, toward the end of his life, he was bored with literature, much preferring the visual arts.

I had hoped, given the countless intellectual references sprinkled throughout Barthelme's stories, that the author of "Kierkegaard Unfair to Schlegel" and "Eugénie Grandet" would be as eager as I was to discuss our favorite authors. As it turned out, asking Barthelme what he thought was like demanding a trade secret, though I never gave up clumsily trying to pry loose his literary opinions. Once, at a brunch, on learning that the Swiss writer Max Frisch, who interested me, was a friend of Donald's, I immediately asked, "What do you think of Frisch's work?" I had either put the question too directly or shown too naked a desire for a glimpse at a higher circle (those writers of international stature, Frisch and Barthelme included) to let my curiosity be indulged, or Donald's feelings toward the Swiss writer were too complex or competitive for him to untangle them in public. Such speculations proliferate in the absence of a definite answer. Donald managed a grudging few syllables, to the effect that he thought Frisch's work "substantial," though "the fellow has a pretty big ego." He seemed much more comfortable discussing the rumor that Frisch might be buying an expensive loft in Soho.

This professional reticence, I should add, was by no means singular to Donald. Part of the larger loneliness of our literary life stems from the fact that writers, especially those who have reached a successful level, tend to shy away from discussing the things one would think mattered to them most—the other authors who continue to inspire them or the unsolved obstacles in their day-to-day composition—preferring instead to chatter about career moves, visiting gigs, grants, word processors, and real estate, all of which become, in effect, the language of power.

Once, when I managed to get Donald off by myself (we were driving to some forlorn suburb in outer Houston to make a fund-raising presentation), he indulged my hunger for candid literary talk. I asked him what he thought of several recent novels by Texas writers of our acquaintance. He didn't mince words; his assessments were extremely pointed and shrewd. It was exhilarating to gain admittance to the inner tabernacle of Barthelme's judgment—not to mention the fact that two writers dissecting the flaws of a third contemporary can bond them in a deliciously fratricidal way. But, to my regret, the experience was never repeated.

Perhaps because Donald had begun as a newspaperman, he still had a fair amount of the journalist left in him, which included not only a topical alertness to fashions but a heavy-

42   drinking, hard-boiled, almost anti-intellectual downplaying of
his own identity as practitioner of serious literature. I remember his boasting once that he'd dashed off a review on a *Super-
man* sequel, a "piece of hackwork for some glossy for a nice
piece of change." Yet when the review came out, I saw that
Donald had, as usual, given good weight, with an elegantly
amusing, well-constructed essay. Barthelme always worked
conscientiously to get the least piece of prose right. But like the
A student who hates to admit he studied for a test, he preferred
the pretense that he was a glorified grub working to pay the
bills. I think he would have *liked* to have been a hack; it was a
persistent fantasy of escape from his literary conscience. He fit
into that debunking, up-from-journalism tradition of American satirists: Twain, Bierce, Ring Lardner. The problem was
that his faux-hack pose made it difficult for you to take your
own writing seriously in front of him, or discuss other literature
with any seriousness.

Barthelme also seemed uncomfortable with psychological
conversation, which was either too intimate or too tattling for
his taste. His writings make it clear that he was quite astute at
character analysis; and yet there was a curious antipsychologi-
cal side to him, or at least a resistance to discussing such things
aloud; in this he was both a gentleman of the old school and a
postmodernist. One time Donald and I were talking after a
meeting about one of our colleagues, who had thrown a fit over
some procedural matter. I remarked with a smile that she
seemed to take a certain pleasure in releasing her wrath all the
way. Donald replied that he'd known people who had had temper tantrums just for the fun of it, but surely not someone as
mature as our colleague. This seemed a perfect instance of
Donald's loyalty: having decided that someone was a "good

guy," he did not like to acknowledge that that person might
still be capable of childish or self-indulgent behavior.

Once or twice a year Marion and Don would invite me to
their house: they'd either give a dinner party or ask my girlfriend and me over for a two-couple evening. Sometimes, after
a particularly happy night of warm, sparkling talk and wonderful food (both Barthelmes were superb cooks) and plentiful
wine, I would think, Donald and I are actually becoming
friends. I would fall under the spell of the man's gruff charm,
morality, intelligence; it was like having a crush; I couldn't wait
to see him again soon and take it further. But there never was
any further.

I would run into him at school and say, "I really enjoyed the
other evening at your house, Don."

"Well, good, good," he would reply nervously, which was
his favorite way of dismissing a topic. Perhaps he was simply
being modest about their hospitality; but I also thought his
uneasy look expressed concern that I would start to get
"mushy" on him, and make demands for a closeness he had
no inclination or ability to fulfill. What I wanted was to re-
move the evening from the category of "dutiful community
socializing that had turned out well" and place it under the file
of "possible developing friendship." But the story of
Barthelme's and my friendship seemed forever stalled in the
early chapters; there was no accrual of intimacy from one time
to the next.

In trying to account for this stasis, I often wondered if it
was a question of age. Twelve years separated us, an awkward
span: I was too old and set as a writer to inspire the parental

fondness he bestowed on his favorite graduate students, but too young to be accepted as a peer. I was the same age, in fact, as his younger brother Frederick, who was enjoying considerable success; if anything, insurgent writers twelve years younger may have seemed to him enviable pups, breathing down his neck. Then again, the appetite for shared confidences often dwindles after fifty; at that point some writers begin to husband their secrets for the page. In any case, I sensed that he'd become used to accepting rather passively the persistent courtship by others (which is not my mode). As a woman novelist said to me: "Donald sits there on the couch and expects you to make a pass at him."

I got a deeper glimpse into his own thinking on friendship one night at a dinner party at the Barthelmes' apartment in Houston. After dinner, Donald and I settled into a rare personal conversation. I asked him if he showed his work to anyone before he sent it off for publication. He said he showed Marion; that was about it. I then inquired if he had any close friends who were his peers with whom he could talk writing. He surprised me by saying he didn't think so. He said he had had two good friends, and they had both died. One was Thomas B. Hess, the other Harold Rosenberg, both well-known art critics. "I started hanging around them in the sixties. They were older than me and they were my mentors, and it was great that we could talk about art and not necessarily about literature. They taught me a whole lot. I haven't learned anything since. I'm still working off that old knowledge. It was distressing how they both died around the same time, which left me feeling rather . . . odd," he said. "What I really want are older men, father figures who can teach *me* something. I don't want to be people's damn father figure. I want to be the baby—

it's more fun. The problem is that the older you get, the harder it is to find these older role models."

A reluctant patriarch, still looking for the good father. Having been on that same search off and on, I understood some of Donald's loneliness. It doesn't matter how old you get, you still have an ache for that warm understanding. He began talking about his own father, Donald Barthelme Sr., a highly respected architect in Texas. His father, he said, had been "very uptight" with them when they were growing up: "I think he was terrified of children." As an architecture professor, Barthelme senior always tried to get the better of his students and demonstrate his superior knowledge. "Well of course we know more than our students, that's not the point!" said Donald.

I thought of his novel *The Dead Father* and wondered whether that title had irked Barthelme senior, who was (and is still) very much alive. The book is Barthelme's best novel and one of his finest achievements. In this part parody, part serious Arthurian romance, the Dead Father is an active character, boasting, complaining, demanding attention. Like a corpse that will not acknowledge its demise, this patriarch who has been "killed" (or at least put in the shade) by his more successful son seems to represent the dead weight of guilt in the Oedipal triumph. *The Dead Father* is an obsessive meditation on generational competitiveness, the division between younger and older men, and the fear of time's decaying hand.

Many of Barthelme's short stories revolve around Oedipal tensions implicit in education, mentorship, and the master-flunky tie. Take, for instance, "The King of Jazz," where Hokie Mokie blows away the young Japanese challenger in a jam ses-

46 sion, or "Conversations with Goethe," where the narrator-flunky is triumphantly put in his place at the end:

> Critics, Goethe said, are the cracked mirror in the grand ballroom of the creative spirit. No, I said, they were, rather, the extra baggage on the great cabriolet of conceptual progress. "Eckermann," said Goethe, *"shut up."*

I always winced when I heard Barthelme read that story aloud (as he often did), partly because of the glee he seemed to express at maintaining the upper hand and partly because of the hint—at least I took it that way—that any friendship with him would have to grow out of an inferior's flattery.

Sometimes it seemed that Donald not only was bored with everyone around him but had ceased to expect otherwise. In Houston he drew his social circle from mildly awed professionals—doctors, lawyers, etc.—who could produce a soothing harmonious patter into which he would insert an occasional barb to perk things up. Mostly Donald preferred to stand back, making sure the social machinery was running smoothly.

In his distance from us, he seemed to be monitoring some inner unease. I suppose that was partly his alcoholism. No matter how sociably engaged alcoholics are, one corner of their minds will always be taking stock of the liquor supply and plotting how to get in another drink without being too obvious about it. I never saw Donald falling-down drunk; he held his liquor, put on a good performance of sobriety; but, as he once admitted, "I'm a little drunk all the time." Sometimes, when he drank a lot, his memory blacked out.

Example: During a spring break Cynthia Macdonald delegated me to phone Donald in New York and find out which students he wanted to recommend for a prestigious fellowship. I called him around eight in the evening, and he gave his recommendations, then asked me a series of questions about departmental matters, raises, courses for next year, etc. A few days later Cynthia called him and mentioned in passing the telephone conversation he had had with me. Donald insisted he had not spoken to me in weeks. Cynthia told me to call him again, this time making sure it was before five o'clock, when the chances for sobriety were greater. The odd part is that when I did call him, we had the identical conversation: he put the same questions in the same order, with the same edgy impatience, quickly voicing one question as soon as I had answered the last. I never let on that he was repeating himself, but it struck me that he must often have been on automatic pilot, fooling the world with rote questions while his mind was clouded by alcohol.

At times he gave the impression, like a burn victim lying uncomfortably in the hospital, that there was something I was neglecting to do or figure out that might have put him at greater ease. Perhaps there is always a disappointment that an alcoholic feels in a nonalcoholic: an awareness that, no matter how sympathetic the nondrinker may seem, he will never really "get" it. That was certainly true for me: I didn't get it. I knew Donald disapproved of my not drinking—or not drinking enough. He once objected to our holding a meeting at my house, saying, "Phillip never has any liquor on hand." Which wasn't true, but interesting that he should think so. The noon meeting took place at my apartment anyhow; Donald arrived with a bottle, just in case.

I also think he disapproved, if that's the word, of my not philandering. When an artist in town began openly having an extramarital affair and most of the Houston arts community sided with his wife, Donald reassured the man that these things happened, telling him comparable experiences from his past. One of the ways Donald bonded with someone was through a shared carnal appetite—what used to be called a "vice," like drinking or womanizing.

In keeping with his Southwestern upbringing, Donald combined the strong, silent dignity of the Western male with the more polished gallantry of the South. He liked to be around women, particularly younger women, and grew more relaxed in their company. I don't think this was purely a matter of lechery, though lust no doubt played its classical part. The same enchantment showed in his delight with his older daughter, Anne, a vibrant, outgoing girl from an earlier marriage, who had been brought up largely by her mother in Scandinavia and who came to live with the Barthelmes while studying theater at the University of Houston. Given Barthelme's own (to use his phrase) "double-minded" language, hemmed in by the ironies of semantic duplicity, girl talk must have seemed a big relief. In his novel *Paradise* (1986), the hero, a middle-aged architect named Simon, shares an apartment with three beautiful young women and seems to enjoy listening in on their conversation about clothes, makeup, and jobs as much as sleeping with them.

In *The Dead Father*, Barthelme shows an awareness of the way a fifty-year-old's interest in young women might look to one's wife:

> Fifty-year-old boys . . . are boys because they don't want to be old farts, said Julie. The old fart is not cherished in this society. . . . Stumbling from the stage is

anathema to them, said Julie, they want to be nuzzling
new women when they are ninety.

What is wrong with that? asked the Dead Father.
Seems perfectly reasonable to me.

The women object, she said. Violently.

Certainly some of the women in the writing program objected to what they felt was Barthelme's preference for the
pretty young females in class. I ended up being a sort of confi-
dant of the middle-aged women students, who had raised families and were finally fulfilling their dreams to become writers;
several complained to me that Barthelme would make short
shrift of their stories, for being too domestic and psychological.
Of course, these were the very materials I had encouraged them
to explore. It's true that Donald once said to me if he had to
read another abortion or grandmother story, he would pack it
in. I understood that what he really objected to was the solemn
privileging of certain subjects over linguistic or formal inven-
tion; but I was sufficiently competitive with him for the students' love that it pleased me to hear their beefs. They also
claimed that his real pets were the talented young men. This is
a standard pattern in the writing program, with its hierarchies
of benediction. I, too, observed how certain of our top male
students would gravitate to Barthelme, and how he not only
would help edit their books—and get them publishers and
agents—but would invite them to hang out with him as his
friend. Perhaps "jealous" is too strong a word, but I was certainly a little envious of their easy access to Donald.

In the classroom Donald could be crusty, peremptorily sitting a student down after a few pages of a story that sounded
unpromising to him—a practice his favorites endorsed as hon-

est and toughening-up; those less sure of their abilities took longer to recover. His true generosity as a teacher shone, I thought, in individual conferences, where he would go over students' manuscripts he had line-edited as meticulously as if they had been his own. Often, as I was leaving, I would see a queue waiting outside his office; he put many more hours into student conferences than I did. I sensed that in the last years his main reading was student work—or at least he led me to believe that. When I would ask Don what he'd been reading lately, he replied, "Class stories, theses. Who has time for anything else?"

Donald loved to play talent scout. When one of his graduate students finished a manuscript he thought was publishable, he would call up his agent, Lynn Nesbit, and some New York editors, maybe start a few fires at *The New Yorker*. I was reluctant to take on this role with students: both because I wasn't sure I had the power to pull it off and because I didn't like the way the writing program's success stories generated a bitter atmosphere among the unanointed. But Donald acknowledged no such side effects: to him, each book contract drew more attention to the program and simply made us "hotter." The students, whatever qualms they may have had about the hazards of Brat Pack careerism, wanted a Godfather to promote them. They were no dummies; they knew that one word from Barthelme could lead to publication.

It's embarrassing to admit, but a few times I also tried to get Donald to use his influence in my behalf. That he had a measure of power in the literary world became steadily clearer to me from remarks he would drop at our lunchtime meetings: how he had helped so-and-so receive a lucrative prize, or had worked behind the scenes at the American Academy of Arts and Letters to snare honors for the "good guys." The Prix de Rome, given out by the Academy, went to several of his protégés in the space of a few years. Well, if goodies were being handed out, what the heck, I wanted some too. Once I asked him shamelessly (trying to make it sound like a joke), "Why don't you ever recommend me for a Prix de Rome or one of those prizes?" After a stunned pause, he answered, "I think they're interested in younger men, Phillip."

Flattering as it was to be told I was past the point of needing such support, I suspected more was involved. During the eight years we taught together, two of my books were published; I sent them to Donald for advance quotes, but he always managed to misplace the galleys until long after a blurb would have done any good. By then I'd had enough good quotes; what disappointed me more was that Donald had not responded to my work.

Months after the time had passed for Donald to "blurb" my novel *The Rug Merchant,* I continued to hope that he would at least read the book and tell me honestly what he thought. I asked him a few times if he had gotten to it yet, and he said, "Regrettably, no." Finally, I must have made enough of a pest out of myself to have an effect. We were sitting together at a party, and by this point in the evening Barthelme was pretty well in his cups. His speech slurred, he said he had read my novel and "it was a good job." He was sorry the main character, Cyrus, had not gotten round to marrying the girl in the end. "Anyway—a good job," he said again, tapping my knee.

In that neurotic way we have of probing a loose tooth, I brooded that Donald didn't like my writing. More likely, he simply felt indifferent toward it. A few times he did compliment me on something I'd written, usually after having seen it in a magazine. But I was insatiable, because his approval meant so much to me—a long-awaited sign of love from the emotionally remote father. The irony is that I so longed for approval from a writer whose own work I didn't entirely accept. Our aesthetics were worlds apart: I was interested in first-person confessional writing and the tradition of psychological realism, whereas Barthelme seemed to be debunking the presumptions of realist fiction. I suppose the fact that this blessing would have come from someone who was not in my literary camp but who represented the other orthodoxy, formalism, seemed to make it all the more desirable. I imagined—craved—a reconciliation, a pure respect between his and my style in some impossible utopian space of literary exchange.

For a long while I felt secretly guilty toward Donald because I did not love his work enough. I respected it, of course, but in a detached way. When I first began reading Donald Barthelme in the sixties, he struck me as a trickster, playfully adjusting a collection of veils, impossible to pin down. Later, when I got to know Donald, I saw that almost every line of his was a disguised personal confession—if nothing else, then of inner weather and melancholy: he was masterful at casting deep shadows through just the right feints, a sort of matador courting and dodging meaning, sometimes even letting himself be gored by it for the sake of the story. Recently, the more I read him, the more I come to the conclusion that he *was* a great writer. Minor, yes, but great at his chosen scale. He could catch sorrow in a sentence. A dozen of his stories are amazing and will last.

The bulk of his best work, to my mind, was done in the sixties: we sometimes forget how energized Barthelme was by the counterculture, the politics and playful liberatory urges of that period. His peak lasted through the early seventies, up to and including *The Dead Father* (1975). After that, his fiction lost much of its emotional openness, devolving on the whole into clever, guarded pastiche. Always the professional, he could still cobble together a dazzling sentence or amusing aperçu, but he became increasingly a master of trifles. There is, however, something noble in a great talent adapting itself to diminished capacities. His 1986 novel, *Paradise*, is a sweet if thin fabrication. Between the lines of its sportive harem plot, one can read an honest admission of burnout. Donald confessed to me that he thought the book "pretty weak," and I hope I had the hypocrisy to hide my agreement. *Paradise* is honest, too, in departing from his earlier intellectual references and in reflecting the creature comforts that engaged him mentally during his last years: food, decor, and sex.

As he got older and was drawn more to comfort, Houston seemed an appropriate choice of residence. It is an easy city to live in—not as stimulating as one might like at times, but pleasant. The Barthelmes lived on the second floor of a brick Tudor house in one of the city's most beautiful areas, the oak-lined South Boulevard. Just across the street was Poe School, an excellent elementary school where his little girl, Katharine, started to go when she was old enough. Nearby were the tennis courts where Marion played regularly. In Houston the Barthelmes enjoyed more of a black-tie, upper-middle-class life than in New York, going regularly to the opera, the symphony, the ballet; Donald became a city booster, telling outsiders that the Houston performing companies were good and getting better every year. Houston proved an ideal place for him to act out his civic impulse: of the ten established writers in town, each one called upon to do his or her community share, Donald was the most famous and most cherished, being a native son. This was what his compatriots in the New York literary world, for whom his resettlement in Texas seemed a perverse self-exile, found so hard to understand.

I remember telling one of Don's Manhattan friends, who was worried that he might be wasting away down there, how packed the literary life was in Houston, how needed he was. Secretly I asked myself whether living in Houston had indeed dried up some of his creative juices. Having never known Barthelme during his "conquering years," I had no way to compare; but I suspect that Houston was not a factor. His creative crisis had already started in the late seventies, when he was still living in New York; if anything, he may have accepted the move to Texas partly in the hope of being shaken out of stagnation and personal loss.

Barthelme's sardonic, Olympian use of brand names in his fiction led me to the mistaken idea that he took a dim view of consumerism, whereas I found him to be more a happy captive of it. He would often talk to me about new types of VCRs or personal computers, a sports car he was fantasizing buying, or the latest vicissitudes with his pickup truck—assuming incorrectly that I knew as much as the typical American male about machines. He was also very interested in food: I would run into him shopping at the supermarket, wicker basket in hand, throwing in a package of tortellini; one time he began talking about the varieties of arugula and radicchio, then added that he could never leave the place without spending a fortune. "They create these needs and you can't resist. They've figured out a way to hook you," he said.

These disquisitions on arugula were not exactly what I had
hoped for from Barthelme. I kept waiting for him to give me
more of his innermost thoughts. But later I began to think: suppose I had been misinterpreting him all along, because of my
own Brooklyn-Jewish expectations of conversation—that mix-
ture of confiding anecdote, analytic "delving," and intellectual
disputation—when in fact he was disclosing his inner self with
every remark, and I was too dumb or incredulous to perceive it.
Maybe he was not trying to frustrate me by holding back the
goods of his interior life, but was confiding his preoccupation
with things, comforts, sensual pleasures.

And why couldn't I accept that? I seemed to have to view
it as a copout, a retreat into banality; I wanted him to stand up
and be the staunch intellectual hero-father. Part of me responded with a line from Ernest Becker's *The Denial of Death:*
"The depressed person enslaves himself to the trivial." Another
part suspected that I, longtime bachelor, was merely envious of
his settled domestic family life. It should be clear by now that
Donald Barthelme was an enormously evocative figure for me.
The difficulty is distinguishing between what was really Donald and what he evoked in me—not necessarily the same thing.
If I came to regard Donald as the prisoner of a bourgeois
lifestyle dedicated to discreet good taste, down to the popular
Zurburán reproduction of fruit above his dining room table,
this probably says less about Donald than about my own patho-
logical attraction-repulsion vis-à-vis the Good Life, or what
passes in today's world for joie de vivre.

No doubt Barthelme *was* often depressed and withdrawn,
underneath all that fixation on obtainable pleasures. But he
also seemed reasonably contented much of the time, at home
with Marion and his two daughters. The younger Barthelme

56 had written scornfully about married life: "The world in the evening seems fraught with the absence of promise, if you are a married man. There is nothing to do but go home and drink your nine drinks and forget about it" ("Critique de la Vie Quotidienne"). The later Barthelme, now remarried, wrote in "Chablis":

> I'm sipping a glass of Gallo Chablis with an ice cube in it, smoking, worrying. I worry that the baby may jam a kitchen knife into an electrical outlet while she's wet. I've put those little plastic plugs into all the electrical outlets but she's learned how to pop them out. I've checked the Crayolas. They've made the Crayolas safe to eat—I called the head office in Pennsylvania. She can eat a whole box of Crayolas and nothing will happen to her. If I don't get the new tires for the car I can buy the dog.

The tires, the baby, the Crayolas, the dog: the tone seems more fondly engaged with domesticity. If the later stories seem to have lost an edge, it's also possible that Donald was simply happier.

His moments of joy seemed most often connected with his child of middle age, Katharine, whom he was smitten by and who was in truth a remarkably adorable, lively, bright little girl. I remember once hailing him as he carried Katharine on his shoulders across the street. "We're just setting off for an ice cream cone," he explained, blushing to his roots as if I had come upon a guilty secret. I had indeed caught him at his most unguarded, a doting father-horsie, without his irony or gravity buckled on.

When Donald went back to New York for the summer

months, he became slightly more nervous and speedy—or, as Marion put it ruefully, he "reverted to Type A"; but for that very reason, I think, I felt closer to, more in harmony with him there. In New York, also, we were removed from the demands of the writing program, and so I found it easier to pretend that we were not only colleagues but friends. The Barthelmes had retained, after protracted warfare with the landlord, their great floor-through apartment on West Eleventh Street: the walls were painted Pompeiian red; a large framed Ingres poster greeted the visitor; the radio was usually tuned to jazz; on the coffee table were oversized art books, often with texts by friends, such as Ann Beattie's *Alex Katz*. Barthelme may have been a postmodernist, but his furnishings held to the scrupulous purity of high modernism, the leather and chrome of MOMA's design galleries. As soon as you entered, Donald offered you a drink, and it was bad form to refuse, if only because your not having one undercut his pretext for imbibing. He was an extremely gracious host, perhaps overdoing the liquor refills, but otherwise attentive as a Bedouin to your comfort.

In May of 1987, by a coincidence having nothing to do with Donald, I sublet an apartment in the same brownstone on West Eleventh Street where the Barthelmes lived. Kirkpatrick and Faith Sale, their writer-editor friends, occupied the garden apartment below them, and I was two flights up in a tiny studio, sublet from an ailing Finn who had gone back to his native country for medical treatment. Though the building had more than its share of literary vibrations and timeworn, rent-stabilized charm, I quickly grew dissatisfied with my bare studio cubicle. It overlooked the street and was very noisy, especially on weekends, when the rowdy packs spilling out of Ray's Pizza on Sixth Avenue clamored up the block.

Donald knocked on my door the day he arrived in New York (I had preceded him by three weeks) and immediately began rearranging my room. "That bed doesn't belong there," he said, pointing to the Finn's futon. "The lamp's in the wrong place too." The interior decorator side of Donald took over; I became passively content to let him dictate the proper placement of objects. He insisted on loaning me some excess furniture from his apartment, and in no time at all I had an attractive Scandinavian rug, a chair ("You can borrow my Wassily chair—it's a facsimile of the Breuer"), a typewriter table, a trunk that would do as a coffee table, and some art posters for the walls. He kept running up and down stairs, hauling pieces from the basement storage.

Donald was a true good neighbor, and I could see he was delighted to have hit upon a way to help me. As long as I expected any sort of intimacy from him, it made him uncomfortable, but if I approached him as one generic human being to another, with a problem that needed fixing, he would be there instantly. If I had a flat tire, if my car engine needed a start-up, if I lacked home furnishings, I knew I could come to Donald for help. This neighborliness and common decency struck me as very Texan. Once, when my apartment in Houston had been burglarized and all my appliances stolen, Donald offered to loan me the little black-and-white television he and Marion used to keep in the kitchen for the evening news while they were preparing dinner. The generosity of this sacrifice I understood only when I returned the set three months later and saw how happy they were to get it back.

In any case, that summer Donald continued to take an active interest in my housing situation; and when I found a charming one-bedroom apartment on Bank Street, three blocks away, and signed a two-year lease, he went with me to have a look. By now I had accepted him as my habitational guru. Through his eyes I suddenly saw it as much smaller than I'd remembered, but he passed over that in silence. "Very nice. Very nice. If I were you, though, I'd have these wall stains removed," he said. "It's simple to do. I can help. Also, if you decide to paint the place, I'm good at paint jobs."

Here was a man who had barely addressed ten sentences to me during the past six months in Houston, and now he was volunteering to paint my house and wash the stains from my walls. I tabled the repainting idea, but I did enlist Donald's help in lugging my belongings the three blocks from West Eleventh to Bank Street. On the Saturday I moved, it was ninety-four degrees, naturally, and several trips were required, and we must have looked a sight, Sancho Panza and the Don with his scraggly beard, pulling boxes roped together on a small dolly. At one point it tipped over and spilled half my papers onto the sidewalk. After that, I let Donald carry the lion's share of the weight, he having a broader back and a greater liking (I told myself) for manual labor, as well as more steering ability. He was hilarious on the way over, joking about the indignity of being a beast of burden, and I must admit it tickled me to think of using one of America's major contemporary writers as a drayhorse. But why not take advantage when he seemed so proud of his strength, so indestructible, even in his mid-fifties?

When I was set up in my new apartment, I invited the Barthelmes over for Sunday brunch. It was both a return for the many dinner parties they had invited me to and a way of asserting that I was now a responsible adult entertaining on my own. Marion, who had just been in Vermont with Katharine, showed up looking radiant and tanned in a sundress. Donald

60 was ill-at-ease that day, as though having to get through an un-pleasant obligation—or else hung-over. I remember there was a direct overhead sun out on the terrace that bothered him into changing his seat several times, and made me worry about the food melting. I had overdone the spread, with so much lox and bagels, quiche, focaccia, orange juice, fruit, pie, and coffee as to leave little room for our plates. But I pulled out all the stops to be amusing, and gradually Donald began to unbend as we sat out on the terrace gabbing about the latest plays and movies and art shows and people we knew. Meanwhile, Katharine had discovered the hammock, and was having a great time bounc-ing in and out of it and performing "risqué" peekaboo fandan-gos. As usual, she and I flirted, Donald pretended to look pa-ternally askance, and Marion was ladylike, furthering the conversation with her journalist's bright curiosity while super-vising Katharine with a light hand.

Whenever, in the face of his opaque silence, I began won-dering if I had fallen out of Barthelme's good graces, someone would reassure me: "Oh, but Don's very fond of you. He always asks after you in an interested way." During the spring semester of 1988, however, I kept having the feeling that Donald was becoming cooler toward me. Interactions that used to take up thirty-five seconds were now clipped to twelve. Nor had I been invited to the Barthelme house for their customary dinner. Had I done something to offend him? I raised the question to Ed Hirsch, who was closer to Donald than I was, and Ed told me that he had detected the same curtness in Barthelme of late—which consoled me, I must admit.

Then on April 15 we received the awful, sickening news

that Donald had had to go to the hospital for throat cancer. His doctor, we learned now, had been treating it with antibiotics, but eventually decided an operation would be necessary, as the tumor turned out to be larger than originally thought. All along Donald had kept his illness secret from us, whether out of privacy or stoicism scarcely matters. I was ashamed that I had been taking his withdrawal personally. We were told he would be in the hospital anywhere from five to fourteen days, but not to visit him there, as he didn't want people seeing him in such condition.

About a week after he had come home from the hospital, and we were informed it was all right to pay a brief visit, I dropped by the Barthelme house. Knowing his love for jazz, I had bought him five archival jazz albums as a get-well present. With his newly shaven chin, Donald looked harshly exposed and rubicund. His eyes were dazed. He had a tube running from his nose to his mouth like an elephant's proboscis; its purpose was to feed him liquids, as his throat was still too sore to take in solids.

We sat in his living room, staring across at each other, having nothing to say. When I handed him the stack of jazz records, he patted them wordlessly, without bothering to examine what they were. Though I knew he must be extremely weak, I still felt hurt: wouldn't he have at least read the titles if someone he liked more had brought them? I told myself I was being ridiculous, the man was gravely ill—put ego aside for once!—and began cranking up conversation. As usual, Donald was the master of one-liners. "Demerol is great stuff." And: "I'm tired of sounding like Elmer Fudd." The tube pinching his nose did make his speech sound gurgled.

He asked testily about our having moved to offer someone

a teaching position for next year while he was in the hospital. Though Donald definitely liked the writer, I sensed an undercurrent of breached protocol. I explained that it was an emergency and we couldn't keep the man waiting any longer. "Well, good, good," he said. I apologized for our having acted without his final input. Barthelme nodded. His daughter Katharine ran into the room, naked and wet. "Don't look at me!" she commanded. "I just took a showw-er!" Donald smiled, followed her with his eyes. I excused myself after another minute or two. A painful half hour.

The next week, though there was really no need for him to do so, Donald came to our Tuesday lunch meeting. He said he was bored hanging around the house. He also seemed to be telling us with this visit: I may be sick but it doesn't mean I'm giving up my stake in the program. Perhaps because he was up and about, and therefore one expected an improvement, his pasty, florid appearance shocked me more than when I had seen him at home. He looked bad. We wanted him to go home and lie down, not sit through our boring agenda.

I could only agree when someone said afterward, "That just wasn't Donald." Not only had he lost his beard, but his glass of white wine. The doctors had told him that from now on he was to give up all alcohol and tobacco; these two habits had probably contributed to the throat cancer in the first place.

Over the next few weeks Donald began to enjoy a remission, and we let ourselves hope that he was out of danger. That summer I moved back to New York, quitting the job at Houston, but I kept tabs on him from mutual friends. They told me he was becoming the old Donald again, except that he seemed miraculously to have given up liquor and smoking—oh, every now and then cadging a cigarette or sneaking a sip of wine at a party when Marion's back was turned.

During the spring of 1989, Barthelme went to Italy, visiting Ed Hirsch, who was there on a Prix de Rome. From all accounts, Donald was in good spirits in Rome. Passing up sightseeing, he preferred to spend his days marketing, cooking, and working on his new novel, *The King*. So in July, when I ran into someone who told me Donald was in bad shape, I wanted to argue that that was old news, no longer current. But it was current. I was stunned, yet at the same time not: when you learn that someone in remission from cancer has had a relapse, it is never a total surprise. I prayed that Donald would somehow be strong enough to pull out of it again.

A week later, waiting by the cash register for a breakfast table at the Black Labrador Inn in Martha's Vineyard, I was turning the pages of the *New York Times* and came across Donald Barthelme's obituary. There was that familiar face, staring at me with unruffled calm. It wore the same expression he wrote about in his story "Critique de la Vie Quotidienne": "you assume a thoughtful look (indeed, the same grave and thoughtful look you have been wearing all day, to confuse your enemies and armor yourself against the indifference of your friends) . . ."

I suddenly remembered the time I had written an essay on friendship for *Texas Monthly*, and I had described a "distinguished colleague" (transparently Donald) whom I liked but with whom I could never establish a real friendship. To my surprise, since Barthelme generally shunned confrontation of any sort, he confronted me on it. "I saw what you wrote about me in that *Texas Monthly* piece," he said, letting me know by his ensuing silence that if I felt there was anything needing to be cleared up, he was willing to give me the opportunity.

"Did it . . . distress you?" I asked.

"I was a bit distressed, yes. But I recognize that that's your style as a personal essayist. You write about people you know; I don't."

"Did you think that what I wrote was . . . inaccurate?"

"No, no, not necessarily. I grant you it's hard for me to make friends. Ever since my two best friends, Tom Hess and Harold Rosenberg, died . . ." and he repeated substantially what he had told me the first time.

After his death a wise man who knew us both said, "Maybe Donald couldn't be a friend, but I think he had deep feelings for all of us." It was hard for me sometimes to distinguish between the taciturnity of deep feeling and unconcern. On my side, I felt guilty for having been one of those indifferent friends who didn't take the trouble to call near the end and ask about his condition. I had told myself, Don't bother them, you're not in the inner circle anyway—a poor excuse.

I have been assessing him in these pages through the prism of my needs, hence probably misjudging him. Certainly it is perverse of me to have manufactured a drama of being rejected by Barthelme, when the objective truth is that he was almost always kind to me—distant (such was his character) but benevolent.

It has not been easy to conjure up a man who, for all his commanding presence, had something of the ghost about him even in his lifetime. My relationship to him all along was, in a sense, with a rich, shifting absence. Donald is still hovering on the page, fading, I am starting to lose him. I had hoped to hold on to him by fixing his portrait. And now I hear him knocking, like the statue of the slain Commendatore in *Don Giovanni,* warning me that I will be punished for my sins, my patricidal betrayals of his privacy.

I have one more memory to offer: the night of the first

fund-raising ball for the creative writing program. When the ball had ended, I could sense an air of letdown afterward as Donald and Marion, Cynthia and I drove in the Barthelme's pickup truck to their house for a nightcap. The event had been pretty successful, but not as large a windfall financially as we had fantasized, after the year's work we had put into it. I tried a few jokes, but I could see the others had invested too much in the evening to jest about it. When we arrived, instead of sitting around having a postmortem, we—began singing songs. Cynthia has a fine trained voice, and Donald had a lovely baritone and a great memory for lyrics: Cole Porter, musical comedy, jazz ballads. It turned into a wonderfully pleasurable evening. Each of us alternated proposing songs, and the others joined in, to the best of our memories. Slowly the tension of organizing the ball seeped away. Donald seemed particularly at ease. There was no need to articulate his thoughts, except in this indirect, song-choosing fashion. It was another instance of Barthelme expressing himself most willingly through an outlet other than his chosen vocation: Donald the would-be graphic artist, the moving man, the decorator, the pop singer.

CONFESSIONS OF A SHUSHER

I am a shusher, which is to say a self-appointed sergeant-at-arms who tells noisemakers in the theater to be quiet. You take your life in your hands when you shush a stranger, since he may turn out to be a touchy psychopath who is reminded of an admonishing schoolteacher he detested. But having been in the past a grade-school teacher, I cannot shake the idea that I am somehow responsible for the correction of these breakdowns in the assembly.

My usual procedure is to start with a glare at the offender. Glares are unfortunately quite ineffective when the noisemakers sit in front of you. Even if they are to the side or behind, a glare may be misinterpreted as rubbernecking. I then proceed to clear my throat, hoping that this signal of civilized discomfit will be understood as a reproach. It almost never is. I then usually undergo an internal struggle, asking myself, Who am I to set myself up as a policer of public behavior? Can't I simply ignore the nuisance? Is it really worth it to emit an ugly sound, which grates on my ears as well, which may distract others from the movie and may draw on my head some physical retaliation against which I am ill-prepared to defend myself, or else some unpleasant curse? These questions are merely a way of biding my time in the hope that the problem will disappear by itself. If it doesn't, I am compelled to graduate to Stage 2: a good hearty "Shhh!" Much as I might want to soften the aggressiveness of this susurration, experience has taught me that a tentative shush is a waste of time—too easily mistaken for some private sigh.

But then, even a lusty shush is frequently ignored. Perhaps it is too comic-sounding, has too much of the sneeze about it, the hyperactive radiator or the ready kettle. In any event, a shush does not obligate its target to recognize that he or she has been addressed, the way normal speech does. What shushes do have in their favor is that, being such a universal signal, they make the reprimand seem less a personal confrontation and more the bubbling up of a communal superego. However, if the offenders continue to talk after several shushes (perhaps even issuing some derisive mimicking shush of their own as a witty riposte), then there is no choice but to come out from behind the anonymity of the shush and, heart in mouth, escalate to a crisp verbal "Please stop talking." This is sometimes followed by "You're not in your living room, you know," if one is feeling pedagogically self-righteous. Whatever statement one makes is likely to produce a furious twisting in the chair by the chief gabbler, to see what puritanical nerd has had the temerity to question his freedom of speech. It is necessary to return the fellow's look with a cool, frowning stare of one's own. Sometimes the shusher senses a small ripple of curiosity among those nearby, like schoolchildren drawn to a playground fight. Their lack of support for law and order is not the least irritating facet of the situation, since you had thought you were intervening at least partly for everyone's sake, and now realize that to them you are merely one more lunatic releasing commands into the indifferent dark.

By now the movie's spell has been broken. I sit boiling, feeling helplessly angry and at the same time frightened of the offender's potential rage. If he falls into a resentful silence, I can calm my heartbeat and tell myself that I have struck a blow for moviegoers everywhere. The problem is that the request to shut up is often taken rather personally. It seems to touch a sore spot in the requestee's dignity. Particularly, I have noticed, if the chief talker is showing off for his date, or his group of buddies, he may continue to jaw all night as a point of machismo, so that what had started out as unconscious rudeness graduates, via shushing, to defiant policy.

At such turns I compose speeches to myself, along the lines of "We did not pay good money to listen to your asinine conversation" or "How can we expect to have a democracy if . . ." But I usually spare them the civics lesson, because by this point I decide to write these people off as hopeless morons. I sweep up my coat and belongings, ignoring the victorious hoots, and allow myself a slow, censorious abandonment of the row. Perhaps a grain of guilt, I tell myself, will lodge itself in their subconsciousness and come to ripening next time.

It would be agreeable to report that the problem ends there. But many times my newly chosen section is also contaminated with talkers, so that I may be forced to move three times in the course of a feature film. In doing so, I incur the risk of being mistaken for a restless flasher, but it is a small price to pay for cinematic peace of mind.

The crux of the problem is that I want to watch movies in movie theaters, as they were designed to be seen, and I like having the company of other bodies, other spectators around me; but at the same time, I have become preternaturally sensitive, during years of devoted filmgoing, to distractions: not just to the conversationalists but to the foot-kickers or those who nervously cross and uncross their legs behind me, each time pressing into the back of my seat; the latecomer who compounds the first fault by making what seems like a deliberately elaborate coming to rest, removing her coat slowly and rearranging her department store bags; the doting parent who keeps feeding his child sourball candy wrapped in maximally crackling cellophane. . . . I don't even like to sit behind bald-headed men, because their domes reflect too much light and detract from the screen's luminescence. (The fact that my own hairline is receding at a rapid pace makes me hope that others are not so pathologically picky.)

The truth is, I can live with the kickers, the candy-unwrappers, the baldies, etc., but I draw the line at prattlers. Is it just my luck to attract them, or have today's movie audiences declined across the board in their capacity to keep silent?

We can always blame television for altering movie-viewing habits. A good many people who attend movies today do seem convinced that they are sitting on the couch at home; others must believe they are in the bedroom, as they snore or make love. You would expect that young people, who have grown up in the channel-hopping, short-attention-span era, would be the worst offenders. But the noisiest, from my observation, are elderly couples, who keep comparing notes on what is happening and why. Maybe hearing loss makes them talk louder, but it is also as if submission to the film experience were a threat to their dyadic bond, and in the end they choose togetherness over immersion.

Audiences of the twenties and thirties were famous—indeed, they were so criticized by intellectuals—for their mass somnambulism as the lights dimmed. Today's audiences are like patients hard to hypnotize; they resist the oneiric plunge. Accustomed to seeing modest-sized images in the convivial, lamp-lit surround of family life, they do not fully participate in the ritual of a sudden, engulfing nightfall. And today's theater owners further dilute the darkness by letting in considerably more ambient light—usually for security reasons—and scaling down the grandeur with smaller, multiplexed screens. The result is an uneasy suspension above the film narrative, the equivalent of a light sleep.

Audience chatter has also been affected by a shifting perception of when a movie actually begins. I was sitting in a movie house recently, waiting for the show to start (I like to get there early, to absorb the atmosphere and compose myself for the descent), and in front of me were two women having a discussion about apples. Granny Smith versus Macintosh, fresh versus baked. It was one of those tedious conversations you cannot help but eavesdrop in on. The lights lowered, the coming attractions started, the women chatted on. Now they were discussing which restaurant they would go to after the show. Coming attractions can be fascinating cultural artifacts, and, in any case, I have a fondness for their tantalizing promise, but I recognize that they are, in a sense, only advertisements, and so the audience has the right to talk through them, resisting these solicitations with skeptical remarks, such as "They couldn't pay me to see that one." However, the titles of the feature film started to appear, and the women continued conversing. Should they go to a French bistro or eat Chinese? But—you will say—it was only during the titles. *Only* the titles? I am curious who is in the cast, who wrote the screenplay, produced it; and even if I were not, I would still think the labor of these collaborators deserved a respectful silence as their names passed before my eyes. Then there is the choice of typeface, no small matter. . . . Above all, the title sequence often introduces the key visual and musical leitmotifs in the film. One school of criticism even argues that the title sequence is a miniature model—encoded, of course—of the movie to follow. All right, I see I haven't convinced you about the significance of the title sequence; but surely you will agree that the first shot of the film is highly important in arousing our expectations—as important, say, as the first sentence of a novel. Yet the women kept talking. This particular opening shot panned across the rooftops of a Sicilian city huddled in the landscape, establishing the drama's larger social context while at the same time expressing certain aesthetic choices (camera movement, angle, lighting) that allowed us to sense the tempo at which Fate would be distributed to the characters. It was a particularly engrossing, well-composed mood-setting shot, undermined by the chatter of my neighbors, and I felt I had no option but to shush. One of the women replied, "Nothing's happening yet!" Mood, location—this was nothing. It was only during the first *dialogue* sequence that they decided something was happening, and finally fell silent.

I want to make a distinction here between what I regard as justifiable audience noise and the kind of chatter I have been describing. I do not expect utter silence in a theater, nor do I necessarily want it. Comedies obviously gain from being seen in a packed, roaring house. If I am at a horror movie and during a frightening sequence some teenagers start yelling "Watch out!" or "Oh, gross!" it's in the spirit of the occasion. If my fellow moviegoers rejoice at a chainsaw dismemberment or at so-called "street slime" being blown away in *Death Wish IX*, I may fear for their souls and their politics, but I do not fault them for improper audience behavior. They are still reacting as a public to the events on-screen, are swept up in the drama. What I cannot accept is the selfishness of private conversation. Even when nothing is audible from a nearby tête-à-tête but a whispering buzz, the mere knowledge that my neighbors are not watching with their full attention dilutes and spoils my own concentration.

For all that one is still a crowd member, moviegoing is essentially a solitary process. To refuse that solitude is to violate the social contract that should be written on each ticket stub. If, indeed, movie audiences of today chatter more during films than they used to, I can only surmise that it has something to do with, on the one hand, a spreading fear of solitude and, on the other, an erosion of what it means to be a member of the public.

There have been times, over the years, when my roles as cinephile and swain have come into conflict. I have had to make it clear to my date, however much I may have doted on her, that I actually did want to watch the movie. I have made it clear to the gabblers around us as well, though one woman who was a perfect lady and to whom I was especially devoted, hated my shushing, which she found an embarrassment and a breach of manners. One time I went so far as to shush *her* when she was talking to a friend who had come with us to the movies, and afterward she let me know, with uncharacteristic directness, that if I ever did that to her again, she would break my arm. She was right, of course—or at least I pretended she was right, because I knew that if I attempted to defend my quixotic position, it would only make things worse. Nobody loves a shusher.

THE MOVIES AND SPIRITUAL LIFE

It is the flattest and dullest parts that have in the end the most life.
—ROBERT BRESSON

The earliest film I remember seeing was *The Spanish Main*, made shortly after World War II had ended. I must have been all of three or four—which is to say, too young to offer the auteurist apology I would now, that the wonderful romantic director Frank Borzage was simply misused in a swashbuckler. I remember a good deal of blushing orange-pink, the color of so many movies by the time a print got to our local theater. But what irritated me were the love scenes, especially the long clinch at the end, when the hero held Maureen O'Hara in his puffy sleeves. "Cut out the mushy stuff!" I yelled.

What children want from movies is very simple: a chair smashed over the gunman's head, a battle with a giant scorpion. They get restless through the early development scenes that give background information, the tender glances, the landscapes. But then a knife is hurled through the air and they are back into it. The kinetic at its most basic captivates them.

This was the initial charm and promise of the medium, as a somewhat astonished Georg Lukács reflected in 1913 after a visit to the motion picture emporium:

> The pieces of furniture keep moving in the room of a drunkard, his bed flies out of his room with him lying in it and they fly over the town. Balls some people wanted to use playing skittles revolt against their "users" and pursue them uphill and downhill. . . . The "movie" can become fantastic in a purely mechanical manner . . . the characters only have movements but no soul of their own, and what happens to them is simply an event that has nothing to do with fate. . . . Man has lost his soul, but he has won his body in exchange; his magnitude and poetry lie in the way he overcomes physical obstacles with his strength or skill, while the comedy lies in his losing to them.

What Lukács could not have predicted was that, side-by-side with this fantastic cinema of movement, would develop a cinema of interiority, slowness, contemplation. Certain directors of the so-called transcendental style, like Dreyer, Bresson, Ozu, Mizoguchi, Rossellini, Antonioni, Hou Hsiao-Hsien, would not be content until they had revealed the fateful motions of their characters' souls on film.

I remember the first time I saw such a movie, in college: Robert Bresson's *Diary of a Country Priest*. The picture follows the misfortunes of a young priest, alienated from his worldly and cynical parishioners, who undermines his health in a quest for divine communion by eating nothing but bread soaked in wine. At the end he dies, attaining grace on his deathbed. Bresson frustrates conventional expectations of entertainment by denying the audience melodrama, spectacle, or comic diversion, offering instead an alternation of tense theological discussions and scenes of the priest alone, trapped by landscape or interiors in psychic solitary confinement. No doubt I identified, in my seventeen-year-old self-pity, with the hero's poetic heartache. But what affected me so strongly at the time was something else.

There was a solitary chapel scene, ending in one of those strange short dolly shots that Bresson was so fond of, a movement of almost clumsy longing toward the priest at the altar, as though the camera itself were taking communion. Suddenly I had the impression that the film had stopped, or, rather, that time had stopped. All forward motion was arrested, and I was staring into "eternity." Now, I am not the kind of person readily given to mystical experiences, but at that moment I had a sensation of delicious temporal freedom. What I "saw" was not a presence, exactly, but a prolongation, a dilation, as though I might step into the image and walk around it at my leisure.

I'm sure most people have at one time or another experienced such a moment of stasis. If you stay up working all night and then go for a walk in the deserted streets at dawn and look at, say, a traffic light, you may fixate with wonderment on the everyday object, in an illumination half caused by giddy exhaustion. Recently, while watching *Diary of a Country Priest* on videotape, I confess I kept dozing off, which made me wonder whether that first celluloid experience of eternity was nothing more than the catnap of a tired student faced with a slow, demanding movie. But no, this is taking demystification too far. Bresson's austere technique had more likely slowed down all my bodily and mental processes, so that I was ready to receive a whiff of the transcendent.

In Paul Schrader's *Transcendental Style in Film*, he accounts for this phenomenon by arguing from the bare, sparse means of Bresson's direction, which eschews drama and audience empathy: "Stasis, of course, is the final example of sparse means. The image simply stops. . . . When the image stops, the viewer keeps going, moving deeper and deeper, one might say, *into* the image. This is the 'miracle' of sacred art."

All I know is that I was fascinated with the still, hushed, lugubrious, unadrenalated world of *Diary*. I kept noticing how the characters gravitated toward windows: could not the panes' transparency be a metaphor for the border between substance and immateriality? "Your film's beauty," wrote Bresson to himself in *Notes on Cinematography*, "will not be in the images (postcardism) but in the ineffable that they will emanate." Perversely, it seemed, he was struggling to express the invisible, the ineffable, through the most visually concrete and literal of media. Yet perhaps this is less of a paradox than it might at first appear; perhaps there is something in the very nature of film, whose images live or die by projected beams of light, that courts the invisible, the otherworldly. The climax of Murnau's *Nosferatu*, where the vampire, standing before the window, is "dissolved" by the rays of morning light, must derive some of its iconic power from self-reflexive commentary on the medium itself.

I noticed at the time that Bresson was also very fond of doors—in much the same way that Cocteau used mirrors in *Orpheus*, as conductors from one world to another. *Pickpocket*, Bresson's greatest film, has a multitude of scenes of a door opening, followed by a brief, tense dialogue between well-meaning visitor and protagonist (the pickpocket), and ending with the frustrated visitor's exit through the same door. This closed-door motif suggests both the pickpocket's stubbornness, his refusal of grace, and the doors of spiritual perception, which (Bresson seems to be saying) are always close by, inviting us to embrace salvation. Bresson's world tends to be claustrophobic, encompassing a space from the door to the window and back, as though telling us how little maneuvering room there is between grace and damnation. Curious how such a chilly idea, which would be appalling to me as a precept to follow in daily life, could prove so attractive when expressed in cinematic form. But part of its attraction was precisely that it seemed an intensification, a self-conscious foregrounding of problems of cinematic form.

A director must make a decision about how to slice up space, where to put the camera. Jean Renoir generously composes the frame so that it spills toward the sides, suggesting an interesting, fecund world awaiting us just beyond the screen, coterminous with the action, if momentarily off-camera; a Bresson composition draws inward, implodes, abstractly denies truck with daily life, cuts off all exits. In many scenes of *Diary*, the priest, let into a parishioner's house, encounters almost immediately a painful interview in which his own values are attacked, ridiculed, tempted. There is no room for small talk; every conversation leads directly to the heart of the matter: sin, suicide, perversity, redemption, grace.

I wonder why this forbidding Jansenist work so deeply moved me. I think it had something to do with the movie's offer of silence ("Build your film on white, on silence and on stillness," wrote Bresson) and, with it, an implicit offer of greater mental freedom. A film like *Diary of a Country Priest* was not constantly dinning reaction cues into me. With the surrounding darkness acting as a relaxant, its stream of composed images induced a harmony that cleansed and calmed my brain; the plot may have been ultimately tragic, but it brought me into a quieter space of serene resignation through the measured unfurling of a story of human suffering.

I could say a good deal more about Bresson's *Diary*, but, first of all, the film has already been picked clean by scholars and academics, and, second of all, rather than fall into the prolixities of scene-by-scene analysis, I want to concentrate on the challenge at hand: to explain how this one movie changed my life.* It did so by putting me in contact with a habit of mind that I may as well call spiritual, and a mental process suspiciously like meditation.

The monks in Fra Angelico's order were each assigned a cell with a painting on which to meditate. It may sound far-fetched to speak of watching a movie as a meditative discipline, given the passivity of the spectator compared with the rigors of Zen or monastic sitting; but parallels do exist. There is a familiar type of meditation called one-pointedness, which focuses the meditator's attention through the repetition of a single sound or mental image. Yet another meditation practice encourages the sitter to let thoughts fall freely and disorientedly, without anchoring them to any one point. The films of Mizoguchi, say, seem to me a fusion of these two methods: by their even, level presentation of one sort of trouble after another, they focus the viewer's mind on a single point of truth, the Buddhist doctrine of suffering; and by their extreme cinematographic fluidity, they arouse a state akin to free fall.

---

* This essay was originally published in an anthology entitled *The Movie That Changed My Life*, edited by David Rosenberg.

At first I used to resist my mind's wandering during such films, thinking I was wasting the price of admission. But just as in Buddhist meditation one is instructed not to brush aside the petty or silly thoughts that rise up, since these "distractions" are precisely the material of the meditation, so I began to allow my movie-watching mind to yield more freely to daily preoccupations, cares, memories that arose from some image association. Sometimes I might be lost to a personal mental thread for several minutes before returning with full attention to the events on-screen; but when I did come back, it was with a refreshed consciousness, a deeper level of feeling. What *Diary of a Country Priest* taught me was that certain kinds of movies—those with austere aesthetic means; an unhurried, deliberate pace; tonal consistency; a penchant for long shots as opposed to close-ups; an attention to backgrounds and milieu; a mature acceptance of suffering as fate—allowed me more room for meditation. And I began to seek out other examples.

In various films by Ozu, Mizoguchi, Naruse, there will be a scene early on where the main characters are fiddling around in the house and someone comes by, a neighbor or the postman (the traditional Japanese domestic architecture, with its sliding shoji, is particularly good at capturing this interpenetration of inside and outside); a kimono-clad figure moves sluggishly through the darkened interior to answer, some sort of polite conversation follows; and throughout this business, one is not unpleasantly aware of an odd aural hollowness, like the mechanical thud-thud of the camera that used to characterize all films just after sound came in; and it isn't clear what the point

of the scene is, except maybe to establish the ground of dailiness; and at such junctures I often start to daydream, to fantasize about a movie without any plot, just these shuttlings and
patient, quiet moments that I like so much. Ah, yes, the lure of
pure quotidian plotlessness for a writer like myself, who has
trouble making up plots. But then I always remember that what
gives these scenes their poignant edge is our knowledge that
some plot is about to take hold, so that their very lack of tension engenders suspense: when will all this daily flux coalesce
into a single dramatic conflict? Without the catastrophe to
come, we probably would not experience so refreshingly these
narrative backwaters; just as without the established, calm,
spiritual ground of dailiness, we would not feel so keenly the
ensuing betrayals, suicide pacts, and sublimely orchestrated dis-
enchantments.

I tried to take from these calm cinematic moments—to
convince myself I believed in—a sense of the sacredness of
everyday life. I even piously titled my second poetry collection
The Daily Round. I wanted the security, the solace of a constant, enduring order underneath things—without having to
pay the price through ecstasy or transcendence. My desire had
something to do with finding an inner harmony in the arrangement of backgrounds and foregrounds as I came across them in
real life; an effort, part spiritual, part aesthetic, to graft an order I had learned through movies onto reality. How it originally came about was this way: watching a film, I would sometimes find myself transfixed by the objects in the background.
I remember a scene in Max Ophüls's *Letter from an Unknown
Woman*, when the heroine is ironing in the kitchen, and suddenly I became invaded by the skillets and homely kitchen-
ware behind her. For several moments I began to dream about

the life of these objects, which had become inexplicably more important to me than Joan Fontaine.

Certain directors convey a respect for rooms and landscapes at rest, for the world that surrounds the drama of the characters and will survive it long after these struggles are over. Ozu frequently used static cutaway shots of hallways, beaded curtains in restaurants—passageways made for routine human traffic, which are momentarily devoid of people. Bresson wrote: "One single mystery of persons and objects." And: "Make the objects look as if they want to be there. . . . The persons and objects in your film *must walk at the same pace, as companions.*" Antonioni also engaged in a tactful spying on objects, keeping his camera running long after the characters had quit the frame. Why these motionless transitions, I thought, if not as a way of asserting some constant and eternal order under the messy flux of accident, transience, unhappiness?

I tried, as I said, to apply this way of seeing to my own daily life outside movie theaters. I waited on objects to catch what Bresson calls their "phosphorescence." In general, these exercises left me feeling pretty pretentious. Just as there are people whom dogs and children don't seem to trust, so objects did not open up to me, beyond a polite, stiff acquaintance. They kept their dignified distance; I kept mine.

Once, I took Kay, a woman I had been dating for several years while steadfastly refusing to marry, to see Dreyer's *Ordet*. It has been as hard for me to surrender spiritually as conjugally; I have long since become the kind of skeptic who gets embarrassed for someone when he or she starts talking about astrology, out-of-body experiences, past lives, or karma. I don't say

I'm right, just that I'm rendered uncomfortable by such terms. And if the exotic vocabulary of Eastern religions makes me uneasy, the closer-to-home terminology of Christ the King and Christianity makes me doubly so—perhaps for no reason other than that I'm an American Jew. In any case, there we were at the Carnegie Hall Cinema, Kay (who is Presbyterian) and I; we had just seen the magnificent final sequence, in which Dreyer "photographs" a resurrection: the mentally disturbed Johannes, invoking Jesus Christ, raises Inger from the dead—which is shown not by any optical trick, mind you, but simply by filming the event head-on, unadorned. One moment the woman is lying in her bed; the next moment she sits up and kisses her husband. I don't know which moved me more, Dreyer's own seeming faith in miracles, his cinematic restraint, or the audacity of his challenge to the audience to believe or disbelieve as we saw fit. The lights went up, and, just as I was wiping away a tear, Kay punched me. "You see, you can take it in films, but you can't take it in life!" she said.

Sometimes I think I am especially inclined to the spiritual, and that is why I resist it so. At other times this seems nothing but a conceit on my part. You cannot claim credit for possessing a trait you have run away from all your life. This does not prevent me from secretly hoping that spirituality has somehow sneaked in the back door when I wasn't looking, or was miraculously earned, like coupons, through my "solitary struggles" as a writer. (It would not be the first time that making poetry or art was confused with spiritual discipline.)

Every once in a blue moon I go to religious services or read the Bible—hoping that this time it will have a deeper effect on me than merely satisfying some anthropological curiosity. I do not, by and large, perform good works; I do not pray, except in desperation. I have never pursued a regular meditative practice, or even meditated under a learned person's guidance (though I have many friends and relatives who described the experience for me). No, the truth is I probably have a very weak (though still alive) spiritual drive, which I exercise for the most part in movie theaters.

It is, I suppose, a truism that the cinema is the secular temple of modern life. A movie house is like a chapel, where one is alone with one's soul. Film intrinsically avows an afterlife by creating immortals, stars. In its fixing of transient moments with permanence, it bestows on even the silliest comic farce an air of fatalism and eternity. All well and good. What I want to know is: Did I purposely seek out the spiritual in movies in order to create a cordon sanitaire, to keep it from spilling into the other facets of my life?

Films have been a way for me to aspire to the spiritual, without taking it altogether seriously. *Diary of a Country Priest* may have helped shape my sense of beauty, but I notice that as a writer I have never striven for Bressonian purity. I am too gabby; such austerity is beyond me. In fact, when I encounter Bresson on the page, in interviews and in his writings, he sometimes seems to me insufferable. Even some of his films, especially the later ones like *The Devil, Probably*, and *Lancelot du Lac*, have passages that strike me as moronically solemn. And, as I am not the first to observe, there is often something mechanical in the plots of Bresson, along with those of other modern Catholic storytellers—Graham Greene, Mauriac, Bernanos (who supplied the novel on which *Diary of a Country Priest* is based)—that stacks the deck in favor of sin, perverse willfulness, and despair, the better to draw grace out of the pile later on. I think even as a college student I suspected this, but the very air of contrivance, which alluded to theological principles I ill understood, filled me with uncertainty and awe.

Another reason why I did not build more on the glimpses of spiritual illumination I received in movies occurs to me belatedly: All the films I was attracted to were either Christian* or Buddhist. I could not travel very far along this path without becoming disloyal to Judaism. Though I haven't been a particularly observant Jew, I retain an attachment to that identity; put bluntly, it would horrify me to convert to another faith. What, then, of Jewish models? Was there no Jewish transcendental cinema? I think not, partly because modern American Judaism doesn't appear to be very big on transcendence. There may be transcendental currents in the Old Testament, the Kabbalah, or Kafka, but Judaism doesn't seem to me to put forward a particular theology of transcendence. Catholicism asserts that death can bring redemption and an afterlife, but it is unclear whether Judaism even believes in an afterlife. In my experience of Judaism, there is only morality, guilt, expiation, and satisfaction in this life. Catholicism insists on the centrality of a mystery. Bresson quotes Pascal: "They want to find the solution where all is enigma only." And in Bresson's own words: "Accustom the public to divining the whole of which they are only given a part. Make people diviners." This language of divination and mystery seems to me very far from the analytical,

---

* Even Buñuel, another early favorite whom I took to be antireligious by his parodies of the transcendent, seems, in films like *Nazarin*, *Viridiana*, *Simon of the Desert*, heavily shaped by a Catholic world view. To turn something inside out is still to be dependent on it.

Talmudic, potentially skeptical methods of Jewish study; as it happens, it is with the latter that I have come to identify.

One of the most beautiful passages in motion pictures is the ending of Mizoguchi's *Ugetsu*, when the errant potter returns to his cottage after long travels and a 180-degree pan finds his old wife sitting there, preparing him a meal. He falls asleep happy, only to wake up the next morning and learn from neighbors that his wife is dead: the woman who had tended him the night before was a ghost. The 180-degree movement had inscribed the loss all the more deeply through its play on absence and presence, invisibility and appearance. Such a noble presentation of the spirit life, common in Buddhist art, would be extremely rare in Jewish narratives, where ghosts are not often met.

If you were to think of a "Jewish cinema," names like the Marx Brothers, Woody Allen, Ernst Lubitsch, Jerry Lewis, Mel Brooks, Billy Wilder spring to mind—all skeptical mockers, ironists, wonderful clowns, and secular sentimentalists. Yiddish films like *Green Fields* and *The Light Ahead* do have scenes of religious piety and custom, but even these celebrate the warmth and sorrows of a people rather than the spiritual quest of a lonely soul straining toward God. Whatever the virtues of Yiddish movies—humanity and humor in abundance—they are not aesthetically rigorous: indeed, it is the very muzziness of communal life that seems to constitute the core of their triumphant religious feeling.

As I look back, I realize that I needed to find something different, something I did not know how to locate in my watered-down Jewish background. I took to the "transcendental style" immediately; it was obviously the missing link in my aesthetic education. Movies introduced me to a constellation of ritual and spiritual emotion that I could willingly embrace so long as it was presented to me in the guise of cinematic expression, but not otherwise. At that point these appeals, these seductions, came into conflict with a competing spiritual claim, indefinitely put off but never quite abandoned: to become a good Jew, sometime before I die.

RESISTANCE TO THE HOLOCAUST

When I was small, a few years after World War II had ended, my mother would drag me around Brooklyn to visit some of the newly arrived refugees; they were a novelty. We would sit in somebody's kitchen and she would talk with these women for hours (usually in Yiddish, which I didn't understand) to find out what it was like. After we left, she would say in a hushed voice, "Did you see the number on her arm? She was in a concentration camp!" I didn't understand why my mother was so thrilled, almost erotically excited, when she spoke these words, but her melodramatic demand that I be impressed started to annoy me. I had only to hear about those lurid arm numbers to experience an obstinately neutral reaction and begin digging in my heels. Maybe I was picking up some of her own ambivalence; beneath my mother's sympathetic sighs, I sensed a little distaste for these victims. Years later she confessed that, when the camp survivors first started coming into her candy store, they were the most difficult customers to please; they had—and here she paused, realizing how insensitive her appraisal might sound, given their tragic backgrounds—a "chip on their shoulders."

Actually, I was touched by her honesty; just because someone has suffered a lot doesn't mean you have to like them, has always been my motto. I used to go into a neighborhood hardware store run by a concentration camp survivor with thick wire-framed glasses, whom I did like but whose superior bitterness gave all transactions an air of mistrust. Once I heard this proprietor say after he had thrown a customer out of his store: "What can he do, kill me? I already died in Auschwitz." This advantage of the living dead over the rest of us seemed unfair.

But I am getting ahead of myself. I want to return to that moment when my mother and I were leaving some poor woman's kitchen and I froze at the demand for my compassionate awe. Let me try to explain by way of anecdote. I once heard of a very liberal Jewish couple whose child would scream whenever she saw a black person. The parents were distressed that their little girl might be learning racist attitudes from somewhere, so they went to a child therapist and asked his advice. After questioning the little girl alone and learning nothing, the doctor suggested that he go for an outing with the family so that he might observe them in an everyday setting. As they were walking along the street, he noticed that whenever a black person approached, the mother would unconsciously tighten the grip on her daughter's hand and the girl would, naturally, cry out. In my case, whenever my mother uttered those magical words "She was in a concentration camp!" the music on our emotional sound track got turned up so loud that I went

90 resolutely numb. Maybe this is the seed of that puzzling resistance I have felt toward the Holocaust all my life.

Before I give the wrong impression, let me interject that I am not one of those revisionist nuts who deny that the Nazis systematically exterminated millions of Jews. On the contrary, I'm convinced that they committed an enormous and unforgivable evil, about which I would feel presumptuous adding my two cents of literary grief or working myself into an empathic lather through the mechanics of writerly imagination. I was not there, I am not the one who should be listened to in this matter, I cannot bear witness. It is not my intent to speak at all about the atrocities of the Nazi era, but only about the rhetorical, cultural, political, and religious uses to which the disaster has been put since then. Of these, at least, I do have some experience.

When I was growing up, we never spoke of a Holocaust; we said "concentration camps," "the gas chambers," "six million Jews," "what the Nazis did." It might seem an improvement over these awkward phrases to use a single, streamlined term. And yet to put any label on that phenomenal range of suffering serves to restrict, to conventionalize, to tame. As soon as the term "Holocaust" entered common circulation, around the mid-sixties, it made me uncomfortable. It had a self-important, strutting air—a vulgarly neologistic ring, combined with a self-conscious archaic sound, straining as it did for a Miltonic biblical solemnity that brought to mind such quaint cousins as Armageddon, Behemoth, and Leviathan.

Then, too, one instantly saw that the term was part of a polemic and that it sounded more comfortable in certain speakers' mouths than others; the Holocaustians used it like a club to smash back their opponents. Lucy S. Dawidowicz states, "The Holocaust is the term that Jews themselves have chosen to describe their fate during World War II." I would amend that to say "some Jews" or "official Jewry"; but in any case, it is one of those public relations substitutions, like *African-American* for black or *Intifada* for Palestinian troubles, which one ethnic group tries to compel the rest of the world to use as a token of political respect. In my own mind I continue to distinguish, ever so slightly, between the disaster visited on the Jews and "the Holocaust." Sometimes it almost seems that "the Holocaust" is a corporation headed by Elie Wiesel, who defends his patents with articles in the "Arts and Leisure" section of the Sunday *New York Times*.

"Shoah" carries over the same problems as the term "Holocaust," only in Hebrew. Both "Shoah" and "the Holocaust" share the same self-dramatizing theological ambition to portray the historic suffering of the Jews during World War II as a sort of cosmic storm rending the heavens. What disturbs me finally is the exclusivity of the singular usage, *the* Holocaust, which seems to cut the event off from all others and to diminish, if not demean, the mass slaughters of other people—or, for that matter, previous tragedies in Jewish history. But more on these topics later.

We need to consider first the struggle for control of the Holocaust analogy. All my life, the *reductio ad Hitler* argument has been applied to almost every controversy. If it is not always clear what constitutes moral action, it is certain that each controversial path can be accused of initiating a slide that leads straight to Hitler. Euthanasia? Smacks of the Third Reich. Abortion? Federal payments make it "possible for genocidal programs as were practiced in Nazi Germany," according to Senator Orrin Hatch. Letting the Ku Klux Klan march? An invitation to Weimar chaos. Forbidding the march? Censorship; as bad as Goebbels. The devil can quote Scripture and the Holocaust, it would appear. We see in the Middle East today how both Israelis and Palestinians compare the other side to Nazis. The Hitler/Holocaust analogy dead-ends all intelligent discourse by intruding a stridently shrill note that forces the mind to withdraw. To challenge that demagogic minefield of pure self-righteousness from an ironic distance almost ensures being misunderstood. The image of the Holocaust is too overbearing, too hot to tolerate subtle distinctions. In its life as a rhetorical figure, the Holocaust is a bully.

The Holocaust analogy has the curious double property of being both amazingly plastic—able to be applied to almost any issue—and fantastically rigid, since we are constantly being told that the Holocaust is incomparable, in a class by itself, sui generis, must not in any way be mixed up with other human problems or diluted by foreign substances.

When President Jimmy Carter made a speech commemorating all those liquidated by the Nazis, which he put at a figure of 11 million, the eminent Holocaust scholar Yehuda Bauer accused Carter and his adviser Simon Wiesenthal of trying to "de-Judaize" the Holocaust. "The Wiesenthal-Carter definition appears to reflect a certain paradoxical 'envy' on the part of non-Jewish groups directed at the Jewish experience of the Holocaust. This itself would appear to be an unconscious reflection of anti-Semitic attitudes . . ." warned Bauer. We Jews own the Holocaust; all others get your cotton-picking hands off.

"How dare they equate using napalm in Vietnam or even

dropping the bomb on Hiroshima with the Holocaust?" one often hears. The underlying sense is: "How dare they equate anything with the Holocaust?" The Holocaust is a jealous God; thou shalt draw no parallels to it.

The problem is that drawing parallels and analogies is an incorrigibly natural human activity. I, too, find it deeply offensive and distasteful when flippant comparisons to Nazi genocide are made. But on the other hand, it does not seem to me unreasonable to regard the Holocaust as the outer limit of a continuum of state-sanctioned cruelty, other points along the spectrum of which might include the French torture of Algerians, Idi Amin's liquidations, My Lai and other Vietnam massacres, the slaughter of the Armenians, Pol Pot. I realize it may appear that I am blurring important distinctions among a genocide, a massacre, and other horrors; but I am not asserting that any of these atrocities was as *bad* as the Holocaust (whatever *that* means), only that the human stuff, the decisions and brutal enactments that followed, may have had much in common. I find it curious for people to speak of the murder of 6 million Jews as a "mystery" and the murder of several million Cambodians as perhaps a more run-of-the-mill open-and-shut affair. The truth is, unfortunately, that there are few things less mysterious and unique in the history of the world than genocide.

It is true that the Holocaust was singular in its hideous anti-Semitism, which made the mere fact of being a Jew grounds for death. But as the historian Irving Louis Horowitz argues in his essay "The Exclusivity of Collective Death": "To emphasize distinctions between peoples by arguing for the uniqueness of anti-Semitism is a profound mistake; it reduces any possibility of a unified political and human posture on the meaning of genocide or the Holocaust. . . . Insistence upon separatism, that the crime was Jewish existence and that this makes the Jewish situation different from any other slaughter, whatever its roots, contains a dangerous element of mystification."

A good deal of suspicion and touchiness resides around this issue of maintaining the Holocaust's privileged status in the pantheon of genocides. It is not enough that the Holocaust was dreadful, it must be seen as *uniquely* dreadful. Indeed, the catastrophe of the Jews under Hitler is sometimes spoken of as an event so special as to sever history in two—breaking the back of history, in effect. "Holocaust stands alone in time as an aberration within history," states Menachem Rosensaft. And Elie Wiesel writes that "the universe of concentration camps, by its design, lies outside if not beyond history. Its vocabulary belongs to it alone." What surprises me is the degree to which such an apocalyptic, religious-mythological reading of historical events has come to be accepted by the culture at large—unless people are just paying lip service to the charms of an intimidating rhetoric.

In attempting, for instance, to resolve the recent "historian's dispute" in West Germany, President Richard von Weizsäcker declared: "Auschwitz remains unique. It was perpetrated by Germans in the name of Germany. This truth is immutable and will not be forgotten." The *New York Times*'s reporter Serge Schmemann goes on to report (October 22, 1988): "Speaking to a congress of West German historians in Bamberg, Mr. von Weizsäcker rejected the attempts by some historians to compare the systematic murder of Jews in Nazi Germany to mass killings elsewhere—like those in Cambodia under Pol Pot or in Stalin's purges—or to seek external explanations for it. Such approaches have been assailed by other historians as attempts to frame the German crime in 'relative' terms."

Mr. von Weizsäcker has been rightly praised for his integrity and statesmanship in this matter—and yet I can't help thinking that he has also engaged in a certain amount of magically placating incantatory language: unique, immutable, never forget, antirelativism. I would have thought that a relativistic perspective was part of the discipline of competent modern historians. Not that history writing is ever entirely value-free or objective; but attempting to situate an era in a larger context still seems closer to normal historical methods than expecting historians to believe there is such a thing as an absolute historical event or an absolute evil. There seems to be a fear that, if we admit there are similarities between the Nazis' war against the Jews and other genocidal atrocities, we will be letting the Germans off the hook. On the contrary, we will be placing them on the same hook with other heinous criminals. And we will be asserting that the forces in history and human nature that brought about the death camps are not necessarily a fluke, so—be on guard.

As Yehuda Bauer has astutely observed:

> If what happened to the Jews was unique, then it took place outside of history, it becomes a mysterious event, an upside-down miracle, so to speak, an event of religious significance in the sense that it is not manmade as that term is normally understood. . . . If what happens to the Jews is unique, then by definition it doesn't concern us, beyond our pity and commiseration for the victims. If the Holocaust is not a universal problem, then why should a public school system in Phila-

96   delphia, New York or Timbuktu teach it? Well, the answer is that there is no uniqueness, not even of a unique event. Anything that happens once, can happen again: not quite in the same way, perhaps, but in an equivalent form.

Let us look at some of the cold figures on genocide in this century. According to Roger W. Smith, in *Genocide and the Modern Age:*

> Turkey destroyed the lives of a million or more Armenians; Nazi Germany destroyed 6 million Jews, but it is often forgotten that it went on to murder other groups as well, so that a reasonable estimate for the total number of victims, apart from war deaths, is 16 million; Pakistan slaughtered 3 million Bengalis; Cambodia brought about the death of 3 million persons; and the Soviet Union first destroyed 20 million peasants in the 1930s and then went on to take hundreds of thousands of other lives in the 1940s with its assaults on various nationality groups suspected of disloyalty.

These numbers may be somewhat high. Barbara Harff, who provides both lower and upper estimates in the same book, rounds out the picture with other twentieth-century genocides: Nigeria's extermination of 2 to 3 million Ibos; the Indonesian slaughter of supposed Communists, 200,000–500,000; the Indonesian action in East Timor, 60,000–100,000; Idi Amin's murder of fellow Ugandans, 500,000; the Tutsis' massacre of 100,000–200,000 Hutus in Burundi; Sudanese against the Southern Sudanese, 500,000; and so on.

The position that the Jewish Holocaust was unique tends

to rest on the following arguments: (1) scale—the largest number of deaths extracted from one single group; (2) technology—the mechanization of death factories; (3) bureaucracy—the involvement of the state apparatus at previously unheard-of levels; (4) intent—the express purpose being to annihilate every last member of the Jewish people. Thus it is argued that, although Hitler killed many, many Poles, he still intended to use the majority of Poles as slave laborers. Some scholars counter that it was Hitler's goal also to eliminate the entire Gypsy population; others dispute this claim. The fact that one's group was not targeted for extermination in toto is a serious distinction, but hardly much consolation to the Gypsies, homosexuals, radicals, Poles, Slavs, etc., whom the Nazis did wipe out.

Alan Rosenberg asserts that the uniqueness of the Holocaust lies above all in "the Nazi abuse of science and technology, the application of bureaucratic techniques, principles of managerial efficiency and 'cost-benefit' analysis." This assessment, with its obvious implications for the present, dovetails with Theodor Adorno and Max Horkheimer's philosophical argument that the systematic, orderly, "Germanic," if you will, manner in which the killings were carried out shows the ultimately debased heritage of Western Enlightenment reason. Certainly much of our abiding fascination with the Holocaust rests on its dystopian, nightmarish use of rational, mechanized procedures. But I wonder how much of the importance we ascribe to these factors represents the narcissistic preoccupations of our Western technological society. Does it really matter so much if millions are gassed according to Eichmann's timetables rather than slowly, crudely starved to death, as in Stalin's regime, or marched around by ragged teenage Khmer Rouge soldiers and then beheaded or clubbed? Does the family mourning the loved one hacked to pieces by a spontaneous mob of Indonesian vigilantes care that much about abuses of science and technology? Does neatness count, finally, so damn much? (And what about the tragic fiasco—not genocide, true, but equally fatal—of the Great Leap Forward during the 1959–60 famine in China, when "anywhere between 16.4 to 29.5 million extra people died during the leap, because of the leap," according to Harvard political scientist Roderick Mac-Farquhar.)

I find it hard to escape the conclusion that those piles of other victims are not so significant to us North Americans as Jewish corpses. Is it simply because they are Third World people of color? How much is social class itself a factor? In so many books and movies about the Holocaust, I sense that I am being asked to feel a particular pathos in the rounding up of gentle, scholarly, middle-class, civilized people who are then packed into cattle cars, as though the liquidation of illiterate peasants would not be so poignant. The now-familiar newsreel shot of Asian populations fleeing a slaughter with their meager possessions in handcarts still reads to us as a catastrophe involving "masses," while the images of Jews lined up in their fedoras and overcoats tug at our hearts precisely because we see the line as composed of individuals. Our very notion of individuality is historically connected with the middle class; on top of that, Jews have often stood for individuality in modern culture, by virtue of their outsider status and commitment to mind and artistic cultivation. I am by no means saying that all the Jews who died in the camps were bourgeois (on the contrary, the majority were poor religious peasants); I am suggesting that, since the bulk of the narratives focus on middle-class victims swept up in the slaughter, this may help account for why the murder of European Jews plays on our sympathies so much more profoundly in this culture than the annihilation of Bengalis, East Timorese, or Ibos. The most obvious explanation may be demographic: there are many more Jews in the United States than there are Ibos or Bengalis.

"What's wrong with you?" I hear certain Jewish readers ask. "Are you not closer to your own dead than to those others? It's understandable for blacks to care more about slavery than about the Holocaust, or Armenians to mourn more for their massacred than for ours. But why do you, a Jew, insist on speaking as if these others mattered the same as our own flesh and blood killed in the gas chambers?" I don't know; I must be lacking in tribal feeling. When it comes to mass murder, I can see no difference between their casualties and ours.

That we must continue to come to terms with the Holocaust is obvious. The questions are: What forms will these commemorations or confrontations take? And addressed to whom? And who will be allowed to speak? And what is the permissible range of discourse?

There exists at present the urgent sense that we must keep up the pressure of commemorating the Holocaust to counteract the poisons of the extremist "revisionist" historians, like Robert Faurisson. To be truthful, I don't believe that the Faurissons and their ilk, who deny that a mass extermination of Jews ever took place, pose a serious threat to altering the world's perception of the historical record. They are the lunatic fringe, which we will always have with us. It makes sense to be vigilant about them, but not so paranoid as to exaggerate their real persuasional powers.

As for the more moderate revisionist historians—such as

Andreas Hillgruber, who has tried to link the collapse of the eastern front with the death camps' greater activity and to propose that many German soldiers were heroically doing their duty—their views may set our teeth on edge with their insensitive tone or alarm us with their usefulness to the far right. But the greater threat they pose to the purity of our outrage is that some of what they say could hold a grain of truth. Is it reasonable to deny that some German soldiers in World War II may have been decent men victimized by the situation? Are we to divide the guilt by battalions—determine, as many are wont to do, that an ordinary German foot soldier may not have been entirely vicious, but that anyone in the S.S. was a sadistic criminal? I can well imagine a kid who didn't know better getting swept up in the mood of the day and joining the S.S. out of idealism. (One may scoff at the seeming oxymoron, Nazi idealist, yet every political movement generates its youthful idealists.)

I know of no event in recent years that has so united educated people in incredulous disgust as President Reagan's visit to the military cemetery in Bitburg, West Germany. At the time, glad to heap scorn on a President I despised, I heartily joined the chorus, although with a slight inner uneasiness that I was too cowardly to express. Now, thinking it over, I would say that it may not have been such a dastardly thing for the visiting President of a victorious nation to lay a wreath on the tomb of his defeated enemy's soldiers. The gesture contains a certain old-fashioned Homeric nobility. *But don't you understand? There were S.S. troops buried in that cemetery! Reagan was "signaling" the neofascists that all is forgiven.* Yes, yes, I remember that argument. To be fair to Reagan, he has also made tributes to the Holocaust. So what was really being objected to was appearances. We could not allow any reconciliation to appear to cloud the distinction between victims and culprits, radical good and radical evil, even if was perfectly obvious to all of us that Reagan was not condoning Nazism. The Holocaust has become a public issue around which Jews must Save Face, must spot anti-Semitism and decry it even when we know that the substance underneath is rather different.

A similar reaction occurred recently when the speaker of the West German parliament, Philipp Jenninger, made a speech in which he tried to show how the Germans were taken in by Hitler. In attempting to re-create the psychology of the typical German fascinated by Hitler's air of success, his irony was misunderstood—in some cases intentionally so by his political opponents—and he was forced to resign. Jenninger, a longtime supporter of Israel, was taken to task for saying honest things at the wrong time and, specifically, for quoting from Nazi speeches and reports without systematic, repudiating interruptions. Yet how is it possible to understand this complex historical phenomenon of the Holocaust without reexamining the Nazi point of view? What sort of intellectual grasp can we have of a historical situation if it is presented only from the standpoint of the horrors inflicted on the victims?

The "sensitivity" quotient operating around the Holocaust has begun to preclude any public discourse that goes beyond expressions of mourning and remorse. And even within that constricted discourse, how greedily we watch for signs of imbalance. Will the Pope single out sufficiently the tragedy of the Jews in his remarks about World War II? If not, Jewish organizations are quick to get on his case. There is something so testy, so vain, so divalike about this insistence that we always get top billing in any rite of mourning. Must every official statement that does not mention the Jews first among the dead be treated as an ominous sign of forgetting? Even if it were true that a certain resentment against the Jews, an incipient form of anti-Semitism, was lurking behind these official wordings or omissions, the result of all our monitoring and suspicious rebuttal is only to leave the impression of a Jewish lobby seeking to control like a puppeteer the language of politicians and Popes.

Whenever I see in the newspaper a story about the opening of yet another memorial or museum dedicated to the Holocaust, complete with photograph of distinguished backers surrounding a cornerstone or architectural model, my stomach gets nervous. What I need to figure for myself is how much this discomfit derives from legitimate doubts and how much it is simply the old fear of making ourselves too visible, drawing too much attention to Jewish things in a world that will never be anything but anti-Semitic. I would like to think, naturally, that there is more to it than cowardice. All right, then, what could possibly be wrong with a Holocaust memorial?

We will start with an obtuse response: I just don't get why both New York City and Washington, D.C., should have to have Holocaust memorial museums. Or why every major city in the United States seems to be commemorating this European tragedy in some way or another. An Israeli poet on a reading tour through the States was taken into the basement of a synagogue in Ohio and proudly shown the congregation's memorial to the 6 million dead: a torch meant to remain eternally lit. The poet muttered under his breath, "Shoah flambé." In Israel they can joke about these matters. Holocaust monuments seem to me primarily a sign of ethnic muscle-flexing, proof that the local Jewish community has attained enough financial and political clout to erect such a tribute to their losses.

In the past, monuments commemorated victories and glory; they were a striving for immortality in the eyes of the polis. But with the very survival of the planet in doubt, eroding our confidence in a future public realm, and in light of our disenchantment with the whole ideal of glory after Vietnam and Watergate, a patriotic equestrian monument raised at this moment would seem embarrassing. Myself, I can easily live without more cannons and generals on pedestals. On the other hand, the dethroning of glory has brought about a tendency to erect monuments to shame and historical nightmare. These monuments have an air of making the visitor feel bad, at the same time retaining a decorously remote and abstract air—all the more so when they are removed geographically from the ground of pain. Auschwitz is one thing: the historical preservation of the death camps in situ makes perfect sense. But it is quite another to allocate the bottom part of a new luxury apartment tower in Lower Manhattan to a Holocaust museum, for which the developer will receive the usual tax abatement.

Snobbish as this may sound, I view museums as primarily places for the exhibition and contemplation of interesting objects. Institutions like Yad Vashem (the Holocaust Heroes and Martyrs Museum) and the Museum of the Diaspora in Israel, which have few artifacts—consisting mainly of slide shows, blown-up photographs, and accompanying wall texts—are, in my view, essentially propaganda factories, designed to manipulate the visitor through a precise emotional experience. They are like a Tunnel of Horrors or a Disneyland park devoted to Jewish suffering. The success of the exhibit depends entirely on entering in a properly preprogrammed state and allowing one's buttons to be pushed.

A woman I know, the child of camp survivors, had grown up with tales of Hitler and Buchenwald at every meal. Finally she got to visit Yad Vashem. She was so bursting with emotion, so ready to be wiped out by the experience that, shortly after entering, she saw a lampshade and thought, Oh my God, that could be my uncle Morty! and ran in tears from the museum. Her companion caught up with her to try to calm her down. "But, Hilda," he said, "those lampshades are part of the exhibit showing a typical Jewish scholar's study, before the Holocaust even began."

In my own visit to Yad Vashem, I was part of a group of Jewish American academics who thought it so "heavy" that I didn't dare open my mouth. Some of the exhibits were undeniably interesting, but it was not an overwhelming experience for me; rather, I was disturbed by what seemed a theatrically partisan misuse of historical methods. I also found it hard to summon the 6 million dead in the face of such ennobling strain. The grounds were a sort of monument park filled with sentimental-expressionist statuary. Our tour guide explained that the steel pillar symbolized a smokestack as well as a ladder of transcendence. All this artistic symbolism talk reminded me of the remark of an Israeli friend: "If bad sculpture could be turned into food, then Israel could feed the world."

Yad Vashem's memorial hall did have a bleak architectural elegance of stone and concrete; but the fire (another "eternal flame") was upstaged by an ugly black organic relief, symbolizing charred bones, I suppose. Someone in my group produced a mimeographed poem, which we read aloud. It was all about the flame being a symbol for the slaughter, of eternal memory, of oppression—a list of pious abstractions clunkily metered and redundant. Why does the poem have to be so bad? I found myself thinking. It is at that level of kitsch doggerel that I start to rebel.

Will the above seem the ravings of a finicky aesthete? I apologize. But remember that it *is* an aesthetic problem we are talking about, this attempt to make an effective presentation of a massive event. The dead of Auschwitz are not buried in Yad Vashem; believe me, I am not insulting their memories. Yad Vashem is the product of us the living and as such is subject to our dispassionate scrutiny and criticism. To project religious awe onto this recently built tourist attraction is idolatry, pure and simple.

In a brilliant essay called "The Kitsch of Israel," which appeared in the *New York Review of Books*, Avishai Margalit wrote:

> Israel's shrine of kitsch is not, as may have been expected, the Wailing Wall, but a place that should have been furthest away from any trace of kitsch: Yad Vashem, the memorial for the Holocaust. A "children's room" has been dedicated there recently. . . . The real significance of this room is not in its commemoration of the single most horrible event in the history of mankind—the systematic murder of two million children, Jewish and Gypsies, for being what they were and not for anything they had done. The children's room, rather, is meant to deliver a message to the visiting foreign statesman, who is rushed to Yad Vashem even before he has had time to leave off his luggage at his hotel, that all of us here in Israel are these children and that Hitler-Arafat is after us. This is the message for internal consumption as well. Talking of the PLO in the

same tone as one talks of Auschwitz is an important element in turning the Holocaust into kitsch.

Another method of Holocaust remembrance takes the form of educational instruction in grade school. The pedagogic problem I have with these Holocaust study units is that they are usually parachuted into the classroom with very little connection to anything else in the curriculum. As someone who worked in elementary and secondary schools for twelve years, I've had many occasions to see how the latest concession to each ethnic lobbying group—be it Puerto Rican Week, Black History Month, or Holocaust Week—was greeted by the students as a gimmick, not to be taken seriously. I remember the morning that the local Holocaust curriculum person came into a fourth-grade classroom at P.S. 75 and in her sweet, solemn voice began describing the horrors of a concentration camp. The children listened with resentful politeness, distracted not necessarily because the subject matter was unsuitable for their age group but because any subject matter introduced in so artificial a manner, with so little relation to their other studies, would be treated as an intrusion.

I realize it may be asking a lot, but we should be attempting to teach the Holocaust within a broader context, as part of an invigorated, general strengthening of historical studies. Why isolate Hitler completely from Bismarck, Kaiser Wilhelm, Adenauer, Stalin? Why teach children about Buchenwald and not other genocides? The Holocaust becomes their first, sometimes their exclusive, official school instruction on death and evil. Of course, kids daily see war and gore on the six o'clock news, but in school we seem to want them to encounter the horrors of mass killing solely through presentations about the fate of the Jews. It is almost as if we Jews wanted to monopolize suffering, to appropriate death as our own. But as Irving Louis Horowitz points out, while Judaism as a way of life is special, there is no "special nature of Jewish dying. Dying is a universal property of many peoples, cultures and nations."

I cannot help but see this extermination pride as another variant of the Covenant: this time the Chosen People have been chosen for extraordinary suffering. As such, the Holocaust seems simply another opportunity for Jewish chauvinism. I grew up in Williamsburg, Brooklyn, surrounded by this chauvinistic tendency, which expressed itself as an insecure need to boast about Jewish achievements in every field, the other side of which was a contempt for the non-Jews, the gentiles, who were characterized as less intelligent, less human, less cultured, humorous, spicy, warmhearted, whatever. All my life I've tried to guard against the full force of this damaging tribal smugness, to protect myself from the weakening lies of group *amour propre* (not that I don't succumb regularly to my own form of it).

"Secularization," Hannah Arendt has written, ". . . engendered a very real Jewish chauvinism, if by chauvinism we understand the perverted nationalism in which (in the words of Chesterton) 'the individual himself is the thing to be worshipped; the individual is his own ideal and even his own idol.' From now on, the old concept of chosenness was no longer the essence of Judaism; it was instead the essence of Jewishness."

There are reasons other than chauvinism why Jews might be loath to surrender the role of the chief victim. It affords us an edge, a sort of privileged nation status in the moral honor roll, such as the Native American Indians have enjoyed for some time. Following Hitler's defeat, Jews had a short grace period in world opinion, pitied as we were and valued as an en-

dangered species. Given the world's tendency to distort and de-
monize Jews in the past, it would almost seem as though there
was no middle ground: either continue to fight for persecuted,
good-victim status or else watch the pendulum swing the opposite way, to where we would be regarded as exceptionally
wicked. But in my opinion, there must be a middle ground, and
it is worth fighting for. In the meantime, is it not possible for
us to have a little more compassion for the other victimized
peoples of this century and not insist quite so much that our
wounds bleed more fiercely?

Theodor Adorno once made an intentionally provocative
statement to the effect that one can't have lyric poetry after
Auschwitz. Much as I respect Adorno, I am inclined to ask, a
bit faux-naively: Why not? Are we to infer, regarding all the
beautiful poetry that has been written since 1945, that these
postwar poets were insensitive to some higher tact? Alexander
Kluge, the German filmmaker, has explained what Adorno really meant by this remark: any art from now on that does not
take Auschwitz into account will be not worthy as art. This is
one of those large intimidating pronouncements to which one
gives assent in public while secretly harboring doubts. Art is a
vast arena; must it all and always come to terms with the death
camps, important as they are? How hoggish, this Holocaust, to
insist on putting its stamp on all creative activity.

On the other hand, reams have been written arguing that
you *can't* make art out of the Holocaust. Elie Wiesel once declared, "Art and Auschwitz are antithetical." Perhaps people
would like to believe that there is some preserve, some domain
that ought to be protected from the artist's greedy hands. Ac-

tually, a whole body of splendid art about the tragedy of the Jews under the Nazis has been made. One thinks right away of Primo Levi's books, the poems of Paul Celan and Nelly Sachs, Tadeusz Kantor's theatrical pieces, films like Resnais's *Night and Fog*, Ophüls's *The Sorrow and the Pity* and *Hotel Terminus*, Losey's *Mr. Klein*, Corti's trilogy *Where To and Back*. . . . Maybe not a lot, true, but then not much great art came out of the debacle of World War I. We should not forget that 99 percent of all art-making attempts are failures, regardless of subject matter.

It has also been argued that the enormity of the Nazis' crimes against the Jews calls for an aesthetic approach of an entirely different order than the traditional mimetic response. This seems to me nothing more than a polemic in favor of certain avant-garde or antinaturalist techniques, hitched arbitrarily to the Holocaust. Yes, Paul Celan's cryptic, abstract poems are powerful approaches to the concentration camps, but so are Primo Levi's direct, lucid accounts. I would not like to think that every stage piece about the Holocaust must perforce follow the stripped, ritualized strategies of Grotowski's or Kantor's theatrical works—effective as these may be by themselves— out of some deluded idea that a straight naturalistic approach would desecrate the 6 million dead.

Art has its own laws, and even so devastating an event as the Holocaust may not significantly change them. For all its virtues, the longeurs, repetitions, and failures of sympathy in Claude Lanzmann's *Shoah* are not exonerated, no matter what its apologists may argue, by the seriousness of the subject matter, as though an audience must be put through over eight hours of an exhaustingly uneven movie to convince it of the reality of the Holocaust. A tighter film would have accomplished the same and been a stronger work of art. Lanzmann might reply that he is indifferent to the claims of art compared to those of the Holocaust; unfortunately, you can't play the game of art and not play it at the same time.

What is usually meant by the statement that the Holocaust is unsuitable for artistic treatment is that it is too vast and terrible to be used merely as a metaphor or backdrop. Certainly I understand the impatience of serious people with the parade of shallow movie melodramas and television docudramas that invoke the milieu of Nazi Germany as a sort of narrative frisson. Indeed, where would the contemporary European art film be without the Holocaust? As a plot device it is second only to infidelity. For the fractured European film market, the trauma of World War II is perhaps the only unifying historical experience to which narratives can appeal commercially. Yet the mediocrity of such "prestige" movies as Truffaut's *The Last Metro*, Visconti's *The Damned*, Zanussi's *Somewhere in the Night*, Malle's *Lacombe, Lucien*, De Sica's *The Garden of the Finzi-Continis*, Szabo's *Hanussen*, among others, illustrates the degree to which—even for talented directors—the Nazi terror has ossified into a stale genre, a ritualized parade of costumes and sentimental conventions, utterly lacking in the authentic texture of personally observed detail. Now we have the Third Reich as dress-up: all those red flags with swastikas, those jeeps and jackboots suddenly flashing in key-lit night scenes, the tinkle of broken glass—accoutrements that seem considerably less menacing in Technicolor, by the way, than they used to in black and white. We have endless variations of the *Cabaret* plot, as characters flounder in frivolous, "decadent" sexual confusion before the evil Nazis announce themselves at midpoint and restore order and narrative suspense in one blow. The Gestapo represents the principle of Fate rescuing the story from its aim-lessness—a screenwriter's best friend. The Jewish protagonists are pulled, at first unknowingly, into that funnel of history, then gradually learn that there is something larger than their personal discontents. Meanwhile, the Christian characters sort themselves into betrayers and noble selfless neighbors, thanks to the litmus test of the Holocaust plot; and the audience read-ies itself for that last purgative scene, the lineup before the trains. . . .

To enumerate the clichés is not to agree with the viewpoint that no art can be made about the Holocaust. Quite the con-trary; it is only to demand that the artist go beyond a senti-mental, generic approach to the subject and find a more com-plex, detailed, personal, and original path.

I have a former student, Bella, whose father was always try-ing to get her to see Resnais's *Night and Fog,* an admittedly fine film about the death camps. The father believed that we must all deal in one way or another with the Holocaust, and his way, as befit an educated man, was to read as many books and to see as many films on the subject as possible. This approach he urged on his daughter. But Bella did not want to see *Night and Fog.* As a child she had had many phobias, and even after she had outgrown them, there was something about the way her fa-ther talked up the film that made her leery. He would try to get her to meet him at a movie theater where it was showing. He kept saying, "But you owe it to *them* to see it." Them: the ghosts, the 6 million.

Bella refused. Since that time she has moved to Israel and is leading, in her own way, a good Jewish life.

What are our obligations to *them?* Whatever they may be, no living person can tell us.

While I also read books or see movies on the Holocaust, I do it more out of a sense of cultural curiosity and desire to learn about history than a religious debt to the victims. I am not convinced that learning history means trying to put oneself emotionally through the experience—or blaming oneself if one is not feeling enough.

I am trying to put my finger on a problem regarding empathy. A Jewish educator recently wrote that we must find a way to make our young people "feel more anguishingly the memory of the dead." But the effort to project oneself into the Holocaust, to "undergo" for a few minutes what others have suffered in the transport trains and the camps, to take that anguish into oneself, seems—except in rare cases—foredoomed. That way generally lies tourism and self-pity. It is hard enough in psychoanalysis to retrieve affectively one's own past, one's actual memories; to expect to relive with emotion invented memories seems overly demanding. Or gimmicky: like those black history courses that made the students crawl along the floor "chained" to each other to give them an existential feel for conditions in the hold of a slave ship.

False knowledge. Borrowed mysticism. By blackmailing ourselves into thinking that we must put ourselves through a taste of Auschwitz, we are imitating unconsciously the Christian mystics who tried to experience in their own flesh the torments of Christ on the cross. But this has never been part of the Jewish religion, this gluttony for empathic suffering. Though Jewish rabbis and sages have been killed for their faith, and their deaths recorded and passed down, Judaism has fought shy in the past of establishing a hagiography based on martyrdom. Why are we doing it now?

In certain ways, the Jewish American sacramentalizing of the Holocaust seems an unconscious borrowing of Christian theology. That one tragic event should be viewed as standing outside, above history, and its uniqueness defended and proclaimed, seems very much like the Passion of Christ. Indeed, in a recent book, *The Crucifixion of the Jews*, Christian theologian Franklin H. Littell has argued that the true crucifixion *was* the Holocaust, not the death of Jesus on the cross, and that the subsequent establishment of the State of Israel was the Resurrection. Littell asks, "Was Jesus a false Messiah? . . . Is the Jewish people, after all and in spite of two millennia of Christian calumny, the true Suffering Servant promised in Isaiah?" And John Cardinal O'Connor of New York wrote, "To say to the Jews, 'Forget the Holocaust,' is to say to Christians, 'Forget the Crucifixion.' There is a sacramentality about the Holocaust for Jews all around the world. It constitutes a mystery, by definition beyond their understanding—and ours." Soothing as all this may sound, it worries me because it shows how easily Judaism can be Christianized—or at least co-opted into a Christian vocabulary—by mythologizing the Holocaust experience.

The theological uses to which the Holocaust has been put by an assimilated American Jewish community are so diverse that the Holocaust has begun to replace the Bible as the new text that we must interpret. There is the danger that the "glamour" of the Holocaust will eclipse traditional religious practice in the eyes of American Jewry—that, in effect, the Holocaust will swallow up Judaism. In the vacuum where God used to be, we are putting the Holocaust.

I first began to notice the usurpation of the traditional Passover service by Holocaust worship at a large communal seder in Houston, around 1982. Though rewritings of the Haggadah were nothing new to me (in the late sixties, the Vietcong were compared to the Jews in Egypt trying to throw off their oppressors), the introduction of references to the Holocaust in every second or third prayer seemed to have a different function. For many of the people at that seder in Texas, the Holocaust *was* the heart of their faith; it was what touched them most deeply about being Jewish. The religion itself—the prayers, the commentaries, the rituals, the centuries of accumulated wisdom and tradition—had shriveled to a sort of marginally necessary preamble for this negative miracle. The table conversation turned to accounts of pilgrimages to Buchenwald and Bergen-Belsen and Auschwitz, package tours organized by the United Jewish Appeal. The ancient Jewish religion was all but forgotten beside the lure of the concentration camp universe.

The importance of the Holocaust for such assimilated Jews must be considered within the broader framework of the erosion of Jewish group memory in the modern period. By group or "collective" memory, I mean simply all the customs, rituals, ceremonies, folkways, *Yiddishkeit*, cuisine, historical events, and so on, that used to be the common inheritance of every Jew. The desperation to hold on to the Holocaust is informed by this larger decay. Underneath these anxious injunctions never to forget, what I hear is "We must never forget the Holocaust because we're rapidly forgetting everything else, so let's hold on at least to this piece."

At first glance it seemed to me a paradox that Jews, ostensibly "the historically minded people" par excellence, should be so resistant to placing the Holocaust in a comparative historical context. But then I came across an illuminating little book by Yosef Yerushalmi, *Zakhor: Jewish History and Jewish Memory,* which argues that antihistorical currents are nothing new within Jewry. The oft-repeated injunction to "remember" is not the same as urging a historical perspective: "Not only is Israel under no obligation whatever to remember the entire past, but its principle of selection is unique unto itself. It is above all God's acts of intervention in history, and man's responses to them, be they positive or negative, that must be recalled."

Yerushalmi points out that for nearly fifteen centuries after the death of Josephus, during the Talmudic period so fertile for commentary about the patterns and meaning of the Bible, there were no Jewish historians. The rabbis felt it unnecessary and perhaps even impious to keep contemporary historical records (except for sketchy rabbinic genealogies), precisely because the Bible was already "sacred history." A brief flurry of Jewish history writing occurred in the sixteenth century, partly touched off by the need to understand the catastrophic expulsion from Spain and Portugal; but these chronicles were not so scientific as Christian histories of the same era; they had elements of messianism and followed a somewhat apocalyptic approach, examining the past for signs and prophecies of an approaching redemption. Even this limited historical activity was submerged, at the end of the sixteenth century, by the greater appeal of Lurianic Kabbalah, which offered Jews "a unique interpretation of history that lay beyond history . . . an awesome metahistorical myth of a pronounced gnostic character. That myth declared that all evil, including the historical evil that is Jewish exile, had its roots before history began, before the Garden of Eden was planted, before our world existed, in a primal tragic flaw that occurred at the very creation of the cosmos itself" (Yerushalmi).

In the modern era, of course, a plethora of Jewish histories and historians came into being, but the new objective methods of analysis have been on a collision course with providential history. "To the degree that this historiography is indeed 'modern' and deserves to be taken seriously," notes Yerushalmi, "it must at least functionally repudiate" two cardinal assumptions of traditional Judaism: "the belief that divine providence is not only an ultimate but an active causal factor in Jewish history, and the related belief in the uniqueness of Jewish history itself."

Forgive this digression; it actually has a point. Our response to the Holocaust must be seen within this broader framework of the ancient Jewish ambivalence toward a historical outlook, which threatens the religious one. The hostility toward anything that questions the uniqueness of the Holocaust can now be seen as part of a deeper tendency to view all of Jewish history as "unique," to read that history selectively, and to use it only insofar as it promotes a redemptive script. Thus, the Holocaust's "mystery" must be asserted over and over, in the same way as the "mystery" of Jewish survival was through the ages, in order to yield the single explanation that God "wants" the Jewish people to live and is protecting them. Being a secular, fallen Jew with a taste for rationalism and history, I cannot help but regard such providential interpretations as superstition. Against them I would place the cool, cautionary wisdom of Spinoza about his own people: "as for their continuance so long after dispersion and the loss of empire, there is nothing marvelous in it."

Sometimes I see the Jewish preoccupation with the Holocaust, to the exclusion of all other human disasters, as uncharitable, self-absorbed, self-righteous, and—pushy. On the other hand, it makes no sense to counsel putting it aside for a while. How can we expect to get over so enormous a tragedy in only forty or fifty years? It takes time, centuries. It took over a thousand years for the Jews as a people to get over the destruction of Jerusalem by Titus, and we may still not have recovered from that. My problem is not that the grief is taking too long but that the orchestration of that grief in the public realm sometimes seems coercive and misguided.

Jewish history is filled with disasters, from which some redemptive meaning has ultimately been extracted. The Holocaust is proving to be a large bone to swallow; it does not turn "redeemable" so easily, and when we try to hurry up that process with mechanical prescriptions and ersatz rituals, compelling governments and churches to pay verbal tribute to our losses in narrowly defined terms, and browbeating our young people to feel more anguishingly the memory of our dead, something false, packaged, sentimentally aggressive begins to enter the picture. Perhaps the problem is that for many alienated, secularized Jews who experience themselves as inauthentic in a thousand other ways, the Holocaust has become the last proof of their own authenticity. If so, they should realize that even this proof is perishable stuff; the further one gets from personal experience, the harder it is to take the spilled blood of history into one's veins.

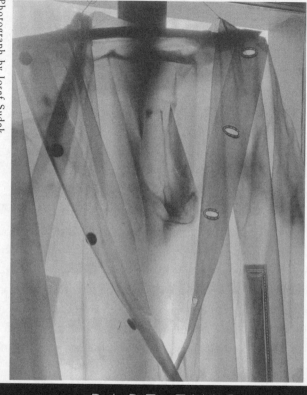

Photograph by Josef Sudek

PART TWO:

THE INESCAPABLE EGO

ON LEAVING BACHELORHOOD

As I stood under the canopy with my beautiful blushing bride, she kept whispering to me to move closer to her. Apparently I was angling sternward—to my mind, merely giving the guests a better chance to see the ceremony, though perhaps some last unconscious resistance also came into play. The rabbi was making his opening remarks to the assembled, and in my wedding stupor I heard him joke, "Earlier tonight, Phillip's publisher agreed to issue a compendium of his essays, to be called *Against Bachelorhood.*" The crowd chuckled, especially those who knew that my previous essay collections had been entitled *Bachelorhood* and *Against Joie de Vivre.* I chuckled too, though I had heard the joke, or variations on it, many times in the preceding weeks and was starting to lose my sense of humor about being the butt of everyone else's.

People seemed to find it vastly amusing that I, "Mr. Bachelor," was being led to the altar. Those who were already married seemed smug in the swelling of their ranks; those who were not, but wanted to, took hope that if I could do it, anyone could; while the single friends of mine who intended to remain solo—even disapproved of marriage on political grounds—wore a superior, shrewd expression that said, "What fools these mortals be."

Why *had* I chosen to leave bachelorhood? To start with, I had never felt like an unregenerate bachelor. In fact, I had been married once before, at the unripe age of twenty; and though the marriage fell apart after four years, the experience had had plenty of tender, rejuvenating moments, and was certainly not bad enough as to sour me off wedlock permanently. So I began looking for another mate. I dated, I had affairs, relationships, call them what you will; in any event, I was serially monogamous, and in between involvements, alone for large chunks of time. What was meant to be a "transitional period" lasted twenty-one years.

Somewhere during this stretch, I concocted a literary persona of a curmudgeonly bachelor, which allowed me to report on the world from an ironic, unattached, mischievous, singular perspective. Though I never advocated bachelorhood as preferable to marriage, I certainly felt sympathy for those, like myself, who lived in isolation. And perhaps, in exaggerating for effect my narrator's cranky refusal to join the desperate American pursuit of happiness, I tended to satirize the bourgeois presumptions of cozy coupledom. Yet all the while, I never lost sight of the fact that this handy literary construct was just that, a construct. All the while, in my hours away from the desk, I kept searching, searching, searching for—a wife.

The world, however (or that small part of it which knew my essays), tended to accept this bachelorly literary persona as my true self. I may even have become a challenge to a certain kind of ambitious or masochistic woman who thought, Aha, here will be an interesting, tough nut to crack! Such an approach provided the woman with a built-in excuse later. When the romance collapsed, her support group could tell her, "What did you expect from a man who writes a book called *Bachelorhood?* He's obviously incapable of sustained intimacy, and terrified of commitment."

To the best of my knowledge, I personally never felt I was terrified of commitment. Cautious, yes, but not quaking. What did give me pause was the thought of marrying someone with whom, I was pretty sure, I would be miserable for the rest of my life. Of course, one could say (and many did) that I was just too picky; I was focusing on the problems because I didn't want to get married. The way I saw it, however, was that I just hadn't found the right person.

I could only marvel at the disparity between the way I saw myself and the way I—and the whole male species—tended to be described. Widely dissected in women's magazines and female gatherings, we men were often viewed as aliens who needed to be trapped, via strategy and stealth, and colonized by a superior civilization for our own good. It was routinely asserted that women were more emotionally honest than men, women made better friends with their sex than men did with theirs (women had genuine friendships, while men had to go through a debased form of intimacy called "male bonding"), women would bring about world peace if enough were voted into public office, women had a more significant role to play historically at this juncture, and women were by and large more interesting and had more character than their male contemporaries. These soothing but by no means self-axiomatic propositions were capped by the assertion that the city was filled with brilliant, accomplished, ravishing single women trying to locate and corral a handful of neurotic, emotionally re-tarded, largely undeserving males, who were glutted with date possibilities.

Why had I not found this to be the case? What was wrong with me that, living in a supposed Golden Age for bachelors, I still found it hard to make a suitable match? Well—many of the most desirable women I met turned out to be either mar-ried or involved with someone; others who were both desirable and available didn't happen to be attracted to me, which was certainly their right; and still others, frankly, weren't all that interesting. I may have had more opportunities, thanks to the demographics of the situation, to go out with women I didn't especially want to go out with than a single woman of my age and cultivation had to date men *she* didn't especially want to go out with. But true love is rare under any circumstances; and if one is at all refined, unique, idiosyncratic, then finding a companion to match one's temperament, interests, and ama-tory tastes is not an easy matter, whether one is a man or woman, straight or gay.

Many women (taking their cues, perhaps, from the slick magazines) tended to adapt a strategic mentality designed to lead an unwitting bachelor step-by-step into matrimony. The problem with this approach was that it was based on the ques-tionable premise that men don't know what they want, so women must manipulate them into it. I once was involved with a woman who went around town telling people (word of which got back to me later) that she was going to marry me as soon as I figured out what she already knew—that I was madly in love with her. I tend to think a man knows when he is madly in love; in any case, that was one wedding ceremony that never happened.

In general, I wonder if men are at all as ignorant of their

emotions, or reluctant to express them, as women claim. There is a type of woman who practices a form of self-deception in the face of a man's emotional honesty by denying what he *is* telling her while claiming that he can't bring himself to say what he is actually feeling. I admit that, as a writer, I may be less shy about uncovering or exposing my feelings than other men. Still, I don't think my experiences are as atypical as all that. There were times when I tried to be truthful about the ambivalent, shifting nature of my feelings, only to be chastised for speaking too "clinically." Another woman told me just to stop when I told her what I was feeling—I needn't be so "brutally frank." Her reaction, while understandable, suggested that it is often less a question of male emotional reticence as of the man's failing to follow the romantic script set out for him.

Just as men are prone to declare the contemporary equivalent of "Dames!" when a love affair ends, so women reassure themselves today with the thought that the men out there are "pathologically skittish." Maybe so; but there are also cases when a man will fight shy of commitment because he suspects—with good reason—that it can't work out. Such hesitations may be based on self-knowledge derived from past experience, which is what we mean by wisdom. The woman tends to think, He just doesn't know his own heart—he'll come around; while the man is thinking, I know what I want all right and this isn't it. I advise women to listen intently to men's expressions of reluctance, and not assume these are simply a form of masculine coyness.

That was, in any event, what I liked to tell myself. I had lots of rationales worked out for this cul-de-sac—a whole philosophy of breakups, in fact. Living through them, however, was a nightmare. Each time I seemed to hit a wall: a claustrophobic, remorseful intuition that, whatever the initial optimism had been, we were doomed as a couple. I fell prey to a system of Gulliverian distortions, which made the woman I was going out with appear, after a time, disconcertingly smaller, more predictable, and more circumscribed than I had first perceived. I would zero in on her insecurities and depressive qualities without acknowledging that, at least in part, what made her so depressed or insecure was the irresoluteness of our relationship, thanks to me.

All this while there was growing in me a stubborn desire to get married—partly just to show 'em and partly to avoid breaking another heart. Up to a point, you can derive a cruel, vengeful lift against the opposite sex from ending an affair; but after a number of such episodes, the excitement flattens out, and you are left with self-disgust. For me, that point occurred, I think, when I had to watch someone I was extraordinarily fond of and close to for years suffer right in front of my eyes, like an animal keeling over in pain. Each time after that, when I anticipated having to tell a woman with whom I'd been intimate that it wasn't going to work out, I felt a self-revulsion bordering on loathing, like a serial killer who can't snap out of his pattern but writes on the wall of his last victim, "Stop me before I kill again." Yes, it was usually I who broke it off, not that that meant much: the women who might have called it quits first had already rejected me at the start, whereas the ones whose love I'd won over had invested too much momentum and pride to throw in the towel. Feminism's best efforts notwithstanding, the structure of contemporary courtship still often dictates that the woman try to wring a marriage proposal or some commitment from the man, regardless of her own inner doubts and aversions.

In any case, I discovered that rejection is a two-edged
sword: it becomes impossible to hurt someone without hurting
yourself. Long after the ordeal of such a parting, I would dread
starting with anyone again if it meant the likelihood of a similar breakup in the future. I was well into my forties; I was thoroughly sick of playing the reluctant partner who could not
come through in the end; the stages of my own romantic disenchantment seemed, even to me, trumped-up and stale; dating's variety had long ago lost its spice; and the prospect of explaining my past to yet another stranger over dinner gave me
the willies.

Then I met Cheryl. A mutual friend introduced me to this
dark-eyed painter with an Italian name, Cipriani, who was in
her mid-thirties and who had been widowed young—a fact
that held a certain imaginative romantic appeal. She had a serious, thoughtful, mature air, which was immediately visible,
and a lively sense of humor, which was not, and it became my
mission to get her to laugh again. She lived in a loft in
Williamsburg, Brooklyn, the neighborhood where, coinciden-
tally, I had grown up. At the time, I had a column on architecture and urbanism in the weekly magazine *7 Days*, and contrived the ruse of getting her to conduct me around the new,
bohemian Williamsburg as my tour guide, while I observed
her.

On this our first "date" (it was one in my mind, not in
hers), a tour of the neighborhood, she told me that she was not
interested in a relationship, or in getting married again, or in
having children. Fortunately, I did not take her at her word. I
pressed on, the next time declaring my romantic interest in
her; she reacted with alarm and said she was not ready for involvements; I pouted; she turned around and pursued. After
several of these advances and retreats, I knew I was in love

with her. She struck me—partly because of her goodness, partly because of her willingness to laugh at herself and me—as someone with whom I could imagine sharing daily life. Beneath her restrained manner, she was gifted with an expressive face that let me know at all times what she was feeling. I trusted her, not only because we shared the same values and enjoyed a strong physical attraction but because I felt the absence of something: that old, dry dread. Not encountering the usual resistance inside me, I was exhilarated to be able to throw myself into a new role. If in the past I had been timid about my amorous verbal expressions, for fear of raising false hopes, now I rejoiced in swamping Cheryl with "I love you"s. It was certainly sincere, but there was also the eagerness to try out a reckless, ardent, active persona. This forwardness was enhanced by the fact that Cheryl is herself more reticent, slower to declare her heart. So I became the aggressive suitor, wooing her and trying to dispel her hesitations, her widow's qualms.

Six months after we started going out, one moonlit night in July at Bennington, Vermont, swept away by love and well-being, I asked, "Will you marry me?" "Yes," she said. One would think such an exchange was unequivocal in its meaning; but the next day, when I was full of joy and pride in the step I had taken, Cheryl went into a deep funk, wondering what she had got herself into, and told me she had only answered "yes" theoretically, in response to what she took to be a hypothetical probe from my side, such as: Would you consider marrying me if I were to ask you?

I somehow managed to convince Cheryl that I had indeed proposed and that she had accepted me. But that was only the beginning of many other negotiable issues: how soon to tell our parents; what date to set for the wedding; whether to have a modest celebration or a large, costly, catered affair; where we would live; whose furniture would go into the joint apartment.

On most of these questions I deferred to Cheryl. All that I asked was that we be married by a rabbi instead of a civil servant, as in my first marriage. It was a hunch, a gut instinct that I didn't know how to explain, since I am hardly religious and Cheryl is only half-Jewish, on her mother's side, and grew up with very little exposure to Judaism. She was nervous that playing the role of the good Jewish bride might involve some hypocrisy, and that the traditional religious wedding service might be sexist or otherwise counter to her taste. But she agreed, largely for my sake, and the rabbi helped to allay her concerns.

We had opted, in the end, for a large, costly, catered affair, to accommodate both sets of friends and relatives. Cheryl, a perfectionist in all matters of visual style, took over the spectacle's mise en scène. Up until the actual wedding day, I was conscious of trying to coax Cheryl out of her anxieties about logistics—Azuma had run out of Chinese lanterns, the sorbet delivery had been delayed, the pepperberry branches were shedding on the floor, the caterer was having a nervous breakdown, and the bride had still not purchased her shoes—and of wondering if underneath these anxieties lay a larger doubt on her part. I think I was suppressing some of my own fears and qualms to set a good example. I became, theatrically, almost bullyingly, the true believer in this marriage. Of course, Cheryl assured me again and again, she also wanted to marry me, with all her heart; but a part of me petulantly refused to believe, accusing her of not being really happy—or happy enough—that we were getting married. It was as though I wanted her to appreciate the huge "gift" that I was bestowing, which I had de-nied so many women before her. I was being insufferable. I was leaving bachelorhood.

Then came the wedding night. Cheryl, serene, beaming, wearing a hunter green gown, looked so happy everyone commented on it. As we took our places under the canopy, I kept slumping and reminding myself to stand up straight. I, the old bachelor, felt disoriented, outclassed by the radiance of her love. I kept stealing glances at the gathering, as though their expressions would tell me whether I was doing it right. Then, in a daze, I would look across at Cheryl and take heart from her smile, the pressure of her hand. How pretty she looked! This was the only thought I could hold on to with clarity as the rabbi read from his texts. Our friend Max Apple came forward with the rings. Everyone seemed moved by the event, oddly overjoyed for us, this unexpected nuptial pair: the hardened bachelor, the stubborn widow. I sensed their approval rolling toward me in disconcerting waves, through the fog and the reflexive skepticism clogging up my head. When I had broken the glass and the last words of the ritual were pronounced, I took my bride in my arms and gave her a long, long kiss. Of all places to hide at that moment, I could think of none better than her lips and her arms.

DETACHMENT AND PASSION

Now that I am securely married, I often think back to my bachelor days, indulging in this candy store of my imagination an occasional mental infidelity with an ex–girl friend who will come around to haunt me for a few days. I will picture her face or skin, recall a scent, try to revive the shock her beauty gave me the first time she undressed; or else the opposite, certain annoying tics, dry Sunday brunches, her betrayals or my cruelties. Lately I have been thinking about Claire. I find her floating in my consciousness more than others who had far more connection with me. Perhaps the very fact that ours was a middling affair makes me brood about her, as over an unsolved riddle. But more likely, it is simply because she died young.

I first met Claire through my sister Molly: they were "dharma buddies" and best friends. Neither Claire's Buddhism nor her friendship with my sister would have been recommendations to me, being a skeptic in both spiritual and familial matters. My inclination was not to go out with any of Molly's social circle. In the best of circumstances, it is a loaded situation: there is something humiliating, not to mention bordering on incestuous, about an older brother preying on his younger sister's friends. If the romance takes, then the sister may feel she has lost a friendship; if it sours, she may have to choose sides.

Added to these qualms were my complicated feelings about Molly. Briefly: My sister is almost exactly to the day a year younger than I am. At times we've been as close as twins. During the period I'm writing about, however, her Billie Holiday, femme fatale, and Kerouac adventuress stages behind her, she was going through a rather shrill, strident period, rationalizing disappointments in love or work with what sounded to me like spiritual eyewash. She had developed the neophyte convert's verbal armor, which gave her answers for every occasion. Granted, I was not as open as I might have been to receiving lectures about compassion from a younger sister; but inwardly I distanced myself from her, against those moments of possession by her Buddhist dybbuk.

Underneath the rigid sunniness of my sister's new-found wisdom, I sensed, she was lonely and depressed. In fact, I liked her much better when she was *openly* depressed: only then did she seem her old, cynical, Marquise de Merteuil self, freed from those Pollyanna smile-faces of her manic positive mode. Of course, it was easy for me to say, "Just be *sad*, for God's sake, stop acting." Perhaps with Molly, the pain ran so deep, the self-criticism was so severe, that any display of serenity, even the most synthetic, should have been preferred.

If I suspected my sister was deluding herself, what did it say about Claire that she hung around Molly? Eager though I was

to discount this Claire, the few times I met her at social gatherings I liked her quick, amusing, unimpinging manner. There
was a pleasing, ladylike coolness about her, embodied by her
smooth, creamy skin. Whatever doubts I may have had did not
stand a chance, finally—especially after my steady girlfriend
and I had broken up and I was once again "available"—before
the fact that Claire was so pretty. She had long black hair that
fell in symmetrical plaits to her shoulders, and a sympathetic,
perky, forties face with a dimpled lipsticked smile, and—this
especially caught my attention—a gorgeous figure. I am sorry
to have been so superficial about it, but there it is. At the time,
I was led into many chagrins and contretemps, allegedly beneath my level of intelligence, by the attempt to sleep with
beautiful women whenever possible. I have since repented.

In any event, Molly brought her friend, looking particularly
ravishing in a blue silk dress, to the book party for my novel
Confessions of Summer, and Claire bought a copy, got me to sign
it, and kissed me on the cheek. That was all the stimulus I
needed.

Having made up my mind to go after her, however, I suddenly felt hesitant about the difference in our aesthetic sta-
tions: she was a beauty and I was—a passable-looking intellectual with glasses. Shortly after the book party, I called Molly
and asked if her friend was seeing anyone at the moment. As
far as she knew, Molly said Claire was seeing several guys, but
none seriously. Not quite the answer I'd hoped for, yet it left
the door open. Did she know if—*were* I to ask Claire out—she
would be receptive or not? Molly guaranteed nothing. "She's in
the phone book. Ask her yourself. What's the worst that can
happen? If she turns you down, it has nothing to do with your
attractiveness; she may be sexually programmed to go for cer-

tain types of guys." This sisterly sagacity irked me; what I'd wanted was inside information. "Couldn't you at least—sound her out? Oh, forget it. I'll make the call."

So I asked Claire to dinner, she accepted, and we began to get to know each other. I found her remarkably easy to talk to. Claire was a freelance magazine writer and, like most journalists, up on just about everything. She played smoothly the traditional feminine role of drawing out the male's concerns and listening flatteringly and flirtatiously, however boorish she might think him. In short, she knew how to "date," as an activity enjoyable in itself, without being consumed, as I was, by the suspense of whether or not we would go to bed together.

It was the winter of 1979. I had just turned thirty-six, Claire was thirty-one; we were both veterans of the liberated sixties. She told me she'd even been a waitress at Max's Kansas City, the downtown art bar, in its heyday; I could picture her wearing a long braid, turning heads wherever she went. "I was never a groupie, but I did have a rock musician boyfriend." How could I compete?

Sometimes, at the beginning of an affair—or to make it *be* an affair—one has to leap into another persona. On our third date we went to an expensive disco supper club, Regine's, on Park Avenue, a place for international jet-setters that ordinarily I wouldn't be caught dead in; but I was trying to show that I could be "fun," not just the bookish highbrow I seemed to be. And Claire told me she liked to dance. So we danced; we drank; we watched with superior amusement the short gray-haired South American (ex-dictator?) rhumba with his statuesque blond starlet partner, the European investment brokers stationed in America trying to boogie, the account executives grinding away like day laborers to Gloria Gaynor's "I Will Survive." New York had narrowly averted bankruptcy in 1975; the memory of that near catastrophe still fresh, we were feeling the start of the Boom, artificially fueled by foreign investments; the bacchanale of the eighties was approaching; and Regine's, now defunct, harbingered an era that promised to be as indestructible as vulgarity itself.

Our amused mood persisted in the taxi, driving through the lamplit Park Avenue snow to Claire's house (she had given the cabbie her address, half the answer to the question I wanted answered), and lust proved a natural outgrowth of margaritas and mirth. But even after we had slept together that first time, I still wondered if Claire was attracted to me or simply being a gracious hostess. Always pleasant, sexy, responsibly conversational, good-humored, she never abandoned her impersonal self-composure. It was not so much what she expressed as what she didn't: urgency, hunger. She seemed more intent on offering me the continuing integrity of solitude and privacy.

For the most part, I took my cues from her, which meant returning tenderness for tenderness, moderation for moderation. We continued to go out, to enjoy ourselves, to perform the act of greatest potential intimacy between human beings; and it continued—not to matter very much.

One night, after we'd made love and I'd fallen asleep, I was awakened by her hand on my penis. It surprised me: not that I'd failed to satisfy her completely, but that she'd brought herself this once to admit a need. I would like to think I honored her request, but memory draws a veil. . . . What I do recall is my overall puzzlement at not being more excited about sleeping with this *dish.* I began to cast about for some way to blame her for my own lack of intense desire; I watched her for subtle indications of "putting me off," as though she were responsible for extruding an aura around herself, like a seducing Circe, but in reverse, a cloud of unexcitement that neutralized her beauty's effect.

I noticed that if, for instance, I complimented Claire on the way she looked, she would reply "You're such a dear" or "You're sweet" with an abstracted, dismissive air, as though she thought I'd been laying it on too thick. Was this simply the reaction of a pretty woman for whom compliments had become boring? Or perhaps she was saying, "What do looks mean, after all, in the larger, karmic scheme of things?" On the other hand, maybe she was self-conscious and critical of her appearance, so that "You're sweet" might be interpreted as *"You* may think I look like a model, but *I* know I have tons of flaws, a bumpy nose, too hippy," etc.

I began to notice also, at first because it seemed another form of resistance to me (as in: "Don't kiss me, my mouth must taste like an ashtray") but later, as a curious phenomenon in and of itself, that she would often complain about something somatically off-register, which kept her from optimum functioning: she had sinus headaches; the pressure of deadlines and caffeine was making her jumpy, or the lack of work, sluggishly woozy; she had slept too much, too little, had insomnia, got up too late, was tired all the time, watched too many late-night movies on the tube, smoked too many cigarettes, hadn't eaten a decent meal all week, felt fat, queasy, bloated, the greasy English muffins were sitting on her stomach, refusing to digest. At first I responded sympathetically, suggesting Coca-Cola to settle the stomach; later, I treated these anxieties as an ongoing subvocal burble that periodically rose to the surface. Were they not also her shield, or a garbled text whose gist was: *You don't understand me, all sorts of thoughts and sensations are going on con-*

stantly inside me of which you haven't the faintest idea. Any woman might think that of any man, and be correct.

Once, out of the blue, she said to me, "You seem like a happy person."

"Happy is hardly the way I look at it," I replied, immediately on guard. Was she trying to assuage her guilt toward me? Getting ready to dump me? "I feel I'm in the middle of my life. I'm absorbed, I'm doing the work I want to do, and that's almost enough for me. What about you?"

"Hmm?" she asked absentmindedly, as if responding to a faulty long-distance connection.

"Are you happy?"

"Oh, sure. I'm basically a happy person. I just wish I felt like you, that I was in the middle of *my* life."

"Well, it took a while to get there," I said smugly.

"I know. I didn't mean you were lucky. I'm sure you're very good at what you do."

"I don't know about very good, but I'm good enough."

We had fallen into the oldest of male-female scripts: I was the grown-up, she the fumbling late bloomer. Had I not been so passive, I might have challenged this flattering schema, which allowed her to hide so effectively from me.

Claire lived in an old building in the East Twenties, near Lexington Avenue, with a slow, tight little elevator that held the curried smells of takeout delivery bags from nearby Indian and Turkish restaurants. We usually stayed at her place; she felt more comfortable there. Even so, she would often express her impatience to fix up the place.

"What's so bad about it? Looks okay to me," I would say,

glancing around at the gray felt chairs, the Mission-style daybed, the plants, the altar, the stacks of magazines. The place had a shabby-genteel air, small, dark, crepuscular: essentially it was one large room divided into four, with the amenity of a Parisian-style skylight.

"The chairs are ratty. I need some blinds. People can look in and see everything. . . . I don't know what to get my mother for Christmas. Look at this plant, it's really pathetic. You should get more sun, baby."

"Maybe the steam heat dries it out."

"No, this one's sick even in the summer. I think it's some sort of scaly disease. Like my chapped lips. Everything's scaly here. I wish I had some new books. I've been reading too many magazines, they're like junk food."

What are people saying when they speak? What are they actually trying to say? It is my lifelong project to figure this out, but I never can decide if someone is speaking literally or metaphorically. With Claire, I tried to follow the emotional thread beneath her random remarks—was she feeling insecure about her reading because she thought me a brain, or did it have nothing to do with me, was she recalling some deferred ambition, or was she hinting she wanted a book for Christmas? By this time Claire would wander into the bathroom and begin blow-drying her wet hair. She had a strong Roman profile, like Penelope in the tapestries. I would relish the flesh peeping through her terrycloth robe—aroused suddenly by her being preoccupied.

"Fascinating, isn't it?" she'd say, catching me spying on her through the door.

"I like to watch you making your *toilette*, like a Degas painting."

"I'm thinking of cutting my hair. It's ridiculously long,
don't you think?"

"I like long hair."

"Would you believe I used to have it cut like Cleopatra?
Shorter in back, with bangs straight across the front. What a
riot. Actually, it didn't look bad. All right, hair, that's enough
for you guys," she'd talk to a strand, then switch to a high,
squeaky "No, no, we're not dry yet!"

Claire did these comic voices, often addressing inanimate
objects. Nothing stayed serious for long. But gradually, in spite
of her rapid shifts, I learned a partial itinerary of her concerns.
She felt bad about taking money from her parents. Not that
there were any strings attached; but as long as they paid her
rent and she only had to earn her expense money, she could remain in this freelance, odd-job life, which felt at times like a
trap. She wondered if she shouldn't get a *job* job, a nine-to-five.
Also, she had been writing articles for a city magazine for over
four years, and wasn't it time they put her name on the mast-
head? She brooded a great deal about how to approach the ed-
itor-in-chief to give her a contributing editor title. The next
minute she would talk about throwing over her magazine work
and writing a book about Tibetan medicine (a project that
struck me as far-fetched, given her lack of both medical training and Tibetan), or else leaving the city entirely and going
into retreat, to a Buddhist monastery/convent in France.

What interested me about these intermittent anxieties was
that they offered an alternative, a counter-Claire (if one could
but understand it) to the calm, detached perspective she, for
the most part, upheld. I was also detached. It had long been my
habit to stand apart from myself, observing, and to "borrow"
excess emotion from the woman, who was usually more ardent

or angry or involved in the prospect of relationship. But this time we were both detached: who was there to keep us emotionally honest?

I knew that my own detachment had come from the need to preserve myself, while growing up, within a family given to operatic hysteria, and later, from a need to protect my writing. But what were Claire's reasons? Had Buddhist practice given her a ground of detachment and poise, or was she drawn to Buddhism because she wanted to find a larger system that would support her characterological equanimity?

Claire kept, as I've said, an altar in her living room, with photographs of her guru, Dujam Rinpoche, surrounded by jewelry and flowers. I assume she meditated regularly before it. She also attended classes at the Tibetan Buddhist center near her house. Yet she never proselytized (as Molly tended to do) or even spoke about her practice, her spiritual progress, her setbacks. Whatever I learned had to be dragged out of her reluctantly. "You don't want to know about all that," she would say, and apologize self-mockingly for her "shrine." She knew exactly how a cynic might regard such trappings; many of her friends were, indeed, cynical journalists, and she tended to keep separate the two spheres of her life. But the less Claire talked about her Buddhist involvement, the more I eyed it for clues to her nature—especially the part I felt her withholding from me.

Here we may invoke Lopate's law of relationships: The less one is getting what one wants from the other person, the more one is apt to fill in the vacuum with interpretation. Claire's mystifying neutrality or reserve inspired several theses in turn: that she was slow to trust men (an all-purpose explanation, always true, up to a point); that she was distracted by various career and personal worries; that there was simply not that much to her, she was bland; that her affect had been "flattened out" by a spiritual practice that valued nonattachment. Others would follow; but for the moment the Buddhist thesis intrigued me the most.

Even without Claire and Molly, I had been coming up against the Buddhist challenge. All during the seventies the New York cultural scene was saturated with Buddhism: benefit poetry readings with Allen Ginsberg, Anne Waldman, and John Giorno; concerts by Philip Glass and other musicians of tantric orientation; conferences at the New School on what Buddhist psychology had to offer Western psychotherapies. Writer friends of mine were conscientiously studying Tibetan grammar. There was a definite upscale chic attached to Buddhism, especially the Tibetan strand—a pedigreed intellectual respectability such as had never burnished, say, the Hare Krishna or Guru Maharaji sects.

The first Buddhist wave had been Japanese: the Zen of the fifties and sixties, introduced by Alan Watts and D. T. Suzuki. The next influx was Tibetan, dominated by the flamboyant, Oxbridge-educated Chogyam Trungpa, whose poet-disciples established the Naropa School in Boulder, Colorado. Molly and Claire looked askance at whiskey-drinking, philandering, bad-boyish Trungpa, preferring instead their aged, gentle lama, Dujam Rinpoche. The old man lived mostly in France; but his American followers had established a center in New York, and every few years he would visit it—to the immense excitement of his devotees.

Socially on the fringes of this scene, I would sometimes be pulled in by curiosity, the chance to witness one more Manhattan subculture. Once, Molly invited me to hear the Dalai

Lama address a packed church. I could barely understand a word of His Holiness's talk, due to the thick accent of his translator and bad acoustics, and the little I heard sounded like platitudes about our need for love and world peace. Now, it may well be that platitudes ultimately contain the highest wisdom attainable. But I was looking for evidence to debunk the scene. I never doubted that Buddhist practices had great efficacy for Tibetans; I was only dubious that the beaming middle-class Americans in the pews around me would ever get beyond their consumerist pride in fingering esoteric traditions.

The American devotees I knew also displayed a parvenu fascination with Tibetan aristocracy (the Dalai Lama and his retinue, the ranks of lamas) that I can only compare to the way Texas moneyed society grovels before the British royals. One night I was taken to an event, at a Soho loft, honoring a group of Tibetan lamas who had just arrived in the States from India. The lamas sat on a raised platform and conversed among themselves, while an awed, handpicked, mostly Ivy League audience, kneeling and lotus-squatting below, watched them eat. What struck me was the determination of the devotees to wring spiritual messages from the most mundane conduct. If a lama belched, it became a teaching: "Don't take anything too seriously." If several lamas laughed (at a private Tibetan joke), the audience would join in gratefully, as though being taught the mystery of joy. Meanwhile, a bevy of *dahini*s, attractive young women chosen to serve the lamas, advanced with dishes and finger bowls. These American women, probably all willing to be identified as feminists, who would have been shocked if asked to perform such duties for their countrymen, were blushing with happiness at the chance to serve the robed contingent. Other women in the audience gasped as one of the tall young head-shaved priests stood up, his saffron robes leaving his muscled arms bare. The monks inspired rock star crushes.

Shortly after the feast had ended and the entire lama delegation had left to go to another party, those remaining milled about, still processing the privilege they'd been given. The Princess of Bhutan and her seven-year-old son were pointed out to me. Much was made of the little boy's playing with a top, as though it were a precocious demonstration of spiritual powers; when the top skittered over the loft floor, everyone oohed and clapped. I wasn't sure whether the child was being drooled over because he had royal blood, because he was mischievous (high spiritual marks for that in *this* crowd), or because he was of an age when future Dalai Lamas are customarily detected.

I was glad not to be won over by this display; it saved me an enormous bother. On the other hand, I could not simply reject an immensely complex, sophisticated tradition just because of some sycophantic behavior on the part of certain followers. The little I knew of Buddhist doctrine actually appealed to me, by virtue of its insistence on the void, on mindfulness, and on the universality of suffering. In fact, I could go along with at least two of its four "noble truths": the first, that existence is suffering, I could accept wholeheartedly; the second, that the cause of suffering is craving and attachment, I was less sure about, but willing to concede. I balked only at the final two: that there is a cessation of suffering, called Nirvana, and that the way to Nirvana lies in dissolving the self and following the "eightfold path." As with Marxism, I agreed with the analysis of the problem, only not the solution.

Buddhism was continually being put forward to me as a doctrine suitable to the agnostic modern age. To my doubts about the necessity for any religion, my sister would repeat,

"I *hate* organized religions. But Buddhism isn't a religion. It doesn't even have a god!" I wasn't sure I liked this, and I had even more problems with Molly's insistence that Buddhism "superseded" Freud, was "vastly superior" to psychoanalysis. It seemed to me she was really saying, in an upwardly mobile, assimilationist vein, that she had no further use for the religion we were born into, Judaism (as represented in my mind by Freud). Not that I pored over the Talmud either; but *were* I to feel spiritual twinges, I would first give my own heritage a chance.

In that sense, I had less problems with Claire's Buddhism, because she was Catholic. It was not for me to judge the theological wanderings of Roman Catholics; moreover, Claire still accompanied her father to Mass like a good daughter. What did it *mean*, though (back to square one), that she was a Buddhist? It seemed such a strenuous, willful act for an American— whose background was Catholic, Jewish, Presbyterian, whatever—to "become" a Buddhist. Did she see herself as a *dahini* (one step away from a Buddhist chorus girl, in my mind)? Or was she actually seeking—what an odd, ambitious idea!—to become enlightened, an illuminated being, to suffer compassionately with all living things, like the bodhisattva? If so, I could well respect her abstracted preoccupation.

Or was there another explanation?

Based on my sister's unforgotten remark, I thought I might not be the only "guy" Claire was still seeing. New Year's Eve, the test, began to loom. When I asked her at the beginning of December, her first response was to hedge: she was thinking she might go out of town, to her parents' house in the mountains. "Can I get back to you in a few days? I won't hang you up. I know, you want a hot date for New Year's Eve," she said, disparaging herself and me in one sentence. I waited a week, darkly imagining her efforts to secure a better offer. The next time, she answered sweetly: "Sure. What did you have in mind?"

I had in mind a movie, Preston Sturges's *Unfaithfully Yours* at Theater 80 (which proved as delicious as I'd hoped), dinner at a good restaurant, and a New Year's Eve party, where I knew there'd be plenty of interesting types. I remember that almost as soon as we entered the party, Claire and I went our separate ways, talking to different people till the time came to leave. This independence was a sign either of a couple supremely comfortable with each other or of one that would soon break up.

Mutual glibness aside, we actually had very little in common to talk about. One of our few conversational mainstays was Molly. Having overcome any scruples about frankly discussing my sister with her best friend, I communicated my worries over Molly's get-rich schemes, which changed weekly, or her then harsh social manner, which turned off men. Claire, to my surprise, agreed. The difference was that when she spoke about Molly, it was not with the overidentifying conflictedness of a family member but with genuine tolerant affection. Her attitude seemed to be "Molly's Molly, that's just the way she gets at times. She'll figure it out—and anyway, isn't she great, on the whole?" Yes, exactly, *that* was what I had meant to say—or feel.

Was it Claire's Buddhist training in compassion that allowed her to enjoy people just the way they were, without troubling about their nuttiness? Or had she simply a good heart?

She rarely spoke ill of anyone; her sympathy was so evenly spread out that I felt, in the end, slighted. She saw the good in me as she would in the next person. I never had the sense she had *chosen* me, or thought of us as an *us*. (Whether I wanted us to be an *us*, in the long run, was a question I put off, too busy being offended that she had not raised it.)

My distrust of Claire grew also from her journalistic work, which caused her to marshal a spurious fascination for the assignment of the moment, and a dazed indifference to the matter once copy had been handed in. I was not the first to suspect this vocation of a built-in shallowness, by virtue of its opportunistic obsession with topicality and trivia. Since then, having been forced to try my own hand at journalism, I have acquired a much healthier respect for the work habits, intrepidity, and antennae necessary to excel at it. At the time, however, I was still appalled at the superficiality of the journalistic enterprise, and I saw Claire's cool aplomb, which kept me at arm's length, as a function of her métier. But even to say that she "kept me at arm's length" falsely implies that I was the ardent, unrequited suitor, when the truth was, I was keeping my distance in my own way, by not respecting what she did.

Our relationship seemed in a holding pattern; and yet it was pleasant enough. Even when Claire became slightly less available than before, begging off because of deadlines and out-of-town trips, we would still get together about once a week. This spared me the necessity of finding a new girlfriend. Busy with my own projects, I viewed our affair as a sort of minimal romantic insurance policy. Then it suddenly ended.

Claire had gotten the assignment to write a story about old, freestanding movie houses in New York. She invited me to

come along on her research; as a film buff, I might find it interesting. When the Saturday for our scheduled tour arrived, I
had the flu. I told her I felt too awful to go out. "Oh, we'll just
wrap you in lots of sweaters. It'll be fun! You'll get to see the inside of all those wonderful old movie houses and it'll cheer you
up." I was about to remark that it wasn't a question of moodi-
ness, but flu, as in "germ theory of illness," when I realized she
was determined—she had arranged this and I was coming
along, period. I suspected she was on deadline and needed my
input. Her selfishness seemed a revelation to me: I thought I
was finally seeing the true, insensitive Claire. For the first time
I got angry with her (though in hindsight, I may have been re-
pressing some anger toward her all along). This bile accompanied me throughout the day while I shivered in the subway up
to Washington Heights, felt my throat swell bronchially under
the February rain, stood on my feet for hours, spitefully and
self-pityingly getting sicker by the moment while perversely
pretending to be all right, as the movie managers took us
around with flashlights to explore the art deco moldings and
cornices in what were now grimy fleapits. I asked the right
questions about the old days, and Claire seemed pleased. "See?
It was fun after all." We took a cab down to my apartment,
where I hoped she would make it up to me by tucking me into
bed. But when we got to my door, she held on to the cab, saying she had an appointment downtown and really couldn't
come inside, even for a few minutes. Once I was alone, my
anger and fever merged in a blaze. Here I was dying, delirious,
and this ***** couldn't even come inside and make me a cup
of tea.

That did it. We were through.

The oddest part was that there was no breakup scene. I sim-

ply never called Claire again, and she never got around to calling me either. It was symptomatic, I thought bitterly, of how
little the affair had meant, that it didn't even need a denouement; we just drifted away like steam vapor.

Shortly after that incident, I was offered a university teaching post down at Houston. I took it, vowing I would find some
nice, sweet Texas girl; I would get away from those hard, self-
serving New York women like Claire, too careerist and too
stingy to love. How could I have thought there was a mystery
about her? Claire became the newest target of my immature
anger, always ready to flare up at women for not giving me the
affection I felt due me.

In the years that followed, I would occasionally hear news
from Molly about Claire. She had completed her book on Tibetan medicine, the first such in English on the subject, and a
small press interested in Eastern religions had published it. She
had quit her magazine work and gone into retreat in France for
several years, fulfilling the required term for Buddhist novi-
tiates at her guru's center. All this dedication and follow-
through could not help but impress me. The closest I had ever
come to making such a commitment was to writing; but writing fed my ego rather than extinguishing it. Self-knowledge I
pursued, at best, without benefit of system, defensively interro-
gating my experiences after the fact, so that whatever wisdom
might stick to me was accidental, like a burr in a forest walk. I
lived for myself, within myself; I had never been able to locate
some Whole or Cosmic Mind that was higher than the individual, inspiring contemplation and admiration. Not that I
wanted to locate any such principle; I was content to follow my

discontented path for the rest of my life. But I tipped my hat to Claire.

The spark of anger I had seized upon to exit from our floundering relationship in fine, self-righteous fettle had long passed; and I mainly recalled Claire's graciousness. Playing back our affair in my mind, I began to think that I may have gotten the whole thing wrong: probably she had liked me more than I'd thought (though clearly not loved me), and the price she had had to pay for getting to know me better, given the only terms I offered her, was to sleep with me and pretend a romantic involvement. This she had done like a good sport. The fact that we had not gone through a breakup scene might be less an indictment of our relationship than a subconscious recognition by our adult selves that there was no need to besmirch with inflationary animosity what had never been more than a courteous, friendly liaison.

So, when Molly informed me that Claire was in New York for a few months, just as I was, and had mentioned she would "love" to see me sometime, I was pleased at this second chance for a more successful closure. I called her and we arranged to have dinner. On the phone Claire sounded much the breezy way I'd remembered her; but as our reunion approached, I began to worry. What had all that meditation work and French country retreat done to our Claire?

She opened the door, attractive as ever, and quickly put me at ease by detailing the latest struggle to hold on to her apartment, which she'd been subletting. The building had been sold to a pair of shysters: a typical New York realty story of the eighties, which reassured me that her street smarts remained intact. Then we went out to dinner together and caught up. Her descriptions of the Buddhist group in France were all amusingly down-to-earth; but she seemed more eager to report gossip about her old American friends, the ones she'd seen in the past two weeks. Fortunately, her practice had not yet purified her of gossip. She also wanted to know everything I had done the past few years; she was hungry for thick narrative detail. Eventually we got around to the subject of romantic involvements. By then we had repaired to a bar in order to prolong the evening's discussion, and were sitting at the railing. I told her about the woman I'd been dating in Houston. She said she was, alas, not in love at the moment, but added that she still saw "various men from time to time." I took this to mean some of the journalist friends she had mentioned earlier. I was working up the courage to ask her about—us.

"What went wrong?" I wondered aloud. "Why didn't we work out as a couple?"

"Well, there was no passion between us," she answered, as though it were the simplest matter in the world. I was glad to hear her put it this way: to distribute the lack equally. She went on to say that passion was rare for her, but of the highest importance. During the period of our affair, she now admitted, she *had* been in love—wildly, reciprocally, with a handsome foreigner, a very important diplomat (she refused to tell me his name) who was, unfortunately, married. Whenever he was in the country, they resumed their secret passion. This affair had gone on for years, until the time that she entered Buddhist retreat.

So! She *had* been keeping a part of herself back. This explained everything—even her stall around New Year's Eve; she was probably waiting to hear from her dashing emissary if he planned to be in the States. I felt a warm contentment, approaching happiness, at receiving this piece of the missing puzzle. I always feel strengthened by learning the truth (however unpleasant) after long being kept in the dark. Besides, it was far too late to feel jealous resentment of this "rival"; happily, he was a diplomat, not a fellow writer, and it pleased me that, by her description, he was very handsome. I made him into Louis Jourdan in *Letter from an Unknown Woman*. It was aesthetic justice that a woman as pretty as Claire should be swept off her feet by an equally good-looking man. I could admire, from outside, the amours of these beautiful people, like a fairy tale one has always believed in. And it exonerated me from any mistakes I may have made in our affair: how could it have worked, she was already in love with someone else?

Finally, there was sweet vindication of sorts in learning that Buddhism hadn't given her any detached perspective toward love, but that—like several other women I had known—she had worshipped at the altar of Passion, kept a votive candle lit to the secret, demon, phantom lover who came and went, holding her in thrall. It pleased me that I recognized the pattern, had encountered it before, and was not alarmed by it, whereas true Buddhist nonattachment would have remained much more opaque and threatening.

Claire drew me out in turn. As she listened shrewdly to my stories of romantic folly, and contributed her own, there was so much good humor back and forth between us that the night took on a sparkle; it became one of the dozen or so charmed evenings in my life. I felt in perfect rapport with Claire. At last, we were meeting as equals, survivors, on a common ground of mutual delight in each other's company. I walked her home; I would have gladly "jumped her bones," as the saying now goes, but I sensed no such invitation. And besides, I feared that making a sexual pass would spoil the mood of the evening. Even if it had succeeded, we would be back in that dry polite corner of two uninfatuated lovers instead of the much richer space (for us) of old friends, which we had achieved for the first time that night. I realized I'd liked Claire far more before and after our time of "intimacy," than during. A love affair, it was borne in on me again, is sometimes the worst way to draw out the best in another.

Claire went off again to her retreat in France. We agreed that we would get together, with pleasure, whenever she came into town. It would be wonderful to leave the story like that, on a high note. But in 1988 my sister told me, trying to keep her voice calm, that Claire was back in New York "for health reasons." Brain cancer had been discovered. She was in Doctors Hospital, receiving chemotherapy treatments.

That Saturday, I made up my mind to visit her. I suddenly recalled all of Claire's complaints about bodily symptoms; could they have been advance warnings? On my way to the hospital, I experienced faintness; there was a "sympathetic" buzz in my head, a fibrillation in my legs. Of course, I often felt that way when I got near hospitals. Still, I seemed to be much more upset about Claire's illness, I was not sure why, than I had expected.

I had debated what sort of reading matter to take someone with brain cancer, deciding in the end to buy a stack of glossy fashion magazines. So I entered the ward, the bearer of frivolous goodies about how to stay young or keep your figure, wondering if Claire had been shaven bald yet or grown emaciated. I first ran into Claire's mother, an Upper East Side matron, looking distressed in the most abject way: she had become deindividualized, the archetypal mother fearing the loss of her only child. Her eyes were already grief-stricken. Claire, she told me, was downstairs in X-ray but would be up shortly.

I waited and looked around the solarium, with its amazing 360-degree views of Manhattan. This was certainly the cheeriest, poshest hospital facility I had ever been in.

A half hour later, Claire entered the ward wearing a quilted robe, moving slowly, gingerly. She still had her beautiful long hair and her striking Penelope profile. But she was thinner; her angles had been purified into ascetic lines, there was now nothing sexual about her. She invited us into her room and sat on the edge of her bed, like a teenage girl. I gave her the magazines. "You're such a dear," she said in that vague way, only this time I was happy to receive the compliment.

I asked her to fill me in. She told me when the pains began; how the diagnosis was made; what her chances were—not good, but not hopeless either. She had discovered a whole network of cancer patients across the country and, like the trained journalist she was, had been keeping up with them via computer, learning all about the latest experimental cures. If she survived this, she quipped, she would go for a medical degree; she'd done three quarters of the work already. I could not help noticing that she bore her suffering with a placid, evolved dignity and determination that were in stark contrast to her mother's panic. Claire was taking it all so calmly that I felt more sorry for her mother at that moment than for her.

I did not want to tire her, so I said good-bye and left. Walking from the hospital, I had the sense of having been in contact with something large—larger than myself. I felt dissolved, borderless, dizzy. A part of me was happy to have seen Claire irrespective of the circumstances. But I was almost certain the cancer would kill her. She would die at forty, still alarmingly fresh and beautiful.

The memorial service was at Frank Campbell's, a traditional Catholic funeral parlor on Park Avenue on the Upper

East Side. Nearly all of New York Buddhism's elite showed up, and there was a touching, if awkward, attempt to mix Catholic and Tibetan ritual, all worked out painstakingly beforehand by the family and Claire's dharma buddies. Many speeches were made, attesting to the deceased's considerateness for others and zestful, life-loving personality. I cannot remember clearly a single thing that was said; in my daze, it was enough to take in that Claire had been one of those popular people, like Frank O'Hara, about whom each best friend learns at the funeral that there were a hundred others. Afterward, at the party at someone's house, I wandered around, eavesdropping on various groups, all of whom were reminiscing and telling Claire stories. I wanted to join in, yet what could I say to them? I never had had the illusion that I was one of her closest friends. I had no way to fathom her deepest commitments. But I mourned her nonetheless.

TERROR OF MENTORS

The word "mentor" has always had an appeal to me, in the abstract. I like its dignified sound, its promised protection, its sense of a craft personally handed down. Only the reality terrifies me. Either because of this fear or a lack of opportunity—the right mentor never came along, as bachelors in the mentor field are wont to rationalize—I had none when I was younger, and now it is too late.

If I speculate on the reason for this nonrelationship, I have to start, as usual, with the family. In this case, the two men in my family: my father and my older brother. Though my mother and sisters had a strong (maybe decisive) influence on me, it has never occurred to me to seek a mentor on the distaff side. The word "mentor" has "men" in it, and has always subliminally suggested, at least to my mind, a ritual process by which a youth takes instruction from a strong male elder and is thereby received into the noble order of men. My own father was too withdrawn, depressed, and obsessed with regarding himself as a failure for him to serve in that role effectually. Perhaps the lack of an early model has inhibited me from growing the receptive apparatus necessary to engage an older, successful man as mentor. This may be part of what Robert Bly is getting at, in *Iron John*, when he talks about the ways the contemporary American father's absence or weakness retards the son's progression into mature manhood.

On the other hand, my older (by three years) brother, Hal, was quite powerful, opinionated, and generous with his knowledge. Whatever he learned about art, books, movies, jazz, and women, he eagerly passed along to me, so much so that I risked becoming his disciple. In matters of taste, particularly, it took considerable stubbornness to resist his certitude. Studying to be a painter, Hal favored an austere, minimalist aesthetic: Piero, Dürer, van der Weyden, Mondrian, Ad Reinhardt. My visual tastes were molded along the same rigorous lines. I remember the night I told him, trembling, that I thought Rubens (his bête noire) was also a pretty good artist in his way. Less heroic was my reversal on Fellini's *La Dolce Vita*, a film I had found bloated and hollow when I first saw it. Hal, away in England at the time, wrote me that it was a masterpiece, and I bowed to his view, saw it again, convinced myself I loved it, and dutifully wrote a long praise of it for the college newspaper. Retrospectively, I can appreciate that *La Dolce Vita* is both riveting *and* shallow; but at the time, it hurt to have sacrificed a gut reaction for my brother's approval.

Freud wrote that at first he missed the thread of the Oedipal complex because his father was a rather mild figure in the household; then he realized it was his forceful older brother who stood in for the threatening king. In my case, my brother had raised me far more than my father had: he took me out to play ball, listened to my reports about school, and taught me the grandeur of art and the facts of life. The debt I owed my brother was so large it compelled me finally to break with his influence. Yet I wonder if some vestigial loyalty to him as my first tutor kept me from following the lure of other potential mentors, even after I had rejected his lead.

There were class taboos as well that restrained me from embracing mentorship. In the tough Brooklyn ghetto where I grew up, we had an indelicate but graphic term for those students who fraternized with teachers: "brownnoses." No one wanted to be a brownnose or a teacher's pet, both of which constituted especial pitfalls for me, since I was the best student in my high school. Often, an unsuspecting teacher, handing back compositions at the beginning of the year, would express her general disappointment, then say, "But there is one paper here that is of college caliber." Already I would be trying to sink under the chair; by the time she had pronounced my name, rather than taking it as a compliment, I felt humiliated. She had shamed me before my peers, threatened whatever chance I had of fitting in; and I did not wait long to take revenge, challenging her authority, organizing the opposition in class against her, seeing, in a word, that she would not make the same mistake twice. As the singling out by adults for praise was something I both cringed at and craved, the only solution was to keep my distance from teachers.

At college I made it a particular point to stay away from those charismatic Columbia professors with large followings. I passed up the opportunity to study with the young, brilliant Susan Sontag in Comparative Religion, the erudite Moses Hadas in Classics, the compellingly witty Kenneth Koch in Poetry, the flamboyant James Shenton in History. . . . What a waste, you will say, and rightly so. But apparently my insecure, emerging writer's ego could not chance exposure to the vortex of some colorful, commanding pedagogue. I witnessed my classmates returning from their seminars with these Pied Pipers, buoyed to the heavens one week by the deity's compliments, devastated the next by his remarks on their papers; saw them imitating their prof's writing style, even his slight stammer, and knew: This was not for me. I gravitated instead to withdrawn eminences like Lionel Trilling, who always looked too basset-hound weary to engage with students, or Eric Bentley, who addressed his dry comments to the farthest crack of the rear ceiling, or Andrew Chiappe, the Shakespeare scholar who threw his glance toward both sidewalls at once. I liked my professors wall-eyed and unapproachable.

Not that I didn't try to snatch some wisdom from these reserved authorities. I would approach them after class, when they longed to sweep up their lecture materials and retire, with a hungry, smarty-pants question, like the other students whose tongues were loosened by the bell. No doubt I made a nuisance of myself at times. But all such encounters were kept within prescribed limits.

It shocked me when I heard of teachers who socialized with their students in the evenings, went to downtown movies, poetry readings, or concerts with them. One professor even invited a favorite student of hers to join her adult writing group—risking the ruin of his talent, I thought, by spoiling him. My objections were both principled and murky. I felt there should be more of a strict separation between "youth culture" (though in the early sixties we didn't call it that yet) and adult culture. I distrusted adults who wanted to poach on the

interests of the young, and I similarly suspected educators who
took their function so seriously they would even bother to cul-
tivate their charges' doughy minds after hours.

My murky objection stemmed from jealousy: I was not the
one chosen. Though presumably intelligent enough, I must not
have given off that special—what?—*scent* that might have inspired professors to offer me their aegis. Perhaps there is a certain look of playful availability or mutual need that passes between potential mentors and mentees. Whatever it was, I
didn't emit it. I was too proud, or too unentitled, to sue for such
cross-generational rapport. The students from more privileged
backgrounds saw nothing improper about friendly confabs with
professors: they were their peers or social superiors. Some were
even the children of academics, raised around professional
adults and comfortable interacting with their parents' friends.
My parents were originally factory workers and, later, clerks; as
their son, I brought a working-class mistrust to the university
environment. College was an extension of class warfare, and
my spy's mission was to extract good grades from these snobbish caretakers of the middle class without falling under their
spell.

But, as I say, no one even tried to put me under his or her
spell. I remember one of my favorite English professors accost-
ing my best friend and making some sort of awkward, open invitation. This professor, though married and living in the sub-
urbs, had a reputation for bisexual yearnings; my friend,
curly-haired and Pan-like, was one of those boys irresistible to
both sexes. The professor said to him, "I'm lonely. When I stay
in town, I have nothing to do but eat a meal by myself and go
back to the King's Crown Hotel to bed. Why don't you take in
a movie or a play with me sometime?" My friend, distressed at

the invitation's innuendo, dodged it. Me, I was jealous. I'd worked so hard in that class; why didn't the professor ever ask me out? Was I simply not cute enough? Not that I'd have taken him up on it, but . . .

Here I confess I have always associated mentorship with an erotic subtext. Teachers who got too close, who viewed us as "human beings" and wanted to be our friends or mentors, posed a threat of violation, psychic or physical; while those students who took up the offer seemed to me at the time incipient hustlers or opportunists. Today, when the academy has become obsessed with sexual harassment, sometimes clumsily defining and crudely trying to extirpate all traces of eros from pedagogy, I see the problem more complexly. As an experienced teacher, I recognize that there is an inevitable, even desirable element of flirtation and seduction in the learning process. At the same time, I think it should be kept within the bounds of metaphor: I disapprove of sex between students and professors, for all the predictable reasons. I am also made uncomfortable by professors who don't get in bed with their students but who encourage a dependency, in the guise of offering limitless counseling, or who become so dependent on youth's enthusiasm to perk up their own desiccated juices that their annual rejuvenation takes on a vampirish cast.

Since I have gone this far, I may as well admit that mentorship—specifically, the surrender of the callower, less-formed mind to the care of the more forceful, developed one—carries in my mind a specifically homoerotic association. I am reminded of the animal kingdom, where the younger, weaker baboon presents his ass as a mark of respect to the older, stronger baboon. When I examine my resistance to mentorship, I find that underneath it is the terror of being dominated, in its most graphic, visceral sense: forced anal sexual penetration.

It helps to know that when I was a freshman in college, perhaps my greatest fear was that I'd turn out homosexual. A gangling adolescent, I had little assurance I could attract women; and I was fascinated with certain of my male friends, the way they looked, the remarks they made, to a degree that the word "crush" would not be inappropriate. Going to an all-male college, and sleeping in the same dorm rooms with other young men, I worried that I might be tempted further. Times have changed: it is as proper now to apologize for admitting I once feared becoming gay as it was then to be relieved to discover I was not.

Having settled that question, I might add, I continued to be a little chagrined that homosexual men never came on to me, just as older professors never offered themselves as mentors. Perhaps these similar outcomes may explain how I got the two crossed in my mind. But no, aside from my own hang-ups, I still detect some objective connections between mentorship and homosexuality, stemming as far back as the Socratic model in ancient Greek culture. The dynamic of younger listener bending to older speaker's will is given a distinctly homoerotic turn in Oscar Wilde's neo-Socratic dialogue "The Critic as Artist." And an older man taking a younger man under his protection, teaching and supporting him, is a familiar pattern in the gay world.

For the younger man, seeking a mentor sometimes involves both homoerotic and parricidal undercurrents. James Baldwin has written eloquently of his own difficulties with his father, followed by a series of mentors who helped him escape from the narrow brutalities of ghetto poverty: first, the white schoolteacher who brought him to plays and movies downtown; then, the various preachers and gangsters who took him under their wing in Harlem; subsequently, the black painter, Beauford Delaney, who taught him self-respect; and finally, Richard Wright, who helped Baldwin get grants and become established as a writer. In "Alas, Poor Richard," Baldwin admits he repaid Wright with a certain ingratitude. According to Chester Himes's account in *The Quality of Hurt*, when the great Wright confronted his disciple for having attacked him in print, "Baldwin defended himself by saying that Dick had written his story and hadn't left him, or any other American black writer, anything to write about." Several drinks later, Baldwin had escalated his defense to "The sons must slay their fathers."

Baldwin's parricidal assertion is typical of a certain pugilistic attitude on the part of postwar American writers, such as Norman Mailer figuratively taking on Hemingway. I bring up this very American view of literary agon between generations—given its ultimate theoretical expression in Harold Bloom's *The Anxiety of Influence*—to shed light on my own terror of mentorship. It so happens (and this was a crucial factor in my development as a writer) that I refused to engage with the literary generation just preceding mine, either by regarding myself as in competition with them or by allowing myself to feel deeply grateful to them. True, up until the time I was a sophomore in college (about the same year that I broke with my brother's influence), I was curious, like any young would-be writer, about the successful authors of the day. I read Bellow, Mailer, Kerouac, Styron, Roth, Salinger, Malamud. Though I didn't think of it back then, perhaps the fact that this period was dominated by New York Jewish novelists made me feel, as Baldwin said about Wright, that they had already used up a good deal of the material from my environment. I could either become obsessed with them or shut them out.

In college I also had plentiful opportunity to read the great, dead writers of comparative literature. My new models became Fielding, Céline, Dostoevsky, Tolstoy, Turgenev, Nietzsche, Flaubert, Stendhal, Jane Austen, Unamuno, Svevo, Tanizaki, Machado de Assis. Years later I took up the essay after reading Hazlitt, Lamb, and Montaigne. My first novel, *Confessions of Summer,* was inspired by reading quantities of Pavese; my second, *The Rug Merchant,* reflected an immersion in the Japanese films of Naruse and the fiction of Narayan and Soseki. All my work has had this tinge of the foreign, the antiquarian.

For me, the prospect of mentorship would mean accepting the literary ethos of the previous generation, as incorporated in the person of the mentor—and this I could not do. I remember in my early twenties going to a talk by Alberto Moravia (whom I then revered) about the crisis of literary modernism and the need to pass on the torch lit by Joyce, Proust, and other groundbreaking experimenters. Moravia was not what you would call an experimental writer, and it seemed to me he was demeaning himself by publicly valuing only the lineage of literary modernism. Somehow, perhaps in defense of Moravia against his own self-dismissal, I found myself thinking, I don't really care about extending modernism; I'd rather read *Dead Souls* and the other juicy classics of the past. Not that I discounted the possibility that literary classics would emerge from the present. Nor was I antimodernist: I enjoyed reading Gertrude Stein and William S. Burroughs, up to a point. But I drew a blank before the imperative of providing the next link in the avant-garde chain. Moreover, the solemnly heroic, self-congratulatory claims of modernism, its founders' myths of struggle to break new wood, started to bore me. And still does: I resist the notion of a progressive dialectic in art. (Hazlitt has a wonderful essay, "Why the Arts Are Not Progressive.")

164   For example, the most influential author on my generation,
the closest one to a Master, was Samuel Beckett. When I was
trying to develop a style of my own, I heard the young writers
buzzing around me: "Beckett's the man, we must study Beckett,
steep ourselves in Beckett, respond to the challenge of his bare
eloquence, we must carry on his noble work." I saw them pen-
ning weak imitations of Molloy or Endgame and getting stuck in
a Beckettian rut, merely because they were sure he was the
most prestigiously radical example to follow. My own choice
was to skip over the previous generation and commune with
the older dead. I assumed, meanwhile, that if I was true to myself as a writer, the results would fit under one or another mod-
ernist rubric without my having to force the issue.

The decision to go my own way, sans mentors or involvement in current literary movements, is a central piece of the
flattering tale I have evolved about my development as a
writer. It should be taken with a grain of salt: no writer, after
all, can escape being shaped by the literature of his contemporaries. At the same time, I do feel out of synch with my literary
times; and I experience real twinges of regret when I encounter
the camaraderie of contemporary fiction writers (such as Ann
Beattie and Don DeLillo), who are like physicists working on
the same set of problems, perusing each others' newest books
for clues to the latest description of contemporary life. I get a
little envious when I read a tender account by Allan Gurganus
about his mentor, John Cheever, or Jay McInerney about his
disciple-friendship with Raymond Carver. These accounts seal
the writer all the more tightly into the contemporary moment
by depicting literary tradition as no more than one generation
old.

"Mentorship has its privileges," to paraphrase the credit

card ad. Not the least of my envies is for a bigshot, a rabbi to go to bat for me when grants and awards are handed out. It is curious that, although I have won my share of competitive fellowships, I have never received a single grant of the type for which one cannot apply, but which must be handed down from above by distinguished nominators. Each year I notice with irritation that some obsequious twerp has been successfully sponsored by his mentor for a MacArthur, a Whiting, a Prix de Rome. At such moments I try to tell myself that at least I have gotten where I am without having had to kiss ass. Oh, I've entertained the thought of doing so from time to time, but I know I lack the patience for that persistent osculation to which the touchy elephant hides of elderly éminences grises are accustomed.

On the other hand, maybe I'm wrong in associating mentor cultivation with toadyism; maybe this is sour grapes. Let us suppose the opposite, that undergoing a mentorship requires supreme character strength, a sense of self-confidence so unshakable that only someone with a very strong ego could request a mentor's guidance. The acknowledgment of need, the admission of personal lack, would in itself signal a stage of maturity. I am reminded of those romantic Hermann Hesse novels I used to gobble down in adolescence, such as *Magister Ludi* and *Siddhartha,* in which the ability to submit to a mentor constitutes the mystical sign of spiritual ripeness.

Of all the arts, writing is the one with the most problematic relationship to mentoring. This is probably because, unlike, say, taking master classes in cello or learning dance from a choreographer or apprenticing in the darkroom to a photographer, there is less teachable technique, less "science" to pass on, and consequently, more need for a magus's seal of approval.

Particularly in poetry, where a ubiquity of candidates meets an uncertainty about what even constitutes a poem, there can be seen a heavy dose of vatic mystification and "laying on of hands" (sometimes literally). The practice whereby established poets pick debut volumes for university publishing series is but one example of this anointing process. Such a plum is the dream of every graduate student in poetry writing, though the odds are long. One of the dishonesties of graduate creative writing programs is that they hold out a fantasy of mentorship to each student, when what is more routinely proffered is a credentialing mechanism.

Now the tables are turned: I am no longer the young man who could not seek out a mentor, but the middle-aged one to whom some young people look for that bond. How do I reconcile my skepticism about mentorship with the fact that I make my living as a creative writing professor? Partly, I think, by denying the degree to which I actually play the role of mentor. I often "pretend" not to see the embarrassing extent to which a student is in my thrall; or I try to defuse the situation with humor and impersonality while continuing to offer concrete assistance. I have had students pursue me with requests for recommendations, blurbs, advice, twenty years or more after they studied with me: some are shamelessly using me, true, but a few actually think of me as their mentor. Yet I have refused the intimacy of that term in my own mind.

Shall I confess one reason why I don't think of myself as their mentor? I have never had a student whom I considered my peer. I have had plenty of students who were talented, lively, perceptive, and great fun to read; but not my literary equals. Perhaps I am being unfair, and the mere fact of their taking writing courses with me disqualified them in my eyes from seeming to possess original power and independence. Perhaps I am being overly competitive with my students. In any case, how could I truly mentor someone I did not believe would ever grow as high as myself? True, one does not normally look to the student body for a soul mate, but to fellow practitioners and friends. Yet mentorship implies at least a potential equality, ripening over time; whatever initial power imbalances attend the early stages of the relationship, the acolyte is eventually supposed to replace or surpass the mentor.

I hope soon to embark on the adventure of fatherhood. If I am so blessed, then all these strands—the desire to have your offspring grow to his outermost limits, counterbalanced by the fear that he will outstrip you; the need to nurture, even if the offspring disappoints—will be tested to the fullest. Against the backdrop of parental experience, I may one day understand more deeply the mentoring role in its idealistic dimension, and come to terms with it more graciously than I have so far been able to do. Until that time, my instinct tells me, I will continue to give mentorship a wide berth.

THE STORY OF MY FATHER

Is it not clearer than day, that we feel within ourselves the indelible marks of excellence, and is it not equally true that we constantly experience the effects of our deplorable condition?

—Pascal

1.

Old age is a great leveler: the frailer elderly all come to resemble turtles trapped in curved shells—shrinking, wrinkled, and immobile—so that in a roomful, a terrarium, of the old, it is hard to disentangle one solitary individual's karma from the mass fate of aging. Take my father. Vegetating in a nursing home, he seems both universalized and purified, worn to his bony essence. But as LSD is said to intensify more than alter one's personality, so old age: my father is what he always was, only more so. People meeting him for the first time ascribe his oddities (the withdrawn silences, sloppy eating habits, boasts, and pedantic non sequiturs) to the infirmities of time, little realizing he was like that at thirty.

A man in his thirties who acts the octagenarian is asking for it. But old age has set his insularities in a kinder light—meanwhile drawing to the surface that underlying sweetness that I always suspected was there. Dispassionate to the point where the stoical and stony meet, a hater of sentimentality, he had always been embarrassed by his affections; but now he lacks the strength even to suppress these leakages. I have also changed and am more ready to receive them. These last ten years—ever since he was put away in old age homes—have witnessed more expressions of fondness than passed between us in all the years before. Now when I visit him, he kisses me on sight and, during the whole time we are together, stares at me greedily, as though with wonder that such a graying cub came from his loins. For my part, I have no choice but to love him. I feel a tenderness welling up, if only at the sight of the wreck he has become. What we were never able to exhibit when he had all his wits about him—that animal bond between father and son—is now the main exchange.

Yet I also suspect sentimentality; and so I ask myself, How valid is this cozy resolution? Am I letting both of us off the hook too quickly? Or trying to corner the market on filial piety, while the rest of my family continues mostly to ignore him? Who is, who was, this loner, Albert Lopate, neglected in a back ward? I look at the pattern of his eighty-five years and wonder what it all adds up to: failure, as he himself claims, or a respectable worker's life for which he has little to be ashamed, as I want to believe? We spend most of our adulthoods trying to grasp the meanings of our parents' lives; and how we shape and answer these questions largely turns us into who we are.

My father's latest idea is that I am a lawyer. The last two times I've visited him in the nursing home, he's expressed variations on this theme. The first time he looked up at me from his wheelchair and said, "So, you're successful—as a lawyer?"

By my family's scraping-by standards, I'm a worldly success; and worldly success, to the mistrustful urban-peasant mind of my father, befogged by geriatric confusion, can only mean a lawyer.

Lawyers, I should add, are not held in the highest regard in my family. They are considered shysters: smooth, glib, ready to sell you out. You could say the same about writers. In hindsight, one reason I became a writer is that my father wanted to be one. An autodidact who started out in the newspaper trade, then became a factory worker and, finally, a shipping clerk, he wrote poetry in his spare time, and worshipped Faulkner and Kafka. I enacted his dream, like the good son (or usurped it, like the bad son), which seems not to have made him entirely happy. So he turns me into a lawyer.

Not that my father's substitution is all that far-fetched. I had entered college a prelaw major, planning to specialize in publishing law. Secretly I yearned to be a writer, though I did not think I was smart enough. I was right—who is?—but bluff got the better of modesty.

The last time I visited my father, he said, "I know what you want to be. *Abogado.*" He smiled at his ability to call up the Spanish word you see on storefronts in barrios, alongside *notario.* So this time I was not yet the successful attorney, but the teenage son choosing his vocation. Sometimes old people get stuck on a certain moment in the past. Could it be that his mental clock had stopped around 1961, right about the time of his first stroke, when he'd just passed fifty (my present age) and I was seventeen? *Abogado.* It's so characteristic of my father's attachment to language that a single word will swim up from the dark waters of dotage. Even before he became addled, he would peacock his vocabulary, going out of his way to construct sentences with polysyllabic words such as "concomitant" or "prevaricate." My father fingers words like mahjong tiles, waiting to play a good one.

Lately he has been reverting to Yiddish phrases, which he assumes I understand, though I don't. This return to the mother tongue is not accompanied by any revived interest in Judaism—he still refuses to attend the home's religious services—but is all part of his stirring the pot of language and memories one last time.

I arrive around noon, determined to bring him outside for a meal. My father, as usual, sits in the dining room, a distance apart from everyone else, staring down at his chin. There are a group of old ladies whom he manages to tantalize by neither removing himself entirely from their company nor giving them the benefit of his full attention. Though he has deteriorated badly in recent years, he still remains in better shape than some, hence a "catch." One Irish lady in particular, Sheila, with a twinkle in her cataracted eye, is always telling me what a lovely man my father is. He pays her no attention whatsoever.

It was not always thus. A letter he dictated for my sister Leah in California, when he first came to this home, contained the passage: "There's a woman by the name of Sheila who seems to be attracted to me. She's a heavyset woman, not too bad-looking, she likes me a lot, and is fairly even-tempered. I'm not sure of my feelings toward her. I'm ambivalent." ("Ambivalent" is a favorite Albert Lopate word. Purity of heart is for simpletons.) "Should I pursue this more aggressively, or should I let things go along at a normal pace?" The last line strikes me as particularly funny, given my father's inveterate passivity (what would aggressive pursuit entail for him?) and the shortage of time left to them both.

It took me a while to give up the hope that my father would find companionship, or at least casual friendship, in a nursing home. But the chances were slim: this is a man who never had nor made a friend for as long as I can remember. Besides, "friendship" is a cuddly term that ill describes the Hobbesian enmity and self-centeredness among these ancients.

"Don't push anything out of the window!" yells one old woman to another. "If anything's pushed out the window, it's going to be you!"

"I want to get out of here, I want to forget you, and I won't forget you unless I get out of this room!" yells the second.

"You dirty pig."

"You're one too."

So speak the relatively sane ones. The ward is divided between two factions: those who, like my father, can still occasionally articulate an intelligent thought, and those with dementia, who scream the same incoherent syllables over and over, kicking their feet and rending the air with clawed hands. The first group cordially detests the second. *Meshuge,* crazy, my father dismisses them with a word. Which is why, desperately trying to stay on the right side of Alzheimer's, he has become panicked by forgetfulness.

Asked how he is, he responds with something like: "It worries me I'm losing my memory. We were discussing the all-star pitcher the Dodgers used to have. Koufax. I couldn't remember Koufax's first name. Ridiculous!" For a man who once had quiz-show recall, such lapses are especially humiliating. He has been making alphabetical lists of big words to retain them. But the mind keeps slipping, bit by bit. I had no idea there could

be so many levels of disorientation before coming to rest at senility.

This time he has forgotten we've made a lunch date, and
sits ready to eat the institutional tray offered him. In a way, I
prefer his forgetting our date to his response a few years ago,
when he would wait outside three hours before my arrival,
checking his watch every ten minutes. As usual, he is dressed
too warmly, in a mud-colored, torn sweater, for the broiling
summer day. (These shabby clothes seem to materialize from
nowhere: where does his wardrobe come from, and whatever
happened to the better clothes we bought him? Theft is common in these establishments.)

I am in a hurry to wheel him outside today, before he becomes too attached to his meal—and before the atmosphere of
the nursing home gets to me.

I kiss him on top of his pink head, naked but for a few white
hairs, and he looks at me with delight. He is proud of me. I am
the lawyer, or the writer—in any case, a man of accomplish-
ment. In another minute he will start introducing me to the
women at the next table, "This is my son," as he has already
done a hundred times before, and they will pour on the syrup
about what a nice father I have, how nice I am to visit him
(which I don't do often enough), and how alike we look. This
time I start to wheel him out immediately, hoping to skip the
routine, when Sheila croaks in her Irish accent, "Don'tcha say
hello to me anymore?" Caught in the act of denying my father
the social capital a visitor might bring him, I go over and
schmooze a bit.

Meanwhile, the muskrat-faced Miss Mojabi (in the caste
division of this institution, the nursing staff is predominantly
Pakistani, the attendants mainly black, and the upper manage-

ment Orthodox Jewish) reminds me that I must "sign the form" to take legal responsibility for our outing. Were Armageddon to arrive, these nurses would be waiting pen in hand for a release signature. Their harsh, officious manner makes me want to punch them. I temper my rage with the thought that they are adequate if not loving—that it was we, the really unloving, who abandoned him to their boughten care.

My father's nursing home, located in Washington Heights, is perched on the steepest hill in Manhattan. After straining to navigate the wheelchair downhill, fantasizing what would happen if I let the handlebars slip (careening Papa smashing into tree), I bring us to a Chinese-Cuban takeout place on Broadway, a hole in the wall with three formica tables. It's Sunday, everything else is closed, and there are limits to how far north I am willing to push him in the August heat. My father seems glad to have made it to the outside; he wouldn't mind, I'm sure, being wheeled to Riverdale. Still, he has never cared much about food, and I doubt if the fare's quality will register on him one way or the other.

After asking him what he would like, and getting an inconclusive answer, I order sesame chicken and a beef dish at the counter. He is very clear on one thing: ginger ale. Since they have none, I substitute Mountain Dew. Loud salsa music on the radio makes it hard to hear him; moreover, something is wrong with his false teeth, or he's forgotten to put in the bridge, and he speaks so faintly I have to ask him to repeat each sentence several times. Often I simply nod, pretending to have heard. But it's annoying not to understand, so, as soon as he clears his throat—signaling intent to speak—I put my ear against his mouth, receiving communiqués from him in this misted, intimate manner.

From time to time he will end his silence with an observation, such as: "The men here are better-looking than the women." I inspect the middle-aged Dominican patrons, indoor picnickers in their Sunday best—the men gray-templed and stout, wearing dark suits or brocaded shirts; the women in skirts, voluptuously rounded, made-up, pretty—and do not share his opinion, but nod agreement anyway. I sense he offers these impressions less to express his notion of reality than to show he can still make comments. Ten minutes later another mysterious remark arrives, from left field, like the one about *abogado*. I prefer this system of waiting for my father to say something, between long silences, rather than prying conversation out of him. If my wife Cheryl were here, she would be drawing him out, asking him about the latest at the nursing home, whether he had seen any movies on TV, what he thought of the food, if he needed anything. And later she would consider the effort a success: "Did you see how much better he got, the longer we spoke? He's just rusty because nobody talks to him. But he's still sharp mentally. . . ." I'm glad she's not here, to see me failing to keep the conversational shuttlecock aloft.

You must have heard that corny idea: A true test of love is when you can sit silently next to the beloved without feeling any pressure to talk. I have never been able to accomplish this feat with any woman, howsoever beloved, but I can finally do it with one human being: my father. After fifty years of frustration as this lockjawed man's son, I no longer look on his uncommunicativeness as problematic or wounding. Quite the contrary: in my book, he has at last earned the right to be as closemouthed as he wants, just as I have earned the right to stare into space around him, indulging my own fly-on-the-wall proclivities.

He eats, engrossed, engaged in the uneven battle between

morsel and fork. With the plastic utensils they have given us, it is not easy for a man possessing so little remaining hand strength to spear chicken chunks. So he wields the fork like a spoon to capture a piece, transport it to his mouth, and crunch down, one half dropping into his lap. Those dark polyester pants, already seasoned, absorb the additional flavor of sesame sauce. He returns to the plate with that morose, myopic glare which is his trademark. My wife, I know, would have helpfully cut up the pieces into smaller bits. Me, I prefer to watch him struggle. I could say in my defense that by letting him work out the problem on his own, I am respecting his autonomy more. Or I could acknowledge some streak of cruelty for allowing him this fiasco. The larger truth is that I have become a fly on the wall, and flies don't use utensils.

Eventually I, too, cut up everything on my father's plate. So we both arrive at the same point, my wife and I, but at differing rates. Cheryl sizes up a new situation instantly, and sets about eliminating potential problems for others—a draft, a tipsy chair—as though all the world were a baby she needed to protect. My tendency is to adjust to an environment passively, like my father, until such time as it occurs to me to do what a considerate Normal Person (which I am decidedly not, I am a Martian) would do in these same circumstances: shut the window, cut up the old man's meat. My father is also from Mars. We understand each other in this way. He, too, approaches all matter as obdurate and mystifying.

My father drops some broccoli onto his lap. "Oh Al, how could you?" my mother would have cried out. "You're such a slob!" We can both "hear" her, though she is some eight miles downtown. As ever, he looks up sheepish and abashed, with a strangely innocent expression, like a chimp who knows it is displeasing its master but not why.

It gives me pleasure to spare him the expected familial re-proach. "Eat it with your hands, Pop. It's okay," I tell him. Who can object to an old man picking up his food? Certainly not the Dominicans enjoying themselves at the next table. Many African tribes eat with their fingers. The fork is a compara-tively recent innovation, from the late Middle Ages; Ethiopi-ans still think that the fork not only harms the food's taste, im-posing a metallic distance, but also spoils the sociability of each eater scooping up lentils and meat with soft porridgy bread from the common pot. Mayhap my father is a noble Ethiopian prince, mistransmigrated into the body of an elderly Jew? Too late: the tyranny of the fork has marked him, and he must steal "inadvertent" bits for his fingers' guilty pleasure.

I empathize with that desire to live in one's head, perform-ing an animal's functions with animal absentmindedness. Sometimes I, too, eat that way when I'm alone, mingling culi-nary herbs with the brackish taste of my fingers, in rebellious solidarity with his lack of manners. Socially, my older brother, Hal, and I have striven hard to project ourselves as the oppo-site of our father—to seem forceful, attentive, active, and se-ductive. But when no one is looking, I feel my father's vague-ness, shlumpiness, and mania for withdrawal inhabit me like a flu.

Across the street from the café, a drunken bum about sixty is dancing by himself on a park bench to Latin jazz. He has no shirt on, revealing an alkie's skinny frame, and he seems happy, moving to the beat with that uncanny, delayed rhythm of the stoned. I point him out as a potentially diverting spectacle to my father, who shows no interest. The drunk, in a curious way, reminds me of my dad: they're both functioning in a solipsistic cone.

Surrounded by "that thick wall of personality through

which no real voice has ever pierced on its way to us," as Pater phrased it, each of us is, I suppose, to some degree a solipsist. But my father has managed to exist in as complete a state of solipsism as any person I have ever known. When he gets into an elevator, he never moves to the back, although by now he must anticipate that others will soon be joining him. Inconsiderateness? The word implies the willful hurting of others whose existence one is at least aware of.

I once saw an old woman in the nursing home elevator telling him to move back, which he did very reluctantly, and only a step at a time for each repeated command. (Perhaps, I rationalized for him, he has a faulty perception of the amount of space his body takes up.) The old woman turned to her orderly and said, "When you get on in years, you have to live with old people. Some of them are nice and some are—peculiar." Meaning my father. When we got off the elevator, he said loudly, "She's such a pain in the ass, that one. Always complaining. I'll give her such a *luk im kopf*" (a smack in the head). His statement showed that he *had* been aware of her, but not enough to oblige her.

My father has always given the impression of someone who could sustain very little intensity of contact before his receptive apparatus shut down. Once, after I hadn't seen him in a year, I hugged him and told him how much I loved him. "Okay, okay. Cut the bullshit," he said. This armor of impatience may have been his defense against what he actually wanted so much that it hurt.

"Okay" is also his transitional marker, indicating he has spent long enough on one item and is ready for new data. If you haven't finished, so much the worse for you.

My sister Molly is the only one who can challenge his

solipsism. She pays him the enormous compliment of turning a deaf ear to his self-pity, and of assuming that, even in old age, there is still potential for moral growth. Years ago, hospitalized with pneumonia, he was complaining to her that nobody cared enough to visit him, and she shot back, "Do you care about anyone? Are you curious about anyone besides yourself?" She then tried to teach him, as one would a child, how to ask after others' well-being. "When you see them, say, 'How are you? What have you been up to lately? How are you *feeling?*'" And for a while it took. My father probably said "How are *you?*" more times between the ages of seventy-five and seventy-nine than in all the years preceding. If the question had a mechanical ring, if he speedily lost interest in the person's answer, that ought not to detract from the worthiness of my sister's pedagogy.

My father's solipsism is a matter of both style and substance. When I was writing an essay on the Holocaust, I asked him if he had any memories of refugees returning from the camps. He seemed affronted, as though to say, Why are you bothering me with that crazy business after all these years? "Ask your mother. She remembers it."

"But I'm asking you," I said. "When did you find out about the concentration camps? What was your reaction?"

"I didn't think about it. That was them and this was me," he said with a shrug.

Here was solipsism indeed: to ignore the greatest tragedy of modern times—of his own people!—because he wasn't personally involved. On the other hand, my father in his eighties is a hardly credible witness for the young man he was. What his reaction did underline was the pride he takes in being taciturn, and in refusing to cough up the conventionally pious response.

As I ask the Chinese waiter for the check, my father starts to fiddle with several napkins in his breast pocket. He has developed a curious relationship to these grubby paper napkins, which he keeps taking out of his pocket and checking. I've never seen him blow his nose with them. I wonder if old people have the equivalent of what clinical psychologists call "transitional objects"—like those pacifiers or teddy bears that children imbue with magical powers—and if these napkins are my father's talismans.

Just to show the internalized superego (God or my wife) that I have made an effort to Communicate, I volunteer some news about myself. I tell my father that Cheryl and I are soon to have a baby. His response is *"C'est la vie."* This is carrying philosophic resignation too far—even good news is greeted stoically. I tell him we have bought a house, and my teaching post is secure. None of these items seems to register, much less impress. Either he doesn't get what I'm saying, or he knows it already and is indifferent.

Hal called him recently with the news that *he* had had his first baby. On being told he was a grandfather, my father's answer was "Federico Fellini just died." This became an instant family joke, along with his other memorable non sequiturs. (If indeed it was a non sequitur. The translation might be "What do I care about your new baby when death is staring me in the face?") Though I could sympathize with Hal's viewing it as yet another dig to add to his copious brief against our father, who has always tended to compete with his sons rather than rejoice in their good fortune, this Fellini response seemed to me more an expression of incapacity than insult. The frown on his face

nowadays when you tell him something important, the repetition of the phrase *c'est la vie*, is a confession that he knows he
can't focus enough to hold on to what you are saying; he lacks
the adhesive cement of affect.

Even sports no longer matter to him. They used to be one
of our few common topics: I was guaranteed a half hour's worth
of conversation with my father, working my way through the
Knicks, Mets, Rangers, Giants, Jets. . . . His replies were curt,
yet apt: "They stink. They got no hitting." He it was who
taught me that passionate fandom which merges with disenchantment: loyalty to the local team, regardless of the stupid
decisions the front office made; never cross a picket line, just
stick with the union, for all their corruption; vote Democratic
no matter how mediocre this year's slate. I would have thought
being a sports fan was part of his invincible core, as much as his
addiction to newspapers. He continues to have the *Times* ordered for him, but now it sits on his lap, unopened, like a ship
passenger's blanket.

Back at the home, I bend down and kiss him on the cheek
before leaving. He says, "I still got more hair than you do." This
statement—untrue, as it happens—no longer can provoke me.
He shakes my hand, to demonstrate how strong his grip is: it's
a stunt he's learned, no indication of his actual strength, but,
like the occasional big word, all that is left in his armatorium
of self-esteem.

"Do you need anything, Pop?"

"Well, I do and I don't."

Not knowing what to make of this enigmatic response, I
say, "Do you need any money?" I hand him two twenty-dollar

182 bills. He takes them uncertainly and bunches them in his hands without putting them away, which makes me think they will not stay long in his care. My father seems much more solicitous of his old napkins than these greenbacks.

"Do me a favor," he says hoarsely.

"What's that?"

"Try to see me more regularly. Once every few weeks."

This request takes my breath away. He's right, of course.

"I'll try. I *will* try. I was insanely busy this past month, but from now on . . ." I lie. Then, to shift the burden elsewhere, I ask, "Did you get any other visits recently?"

No, he shakes his head. I know this is not true: my brother visited him last Sunday. He gets no brownie points; Pop's already forgotten. Which means he won't remember my visit either by tomorrow.

2.

"If I wrote my life down, I would have to title it *The Story of a Failure*." This is, in old age, my father's idée fixe. Ask him for particulars, he will reply tersely, "I was a failure. What else is there to say?" Being a failure apparently grants one the privilege of taciturnity (just as being a success must condemn me to garrulity).

Many times I have argued with him: "What makes you so presumptuous or so arrogant as to judge yourself a failure, when you accomplished no less than ninety-five percent of the rest of humanity?" He will not hear of it. He thinks I am trying to reassure him. Besides, he seems at times proud to be labeled a failure, to partake of its peculiar romance. Nineteenth-century Russian fiction perfected this defense of the failure as the underground man, the marginal, economically redundant, passive intellectual, for whom superfluousness was a mark of superiority. The less you accomplished, the more you built up your store of latency, and the purer your integrity remained.

About a year ago my wife and I were driving my father to a midtown restaurant, just to give him an excursion. In the car he was telling us he considered his life a failure.

I had heard this too many times to comment, but Cheryl said, "Why? You worked every day of your life, and you raised four children and they turned out fairly well."

"But I was always doing what I shouldn't have been doing, and not doing what I should have," he replied.

"What do you mean? You were supposed to go to work and you did."

"Yeah, but even though my bosses said I was a good worker, they didn't pay me well."

"Then it's their failure, not yours," said Cheryl. "They failed to do the right thing."

"What do you think you should have been doing?" I interrupted.

"Writing," he said.

"What kind of writing?"

"Fiction."

I never knew he thought of himself as a failed *novelist*. "Fiction?" I demanded.

"Or semifactual," he reconsidered. "I always wanted to be a writer, or something of that sort, and in some respects you fulfilled my ambition. Vicariously, I am *kvelling* in your success as a writer." He added that lately he had been having "hallucinations" that he wrote a book, or rather, stole it from me, and in so doing brought shame and dishonor on us all.

This confusion between his and my writing achievement has been there right from the start. Growing up, I was impressed by my father's large vocabulary, his peculiar, formal, crisp feeling for language. I submitted my first short story (about a gangster shot in a dark alley) for his criticism, and watched as he struck out the unnecessary words and told me, "Write what you know." Still trusting his infallibility in writing matters, I was graduating from junior high school when my teacher asked me, along with four other students, to compete for valedictorian by writing a speech. Since I had the highest grade average in the school, everyone assumed I would win the contest. But I had no idea what a valedictorian's speech was supposed to sound like, and so—oddly enough—I asked my father to write mine for me. He complied, employing his fanciest vocabulary and dwelling on the *parents'* feelings during such an occasion (using words like "vicarious" and "progenitors"). The speech laid an egg, and a chubby girl named Andrea Bravo, who expressed herself earnestly if tritely, got chosen instead. After that, I was warier about asking for his writing help.

I remember when I told my father back in 1971 that my first book of poems was about to come out. His only response was "I haven't been writing any poems recently." I was struck then by how little feeling he seemed to have for me. Yet my siblings claim that I am my father's favorite—that he brags about me more to strangers, or, to put it another way, that he pays even less attention to them than he does to me.

"The possum," my mother calls him. "He plays dead. It's an act, he thinks the Angel of Death won't notice him if he lays low. The old man's stronger than you think. He'll outlive me, you, everybody."

All my life, it seems, I have been rehearsing prematurely for the death of my father. At eleven years old I woke from a dream in which he had been killed; I got up like a sleepwalker and, as if by dictation, wrote down a poem of grief over the vision of him laid out on a bier. My mother took it to her analyst, Dr. Jonas in the Bronx, and he told her that dreams were wish fulfillment. She broke the hard news to me: it wasn't that I loved my father so, it was that I wanted him dead in order to marry her. This made little sense at the time, but I have always been willing to believe the worst about myself, and began to accept the possibility of harboring a parricide within.

("Parricide," incidentally, was a concept very much in the air when I grew up. My father had no love for his father, and his favorite book was *The Brothers Karamazov.*)

I must say, never for a conscious instant did I wish my father dead. But that may be because he seemed, as long as I can remember, already suffering from a mortal wound. One of the movies that left the deepest impression on me in my youth was *Odd Man Out,* in which the sympathetic IRA operative, Johnny, played by James Mason, has been shot and spends the rest of the movie trying to stay alive. Somehow you know just by looking at him that he is bleeding to death. James Mason (cerebral, ironic, solitary, drawn) was a sort of idealized version of my father. Wiry and gaunt, my father would come home, his job having consumed his stamina, and sit like a zombie, halfdozing, letting the cigarette ash grow dangerously, while a ballgame sounded on the radio.

Avoiding pain and love, he withdrew into that dreamy, numbed zone that Schopenhauer (one of his favorites) called "the lost paradise of nonexistence." These withdrawals, this maddening, arms-folded passivity of his, infuriated my mother, goading her into ever-stronger provocations. We, his four children, also provoked him, wanting him to notice us. It was like baiting a bear; occasionally he would treat us to a smack, but for the most part he shrugged us off, with a half-smile that said, You can't get to me.

I have never known a man who was criticized as severely as my father. You would think he had committed some heinous crime. Hour after hour, he would be told he was uncouth, insensitive, thoughtless, gross. It made no difference in his behavior: he didn't get it, or he didn't want to get it. He continued to do things in what seemed like an alien, oafish manner—not to mention the things he didn't do, such as: talk to us, buy us birthday presents, show us affection, compliment us, even go to the hospital when my mother gave birth. By today's sensitive-male standards, he was certainly a washout. On the other hand, I wonder if he was really so different from many men of his generation.

Just for variety's sake, if nothing else, I would defend him in the family circle. But then he would say something mean to me as well that would catch me up short and make me realize what hostile bitterness had collected behind that carapace of silence. It was the custom for my father to take us to the museum on Saturdays when he didn't have to work—usually after much badgering by my mother, who wanted some time to herself alone. One Saturday morning when I was about ten years old, we were all hounding him because he wouldn't take us anywhere; and this time I joined in the assault. Suddenly he lashed out at me with rabid fury: "You! You stay out of it, you're a cold fish." It was as if he were rebuking me for not having attacked him "warmly" enough in the past. I think he liked being attacked, or at least knew how to convert that coin into love more dependably than direct expressions of affection.

"Cold fish" is an awful judgment to hang on a ten-year-old kid. But give him his due, he could have had a prescient insight: I often think there is something cold and "fishy" about me. Or perhaps he was really saying, "You're like me, detached, unemotional." An inverted compliment.

So I became a writer.

But this is not about me; I must restrain myself from turning my father into a repository of clues to the genesis of my own development. I must get back on track and try to tell the story of this tight-lipped man's life, attempt to discover its underlying meaning. Why had he gravitated toward death-in-life? What made him throw in his hand so quickly? Or did he, really? There are organisms, such as barnacles, that manifest the most dogged willpower through a strategy that looks initially like weakness or dependency.

Albert Donald Lopate was born on September 2, 1910. He grew up in Jamaica, Queens, with three older half-siblings and one full brother. He felt unloved by both his mother and his father, with good cause.

My grandmother Sophie died before I was born, so I cannot describe her from experience. (I am told that she spent her last years looking out the window spotting car makes, went mad, and died in a mental hospital.) But I remember my grandfather Samuel Lopate quite well. He was a *character*, a Jewish Fyodor Karamazov in his appetite for women and money, and his utter indifference to children.

My grandfather was born in Russia; when he was about ten, his parents fled the pogroms, via Turkey, to Palestine. Family legend has it that they were thrown out of Palestine because he pissed on the Wailing Wall. My father says, more conservatively, "He did something which caused the Arabs to expel them. He made fun when the Arabs were praying at the wall, and they were outraged."

The next we hear of my grandfather, he has come to New York and married, for love, a woman who dies in childbirth. Soon after, for economic security, he latches on to an older widow, Sophie—a second cousin of his—with three children and a dry goods store. He goes to work in the store and wrests it from her. He sires two sons, Arthur and Albert.

Sophie was almost fifty when she had my father, and felt so lukewarm toward this child, whom she had tried unsuccessfully to abort, that she would not even look at him. Afterward she used him as her servant, making him wash the floors every Saturday. She favored the offspring from her first husband, the love of *her* life.

My father's parents fought openly. Sophie called Samuel a *trumernik* (loafer, bum, philanderer). My grandfather was, in truth, something of a ladykiller. He had one talent that would knock women dead: he could cry at will. The sight of those plump crocodile tears rolling down his émigré cheeks melted many a female heart. (This led my father to the unfortunate conclusion that being emotionally undemonstrative was a mark of sincerity.) All told, Samuel buried three wives, which gave him the reputation of the family Bluebeard. The last wife, Esther, I knew as a child. She was sweet, gave us oatmeal cookies, and was a reader (by which I mean she subscribed to the Book-of-the-Month Club). My mother, who despised her lecherous father-in-law, used to say, "He'll drive her into a grave too, like the others." Sure enough, Esther died, leaving Samuel a chunk of money, and us a box of books, which included Goren's *Contract Bridge*, *Thirty Days to a More Powerful Vocabulary*, and Henry George's tracts on social economy, which I tried in vain to penetrate.

I remember Samuel in his widower dotage: a cranky, cold, bald-headed, fat old man who would sit on his porch in Ozone Park, his bulging pants held up with suspenders. The only time I ever saw him pleased was when he took out a rainbow-speckled Irish Sweepstakes ticket, ornate as a stock certificate, and stared at it. He was convinced he would win, and not have to enter an old-age home; but he didn't, and soon he was complaining from the much smaller confines of half a room in the Rogers Avenue Nursing Home. My father would take us there to visit, perhaps in the hope that Samuel's grandparental warmth would be belatedly awakened and he'd leave us something. We were all very conscious that the longer he stayed in that nursing home, the more our possible inheritance was being eaten up.

I tried to encourage Grandpa to go out into the little garden and take a constitutional. He never listened to me, any more than he did to my father. My sister Molly alone knew how to handle Grandpa. Whenever she needed money for the movies, she would pay him an impromptu visit and wheedle a dollar bill out of him. This game he understood; he had played it on women often enough.

But to return to my father's youth. He used to sit in the back of his parents' dry goods store and read for escape. Dumas, Hugo, *The Count of Monte Cristo*. At school he was skipped ahead, and a sympathetic teacher helped him to catch up with the older kids; by the end of the term he had the highest average in the new class.

The next year my father, a natural lefty, had a less understanding teacher, who tried to force him to write right-handed. He developed a stammer, and his grades suffered when the teacher couldn't decipher his penmanship. Defiantly, he went back to writing left-handed.

In high school he continued to read voraciously on his own, meanwhile ignoring the assigned schoolwork. Later in life he would brag about his scholastic exploits in high school: acing a Latin test he hadn't studied for, or frustrating teachers with his nonchalance. "I had a math teacher who would open up the class with a question, 'Lopate, did you do your homework?' And I would say, 'No, ma'am.' And she'd write down a zero in front of my name. Then I got 96 on the final, and she gave me a 69 for the course. I said to her, 'How could you give me a 69, when I got 96 on the final?' So she showed me all the zeroes and when she averaged them out, I got a 34. I said, 'Why don't you give me a 34, then? What you're doing is dishonest.' "

He was proud of being an intellectual dark horse—a "gifted underachiever," as it would later be called. I asked him once why he took such pleasure in flouting the teacher's authority, when he must have known he would get punished for it. He said, "I didn't give a good goddamn what she thought, so long as I knew I understood the math."

His rebellion extended to rejecting his own family's Orthodox Judaism and Republican politics. They thought him a Socialist, and at least temperamentally he was pointed that way. "I thought of money as evil. I became an intellectual snob. I *eschewed* financial gain," he boasted. He wanted to go on to college and asked his mother for a loan, and she turned him down, "although she had the dough," and although she had already subsidized his brother Arthur's higher education. He knew enough not to ask Samuel. "My father never treated me with the proper respect." The only one in his family who saw he had a brain, and encouraged him to continue learning, was an older half-brother, Charles. But Charles obviously could not foot his tuition bill, so my father went to work, with the notion that eventually he might save enough to pay for his own college education.

He was drawn to newspapers. His first job was taking ads and running the switchboard for the *Long Island Press*. From there, he tried out for a job at a trade magazine, *Editor and Publisher*. Typical of my father's somewhat self-destructive integrity is that he made a point of telling the interviewer he was Jewish (he does not look noticeably so), at a time when discrimination against Jews was widespread. They hired him anyway. After that, he became a reporter for the *Queens Evening News*: his beat was to cover the political clubs and civic organizations in different neighborhoods and drum up stories. Though I find it difficult to imagine my father engaged in anything so extroverted, these cub reporter days were happy times for him. His terse style suited the newspaper format.

Having saved enough money, he enrolled in night school classes in journalism. But, after the long workday, he would fall asleep in class. So he dropped out of college in his freshman year, focusing on reporting instead.

"Then the Depression came, and the paper folded up, and there were no more journalistic jobs to be had." (Whenever my father would say, "Then the Depression came," the historical, capital *D* event always carried an echo of clinical, small *d*.) He took the only job he could get: a stock clerk for six dollars a week. As this was not enough to live on, he augmented his salary by playing poker at night. My father has always disliked gambling; but he was blessed with a poker face, and always believed himself smarter than others, and so, by cautious, close-to-the-vest playing, he would pocket a few extra dollars.

It was still not enough to make ends meet, so he asked his boss for a raise. "I was told, 'I can replace you with a college graduate who will willingly take your place for the same salary.'" My father answered, "In that case, you can get someone else." Years later he recalled vividly the boss's utter power over him; in that encounter, despite his shaky bravado, he was traumatized into a lifelong fear of unemployment. He reluctantly took the step of going to work for his older brother Arthur, on the assumption that a family member, at least, would never fire him.

At this moment in the story we may pause and note two things: (1) my father's capacity for defiance and self-assertion was still operating; he had not yet joined the legion of the defeated; (2) his explanation that the Depression had closed down his journalistic options, true as it may be, does not explain why he never tried to reenter this beloved milieu when the economy improved. His fatalistic statement, "Then the Depression came," became one of those family myths that remains to this day sacrosanct, unquestioned. On the other hand, I have no business judging him on this score, never having lived through such an ordeal. The critic Manny Farber once told a younger man, "You know, I'm not someone who ever survived the Depression. It's not the sort of experience you ever really get over."

In any event, my father despised his powerful older brother, so that to go to work in his ribbon-dyeing factory, Parkside, meant no small swallowing of pride. The source of this fraternal dislike must have had roots in childhood, but my father always harps on a later incident. "When my brother Arthur got married, he started catering to my mother, he played up to her, and he got a good present for the wedding. I thought he had prostituted himself to get some dough, because he didn't give a damn about her. I don't think he cared at all about her, he didn't have one iota of feeling."

"Did *you* care about your mother?" I asked him.

"Not really. But I wasn't ready to prostitute myself."

As people are rarely entirely unselfish or sincere, I could never understand my father's enduring shock at this bit of filial pretense (if it was that). His outrage had something primitive about it: Arthur had stolen the "blessing" of their mother, through guile, and Albert had gotten nothing. Jacob and Esau all over again.

It was also said in my family that Arthur "cheated" my father by skimping on his salary. I have a feeling he paid him the going rate, no more, no less. My father liked certain manual labor aspects of the job: lifting hundred-pound bales, going out with the drivers on delivery. One time, however, the workers struck; my father was sympathetic to their cause, but felt an overriding family loyalty. When the labor trouble was settled, everyone got a raise, except my father, who was not in the union and was treated, conveniently in this instance, as management. To compound the indignity, Arthur "threw me a few extra dollars from time to time, to keep me quiet."

If Uncle Arthur had that family knack of treating Albert with insufficient respect, my father also seemed quick to take offense. In recent years he would tell of running into Arthur at the funeral of a relative. Arthur took him aside and said, "We're the only ones left. Let's stay in touch. Give me your phone number." My father pulled himself up with dignity: "You should know my phone number. It has been in the book for years." He offered this story as proof of Arthur's hypocrisy: "He was phony as a three-dollar bill." Of course, my father could have just as easily phoned Arthur all those years, and didn't.

It strikes me as curious that, though my family has been willing to mock my father at every turn, it has never questioned his judgment of Arthur. In our family myth, Uncle Arthur is the Evil One, the vulgar Capitalist, like the figure of the watch-chained plutocrat in left-wing cartoons. On the few occasions we visited Arthur in his spacious Queens home, usually for his children's bar mitzvahs or engagement parties, he struck me as a typical hail-fellow-well-met type. I remember his prosperous, well-fed look, the rosy spots on his cheeks—and the well-founded report that he had a mistress.

That he kept a mistress made me like him. I dreamed of attaining the same worldliness as a man. Over the years, in fact, I developed a blasphemous feeling of identification with Uncle Arthur, partly because I did not myself "eschew" financial success and partly because I took with a grain of salt my impoverished family's self-serving antagonism toward him. Maybe Arthur really was a shithead, maybe he was a decent guy, I have no idea. All I know is the role he played in the family mythology. After he sold the ribbon-dyeing plant, he went into "the oil business." Probably what was meant was some sort of fuel delivery, but I always liked to fancy him an oilman, the Queens equivalent of a Texas millionaire. If I secretly identified with Uncle Arthur, I also suspected my father associated me with his older brother. He had been told when they were growing up that Arthur was the handsome one, and he, not; he has often described me, with mixed pride and rue, as "a good-looking guy." At such moments I feel myself lumped with his nemesis. The glib-tongued charmer. The lawyer.

My father, from the photographic evidence of his young manhood, seems to me to have been quite good-looking, in that brooding, sunken-cheeked way of Lincoln, Joseph Wiseman, Jack Palance, Cesare Pavese, and an Appalachian farmer in a Walker Evans photograph. But what matters is what my father thought; and when my father met my mother, he thought himself ugly. At twenty-seven, he had never been in love; he had never slept with a woman who was not a prostitute. My mother, Frances, was working in a beauty parlor when they met. She was sexy, she had a voluptuous figure, and all the guys wanted her, or at least, as she puts it, wanted to fool around with her. But she was attracted to brains; and in their Jamaica, Queens circle, Albert was the intellectual. He wooed her with talk about politics, books, art, Bach. He taught her. He saw in my mother an unformed intelligence—but an intelligence. "All of Fran's siblings kept saying she was the dummy in the Berlow family. I took one look at her family, and I said, 'You're not stupid. They are.' "

Bonding on the resentful basis that they were both insufficiently respected by their families, they married. Many good marriages have been founded on less. In their case, however, it was not enough.

My father tells it one way, my mother another. The difference is that my mother's version is livelier and more voluble; my father's, extremely laconic. (I once tape-recorded my mother telling her life story: it took six sessions and twenty-two

sides. My father's took less than an hour.) As long as I can remember, my mother has been honing and expanding the story
of his husbandly wrongs. According to her, the problems began
while they were still courting; he had laughingly allowed a jibe
at her by Arthur's son ("Gee, you got a big nose!") to stand,
and she never forgave him his lack of gallantry. My mother had
notions of a gentleman's behavior toward women that my father violated at every turn: he did not pay enough attention to
her on their honeymoon, he lacked the proper romantic approach to lovemaking. Later, back in the city, he would come
home from the factory, reeking with sweat; the odor turned her
off. She would make him take a bath immediately. His personal
hygiene standards, she felt, left much to be desired; his sexual
technique, likewise.

My father says: "Look, Fran was not a virgin when I married her. She insisted that I wasn't 'liberated' enough, that we
weren't sexually 'compatible.' Although we managed to have
four kids, supposedly we weren't 'compatible.' "

Juxtaposing their testimonies, I can still hear the sound of
two people not listening to each other—the sound that dominated my childhood.

My mother says now that my father missed out on the joys
of fatherhood by not involving himself in changing diapers,
preparing bottles, cradling us, and so on.

By his own account, he kept a distance from childrearing:
"When Hal was born, we used to have a next-door neighbor
named Herman. And Hal would say 'Herman, Herman' before
he said 'Daddy.' " My father's deadpan voice on the tape betrays
only a quiver of the pain this memory must have caused him.

"How come?" I hear the interlocutor (myself) ask.

"I don't know. Maybe I wasn't exactly a loving father like

most fathers are. And this man paid a lot of attention to the kid, and the kid reacted to it."

"Do you think it was because you hadn't gotten any example of love from your own father?"

"Probably. Same thing happened all over again."

By my father's admission, he was ambivalent about having children. The first one he accepted philosophically. "When we had the second and third, I became a little leery."

Understandably, since there was never any money, and he had found himself indentured to the economic burdens of a large family. He took them on without complaint, working six days a week. At home he was both an ineffectual and a scary figure. I remember as a boy being physically frightened of my father. He was much more prone to hit my older brother than me, being more jealous of Hal, I suppose. And Hal was more willing to trade blows with him: they would go at it, crashing into furniture, with my mother in the background, screaming at them to stop. I felt it taboo, unthinkable, to raise my hand against my father. He could have killed me. I kept my distance, knowing he could hurt just as easily through absentmindedness as intention. One time we were waiting to be served in a bakery, and he accidentally let a cigarette ash drop down my back. For years I felt that ember on my back with wincing reflex.

By the time I was six, the fighting between my mother and father had become so severe they almost split up. This is how he told it to me on tape:

"Let's get to the nitty-gritty. When I was first married, your mother was unfaithful to me. And I found out. And one day I found myself choking her. Then, in the middle of it, I stopped short. Because I said to myself, 'Why am I doing this? This is not me. I am not a violent person. I'm not a person of action.' And I stopped. That's when your mother had me. Because she had something she could always hold against me, that I tried to choke her."

My father had very consciously set up this experience as the key point in his oral autobiography, although, with his usual self-absorption, he was unaware of the repugnant effect this confession—that he wished he had strangled my mother—might have on me, her son.

"Why didn't you leave her instead?"

"That's the story of my failure. Because I couldn't leave her. I'm not saying this in defense of myself. I *said* I made my mistake: I should have killed her, and it would have ended then and there. I would have been tried and sent to prison, and that would be that. This way I let everything linger on, and solved nothing."

"So your greatest regret in life is that you didn't kill her?"

"Yes. That I didn't stop the thing—the condition."

"And that would have been the only way to stop it?"

"I don't know whether it was the only way, but it was a solution. Whereas what ensued was not."

"How would you characterize what ensued?"

"Years of nothing. Of numbed nonexistence." (I was surprised to hear my father himself acknowledge this death-in-life state.) After a long pause, he said, "I want to amend that. The only encouraging thing was that we engendered four children whom I think in some ways have embellished my life." He paused. "I realize, of course, that Leah is not my kid. But I never told her, and I never acted as if I knew. I acted as fairly as possible, because I said to myself, 'This is not her fault, why should I hold it against her?' "

In fact, he succeeded, to the degree that he showed more fondness for Leah as a child than for the rest of us. What does it say about this man, that he would dote on the one child that was not his own? Self-hatred? But Leah was also the youngest, she was very winning, she was a girl (hence less threatening to him than his sons), and she was quiet, soft-spoken like him. Whatever the reasons, his decision to treat her as his own, without ever letting her know she had a different father (the truth came out eventually, but not through him), seems admirable in retrospect. It may be the most noble, disciplined-heroic thing he ever did. A shame we never gave him sufficient credit for it.

But something was bothering me: "How is it that you and Mother were so sure Leah wasn't your kid?"

"I wasn't that sure until your mother told me. . . . Look, it doesn't make any difference, that's the way I felt."

"Still, it's a hard thing to know for sure unless you take blood tests."

"At first she looked a little different than the Lopates. Don't get me wrong, I think Leah is, in her way, a wonderful girl."

He spoke about the summer that had led up to her birth. "We went upstate on vacation, and we lived in a bungalow colony—a *kuchalein*, they called it, because you did your own cooking. At that time I used to play cards. I spent a little more time with cards than I should have. That's when your mother took up with this fellow. Benno. He was supposed to be related to one of the big-shot families in the Israeli government. He was a nice guy. He must have aroused a spark in the old lady.

He didn't seem too bright to me. But that judgment may be qualified by the fact that I resented him. Actually, I spent too much time with cards, and I shouldn't have."

"So you blame yourself partly?"

"Oh, yes. The old lady wasn't entirely wrong."

This responsible, mature perspective somehow manages to coexist with the regret that he did not kill her.

My father's emphasis on the choking incident spooked me because I had already used that episode as the climax of my story "Willy." After the story appeared in my book *Bachelorhood*, my mother informed me that I had exaggerated the ferocity of his beating. "I wasn't afraid of him for one second. If he'd really tried to hurt me," she boasted, "I could have broken him in half." (My mother is a stout woman and, in fact, outweighs him.) My father, on the other hand, was so impressed with the story's denouement that he seemed to have appropriated it as his central myth. I'm not at all convinced he saw his whole life as leading up to and away from this failed homicide until he read my story, which could have put the notion into his head.

Around the same period that I tape-recorded him, when he was in his mid-seventies, my sister Molly asked him, point-blank, "When did you decide to become a vegetable?"

He answered her: "When I had my hands around your mother's throat, I was so horrified at the violence this evil woman had provoked in me, when my nature is not violent, that I decided then and there to punish her by becoming passive."

To Molly, this answer confirmed her belief that he had deliberately created a passive persona—out of spite. I remained skeptical. For one thing, it was almost word for word what he'd said to me, and sounded too canned. For another, I could never accept the family's idea that my father had sinisterly willed himself to be a "vegetable." This gave him too much credit for intent; he was trying in the final hours to pretend he had caused the shambles of his life, rather than acknowledging the more common fate of limitation and deterioration.

But Molly took him at his word. Her response was funny if harsh: "If you want to be a vegetable, you gotta be sent to the farm!" (i.e., the nursing home).

My mother's tendency was always to speak of my father as a needy child. "I got five kids at home, you four and Al. He's the biggest baby of all." Or: "He doesn't want a wife. He wants a mother. A nursemaid," she would say bitterly. She is a large-bosomed woman, and I took her comment to mean she found something infantile about my father's fixation on that part of her anatomy. But what is so unusual about a man looking for Nirvana at a woman's breast? Freud argued that fantasy had its origins in an irrecoverable experience of bliss at the mother's breast, and that all later gratifications, including sex, are bound to be incomplete. In my father's case, his own mother had been cold toward him, so his search was all the more imperative, if tinged with the expectation of rejection.

Many of the dozen or so poems my father wrote my mother, in an effort to win her back when she was seeing another man, speak to this pathos of unsatisfied desire, the distance between coitus and possession.

DILEMMA OF LOVE

I made love to you and you sighed
And violently clawed my heaving flesh.

This should have been ecstatic joy,
But both you and I know that
Tho I possessed your body, I had
Penetrated only to your outer shell.
Deep inside there remained the
Suppressed mask of discontentment
The ever-present search for
I know not what. But not for me.

I make no claims for my father's verse—he was clearly a
self-taught, Sunday poet—but what mesmerizes me is the
Cavafyan dryness, the refusal of consolation that pops up in the
last line. Another poem is again about sex; this time he is the
onlooker. It begins:

Last night you were entwined with another.
I saw your passionate embrace
And heard your deeply contented sighs,
And I fondly remembered that there
I had once joyously nestled.

"Nestled"—so fitting a word for the infant at the breast. He
then seeks to recall her to their happy hours together: mean-
derings through Central Park and Coney Island, long conversations on her stairs. The poem ends:

Even tho you presume not to remember,
And your thoughts are concentred on him,
I can never obliterate them from my mind—
And neither can you.

That menacing last line—no wonder these poems did not
do the trick of winning her over! Reading through them, I am

struck by their narrow range of lament at love's inconstancy. However, as Faiz once said, "the proper subject of poetry is the loss of the beloved." Certainly there is something moving about a pain so unbearable it could find expression only in po-etry—and then only once, during the initial marital crisis.

That early threat of losing her had elicited, then, two ex-traordinary responses: the poems and the choking, that violent aggression finally coming to the surface. After that, he was spent, for the rest of his days, or so he says. But isn't this too pat, too "literary" an interpretation of a man's life? Are there really such crossroads of decision in life, like a well-made Chekhov story, after which the person who has chosen un-wisely drags on to the end like a ghost of himself? Is there such a limited supply of life force in a human being that it can be consumed at one go?

Interestingly, my mother dates his giving up to an earlier point: the marriage itself. "He didn't read as much after he got married. He started quoting what he'd already read." Since she had married him for his brains, this relaxing of mental striving caused her understandable chagrin. Still, it means he stopped trying to expand his range not from jealous spite but from re-lief of the sort that follows accomplishing a goal. Supposing this lonely, cerebral young man had yearned for "normalcy," marriage and family, and, having attained this plateau—like the woman who lets her looks go after marriage—he had less need to develop his intellect as a lure.

All the while that he was working at his brother Arthur's factory, my mother was always goading him to improve his sit-uation in life. Among other things, she urged him to become a life insurance salesman. One of her beaux sold insurance, and said he would put in a good word for Al. My father went so far as to enroll in a training program. At night he would practice the standard pitch, the euphemisms sticking in his craw ("Should one of your loved ones drop out of the picture . . ."), using his children as audience. But he had such a mournful countenance that one could not imagine him selling anything, much less insurance. When he took the aptitude test, he scored high on the intellectual portion, as expected, then was disqualified by a disastrous personnel interview.

According to my mother, he kept resisting advancement. After he left his brother's plant to work in another factory, he took a test for a foreman's position and scored very high, only to see a man with a lower grade but more seniority hired. "Instead of telling himself, 'Okay, I'll get it on the next opening,' he gave up. He was defeated before he started," she says.

My mother is, if anything, the opposite: she had a lifelong dream to become an entertainer, and, after she was fifty, did succeed in getting acting jobs, doing commercials, playing Golda in road productions of *Fiddler on the Roof*. Perhaps she had so much life force, so much determination, that he receded before it, feeling that that department was already being looked after. He was content to support her efforts to enter show business.

I think another reason for his resistance to climbing the managerial ladder was that he already had an ambition—to write—and, failing to achieve it, didn't wish to substitute a less compelling one. All this is speculative; my father himself has offered only the murkiest explanations about this area. I asked him once, "Did you *want* to be promoted to manager at the plant?"

"I didn't know what the hell I wanted. I was so confused at the time."

Eventually he followed my mother into the white-collar side of the textile industry, becoming a shipping clerk in midtown Manhattan. He was an excellent clerk, perfectly suited for the duties of keeping track of numbers and shipments, by virtue of his phenomenal memory. Sometimes he could not resist showing off his intellectual superiority, as when he sent a telex to the North Carolina plant in Latin: *"Que usque, Catilina, abutere patientia nostra?"* ("How long, Catiline, will you abuse our patience?") That must have gone over big.

Though my father continued to read, often picking up the novels my brother and I introduced into the household, his main intellectual activity became doing the crossword puzzle. Increasingly, the less respected he felt in the world, the more he took to boasting about his mathematical shortcuts or word power. Or he would go on about how he was the first in our family to appreciate, say, Bessie Smith or Stroheim's *Greed*. Even as a child I was embarrassed by these threadbare boasts; for if this was all a grown man had to feel good about himself, he was clearly in trouble.

As he grew older, the boasting anecdotes began to substitute for an active memory. He would tell for the thousandth time how he had responded to *Greed* before anyone else knew it was good. "The thing that made it so unusual was that they cast against type. They took ZaSu Pitts, who was known as a dizzy comic, and made her play the mean, calculating bitch. Then they got George O'Brien, this romantic lead, and made him play a stupid lunk."

(One time, overcome by impatience at hearing this broken record, I interrupted: "Actually, it was Gibson Gowland who played McTeague, not George O'Brien, and what makes *Greed* so great is the physical detail of the film—the direction, not the casting." He looked miserable. "I don't know, I probably got it confused." Instantly I regretted not having let him ramble on. It was too easy to slay this father.)

Bragging is a Lopate family trait; not only my mother and siblings, but I succumb to it all too often—especially under stress. As soon as I start to brag, though, I hear my father's voice, and flinch at the futility of bestowing on oneself the admiration one craves from others.

The other negative of his bragging was that it deepened his obsession with being a failure. Had he not insisted so on his superiority, he might not have been so hard on himself about the way his life had turned out.

3.

Each year the nursing home invites family members to a staff meeting to discuss the resident's overall condition. I have been to several of these: the psychologist always says, with concern, "Your father seems depressed," as though such reaction to being locked away in a nursing home were peculiar. Each year I answer, "My father has been depressed all his life." The statement is greeted with meaningful nods, but has little lasting effect: the training of those in the caring professions seems to obligate them to treat melancholy as a temporary aberration. The psychologist working with my father is a behavior-modification enthusiast who is convinced that if you can get people to frame their statements in a positive form, they will feel better about themselves. The clinical equivalent of a "Smiles" face. It is even more futile in this case, given my father's vanity toward his pessimism. But I appreciate that they are trying their best: the concern and good intentions of the staff are evident. They tell me (first the good news) that my father is an "attractive," well-liked resident, who makes a strong impression. But (the bad news): "He does not eat. He is losing weight. He shows very little appetite, and he won't even let us feed him." All present look frowningly in the direction of the wheelchaired old man, head sunk on his chest, who, as it happens, has been there throughout his case discussion.

I do my part to scold as well. "Pop, you're intelligent enough to know that if you don't eat, you'll get sick. Do you want to be sick?"

He's heard it before. Unimpressed. He keeps his counsel: silent, deep, unfathomable.

"Mr. Lopate," asks a social worker sharply, in such a way as to demand an answer, "what do you make of all this?"

"I'm trying to figure out," says my father, "how the hell to get out of here."

When he was in his early fifties, my father had his first stroke. I was still living at home, going to college, and I remember the shrieking in the middle of the night as my mother tried to restrain him from getting out of bed. "Please, Al, don't move, the ambulance is coming!" He had it in his head that she was trying to kill him, and he had better get up or he would never rise from the bed again.

Tanizaki's novel *The Key*, which had been making the rounds of our house, lay on his night table: this perverse story of husband and wife plotting to do each other in may have fueled his suspicion. Then again, my mother had so often declared she wished he was dead that I, too, watched her uneasily that night.

After the stroke he never recovered the full strength on his right side. And it threw a fear of death into him that made him even more inert, as though by doing next to nothing he would conserve strength and live longer: the possum strategy.

On the plus side, he was no longer frightening to me after his stroke. His new harmlessness enabled me to nurture feelings of affection and pity for him: I came to a fondness for the idea of my father, especially in the abstract. I admired his dutiful work ethic, his dry sense of humor, his love of reading, his gentle, long-suffering air, his ethical values, his progressive politics. Moreover, we looked a lot alike—had the same rangy build, shy grin in company and set grim mouth when alone, along with several dozen physical gestures we shared or, I should say, he had imprinted on me.

After I was set up in my own life, I had a persistent if undeveloped fantasy that I would somehow rescue my father. It seemed to me I was the only one in the family who actually liked and understood him. So I would go out of my way on occasion to be nice to him, or to treat him with the deference and respect to which I imagined a "normal" father might be entitled. These good intentions were fine as long as they stayed largely in the abstract and were not tested by reality.

In the spring of 1969, when I was living in California, I invited him to stay with me for a week. My first marriage had collapsed, I had run away to Berkeley, and I was trying to throw myself into teaching children creative writing, while waiting for the pieces of my shattered ego to reknit. My father arrived, and soon let it be known that he was unimpressed with the Bay Area: it had fewer pizza parlors, barbershops, and newsstands than New York. On Saturday afternoon I took him to Candlestick Park to watch a ballgame. His response was lukewarm: too windy. A classically provincial New Yorker, little-traveled, he shielded himself against feelings of unworldliness by making a point of appearing unimpressed with new experiences. I knew this. Still, his phlegmatic sourness began wearing me down: after the first few days I left him more and more to himself, especially during the day, while I went off to my teaching job at a private school. At night I would come home bearing excited tales of battles with the school administration and of the kids' responses to the creative writing assignments I had just cooked up. My father cut off my enthusiasm with the comment "Those who can, do. Those who can't, teach." It had not occurred to me—so sure was I that all this pedagogic turmoil would one day be grist for the literary mill (as indeed it was)—that, at twenty-six, I was already a failure in his eyes. Like him.

He continued to work at the textile firm of M. Lowenstein & Sons, rarely missing a day, until he turned sixty-seven and the company forced him to retire. It was retirement that withered him. Without the focused identity that his desk and shipping orders brought, he became hollowed-out. About a year after his retirement, he came down with pneumonia. I visited him in the hospital, where he was hoarding a pile of hospital menus—long green slips with boxes for checking off the desired entrées. Disoriented, he thought they were shipping orders, "work" he had to finish while recuperating.

I remember the urgent phone call from my mother at the start of that illness. "Come quickly, he's very ill." I thought, This is it. On my way over, I began preparing for the worst, rehearsing my funeral oration, letting my stomach's churn dredge up the proper words. His death, I secretly hoped, would deepen me. I was always waiting for life to become tragic, so that I would merely have to record it to become a powerful, universal writer.

"He's always been such a stoic," my mother said, greeting me at the door. "So when he said he felt a little pain, I knew it must be bad. Poor Pop, it hurt him so much he was doubled over, he couldn't lie down, he had to sleep all night in the chair. I can't bear to see it happening to him. He's like a—great tree withering in its branches."

A great tree? My mother, a professional actress, tends to dramatize. Still, I was pleased to hear her invoking this se- quoian imagery in his behalf, instead of the usual scorn. We helped him on with his trousers; I kneeled at his feet to strap on leather sandals over phlebitis-swollen ankles, enacting my Cordelia fantasy. There *was* something grand, Lear-like about him that morning, a frail, bundled-up survivor lifted into a taxi in the freezing cold, skittering across iced sidewalks.

Once stationed in a ward, however, he became a hospital thing. I visited him two days later: sunk in a bed-wet trough, he was gray-stubbled, bone-protrudingly thin, his complexion white as celery. Amber traces oscillated on the EEG screen: which will it be, life, death? life, death . . . ?

"If I don't talk, it's not because I'm not happy to see you," he said.

"Please, no need to talk. You can even sleep; I'll still be sit- ting here." Frankly, I would have preferred he slept; talking was never easy between us. His eyes kept opening and staring at me—accusingly, I thought, though perhaps this was only his myopic stare.

"Don't worry, Pop, tomorrow they'll give you a shave. You'll look a million times better. You want your glasses?" No, he shook his head. "Why don't you put on your glasses?" I repeated. Somehow it seemed to me that everything would be fine if I could just get him to wear his glasses.

"I'm saving my eyes," he said.

"What are you saving them for? A rainy day?" I joked.

The glasses were smudgy with thumbprints; I washed them off with water from the tumbler and placed them on him.

"What are you thinking?" I asked, in the silence.

"I'm thinking, Why me?"

In those days I still hoped for some sort of wisdom from my father, poised at the maw between life and death. "Why me?" was not the illumination I had in mind. But "Why me?" was a curt summary of what he felt.

"Gimme that thing." He pointed his bony finger toward a plastic bottle that he kept by his side constantly.

I watched, heard him, pee into the bottle.

"Got any pretty nurses?" I asked. "I saw one outside your door, she looked like a cutie."

He stared at me sternly, reproachfully, with sea-green eyes. "Take my word for it, this is the most—emasculating experience you could ever have," he said. He swallowed hard; then he rubbed his forehead, looking pained.

"What's wrong, Dad, got a headache?"

No, he shook his head.

"Do you want to hear the news?"

"What difference does it make?"

"What do you think about, lying here all this time?" I tried again.

"Nothing. When you're in pain, that's all you think about."

Again, he was telling me something important, but I didn't know how to listen to it.

4.

My mother and father had once taken a magazine quiz: "Do You Know Your Mate?" She had been able to fill out everything about him, from his Social Security number to his mother's maiden name, whereas the opposite was true for him. "He didn't even remember my mother's maiden name! I realized I was living with a stranger, who didn't care at all about me as long as I fulfilled his creature comforts." What my mother says is true, up to a point. My father is a stranger to everyone. On the other hand, his not knowing her Social Security number does not negate the fact that he was completely attached to her, and would have undergone any amount of humiliation to keep living in her presence.

Ten years ago, when my father was seventy-four and my mother sixty-eight, she divorced him so that she could put him in a nursing home. She was candid about not wanting to spend her remaining years nursing an old man she didn't love, and it was clear that he could no longer take care of himself. Apparently the nursing home's regulations stated that a prospective lodger could have no other recourse before being taken in: hence, the necessity for divorce.

After the divorce went through, there was an interim period when my parents continued to live together, waiting for an opening at the nursing home. During this time my father was "on probation," as it were, and if he behaved well, it seemed my mother might reverse herself and allow him to stay with her. In the midst of that limbo period, I was in New York for a few weeks (I had taken a regular teaching job in Houston) and called on them. My mother sent us out to breakfast together so that we could talk "man-to-man." Since he is so laconic and apt to drift into withdrawal, I could only smile at my mother's fantasy of a "father-son powwow." We stopped at the corner stand to buy a newspaper; I was tempted to buy two newspapers, in case we ran out of things to say. It was raining as we walked across the street to the coffee shop, a greasy spoon joint, for breakfast. The breakfast special was $1.55, "Hot Pastrami Omelette." Since he was treating, I had chosen the cheapest place around.

"How's . . ." my father began, then lost his train of thought.

"How's Helen?" I prompted, offering the name of my then-current girlfriend.

"I thought the other one was prettier."

"What other one?" I asked irritably, knowing he meant Kay, a previous flame who had two-timed me and whose prettiness I did not relish being reminded of at the moment.

"You know, I had a funny dream last night," he said, changing the subject. "I dreamt I was sick and there were about ten people in the hospital room who came to see me. One of them was my brother Bernie. Now, I know my brother's been dead for years. I don't understand the significance of his being there."

"I don't either. What happened in the dream?"

"Nothing. Your sister Leah was in the room, and her friends. That's another thing I couldn't understand. Why wasn't Molly in the dream? Or you and Hal? Your mother would have a interpretation."

"Probably." A long silence fell. "So, you and Mom seem to have made peace with each other."

"You know, your mother and I got divorced."

"I know. Does it feel strange, living together after you're divorced?"

"Yes it feels strange."

"Did you sign the papers too, or—"

"I signed it," he said. "It was a joint divorce. Because your mother was going to go through with it anyway. One of the reasons for the divorce was to get a better tax break. And now they've changed the law, so it wouldn't have made any difference anyway."

"I thought the divorce was so that they wouldn't take Mother's income if she put you in a nursing home."

"Yes. But I don't want to go into a nursing home. My father, my brother, and my sister all went into nursing homes, and I don't have fond memories of them."

I liked the understated way he put it. "What I don't understand is, is it your legal right to stay in the apartment now, or are you there at Mother's sufferance?"

"I think it's the second. Besides, she doesn't want to have me forcibly removed."

"So you're on your best behavior now? And you're getting along?"

"Well. . . . There have been some peculiar things lately."

"Like what?"

"We were at a gathering, and your mother was talking as if I had nothing to do with the way you kids turned out," he said, holding his fork in midair and glancing up at me sideways. "She was saying 'My son does this' and 'My other son does that' and 'My daughter is such-and-such.' She was taking all the credit, as if I had no influence on you."

"Well, that's not true. We all feel you had a big influence on us." For better or worse, I added in my mind.

"I'm not saying I was the only influence. But I did have a little."

"Of course. She was just bragging, Pop. Like you do."

Another long silence, during which I watched the flies buzzing around the Miller beer sign.

"What have you been thinking about lately?" I asked.

"Nothing. I've been slightly depressed," he said.

"About what?"

"Nothing special."

"Your health all right?"

"My health is as good as can be expected for a man my age. I'm actually in good physical shape, except I have emphysema. I haven't smoked for years, but I still have emphysema from all the smoking I used to do."

"Are you still on medication?"

"Just vitamin pills."

"That's great!" I said with false, hearty enthusiasm.

"And half an aspirin a day for my heart."

"You get any exercise at all? Do you walk?"

"No, I don't walk much." He shook his head.

"You used to love walking."

"But now I walk so slowly. I used to walk real fast. Now your mother walks faster than I do, and she gets impatient."

"You can take walks alone."

"But I walk so slowly that it bugs me. Put it this way: My *halcyon* days are over," he said, grinning at his use of the unusual word.

"When were your halcyon days, Pop?" I asked skeptically.

"Before I got my stroke. I thought I was immortal. I was healthy as a horse. I used to work all day and night without stopping. I never even took a sick day. Then I got the stroke and I couldn't get out of bed. I don't know if you could understand unless it happens to you. You try to stand up and you can't. That frightened the hell out of me." Now he was warming up. "And I had this internist. Supposed to be one of the top internists in the city. At least that's what he told me. He prescribed Dilantin and something else. The two medications canceled each other out. Later on, someone told me that I could have sued him for malpractice. But someone else said that if he was such a big internist, then I couldn't win. So I didn't sue."

"Just as well."

"He's still practicing. Cut down on his hours, though," he added.

"But that was over twenty years ago. A long time to get over a fright."

"A lot of people at the Senior Center had strokes. So they understand. That's one good thing about that place. The problem is . . . that the two men I played canasta with, one is sick and the other man . . ." he mumbled.

"I'm sorry, I didn't hear."

"The other man passed on."

"That's too bad. So you have to make new friends."

"It's not easy for me. I'm not the gregarious type."

You could say that again. "Why is that, I wonder?"

"Your mother was the gregarious type, but I wasn't."

"What about when you were younger, before you met Mom?"

A pained look. "I didn't have too many friends."

"Were you shy?"

"Probably I am shy."

"Why is that?"

"I didn't have any confidence in myself."

The truth in a nutshell. Another silence. "Well, you don't have to make friends with the people at the Center, you just have to play cards."

"I do. I play rummy. And I find I'm better at rummy than I was at canasta— Eat slowly, take your time," he told me. My French toast was so awful that I was trying to get through it as fast as possible.

"Does the Center ever go on outings?" I asked.

"They go to Atlantic City. That's not my style. I don't bother going."

"I was once in Atlantic City," I reminisced, "and I enjoyed it. The ocean, the Boardwalk."

"The hotels expect you to gamble. I'm not a gambler."

When he was finished, he started to get up, and reached ever so slowly into his raincoat, which was hanging on the hook behind him, for some money. He found only a dollar. Puzzled. His hand traveled with incredible hesitation across to the other pocket. Nothing in there. A look went across his face, like that of a child who has accidentally lost something and expects a beating. He put his hand in his shirt pocket. Pulled out a twenty-dollar bill. Satisfaction. The check came to $5.60.

"You pay the tip," he said cheerfully.

A week later I asked my mother how Pop was doing. "He fell out of bed again. I didn't help him up either. He's got to learn to do for himself. What if I go on the road again? It's what I learned when I was working with those retarded kids—same principle. You've got to teach them to be independent."

"It's not very nice to compare him to a retarded kid."

"Don't worry," she sighed, "I'll do what's right. Because I don't want to live with guilt. I've lived with guilt before and it's no fun."

But fighting broke out between my parents constantly. Before I left the city, I visited them again. My mother was telling me about her stocks. Considering how poor we had been, and how she is still living in government-subsidized housing, having stocks, even worthless ones, is a status symbol. "This stock went from fifty cents to four dollars, I didn't sell, and now it's down to a dollar."

"If it reaches four dollars again, you'd better sell," I said cautiously.

"What's the difference? It only cost me a few hundred bucks. If I can't afford to risk that much, forget it."

My father interjected, in his phlegmy growl, something about the Mindanao Mother Lode.

She blew up at him: "You'll see, you're not getting a cent of that money! Even if the lawyer did say you were entitled to fifty percent of our property after the *divorce*. I'll fix your wagon!"

My father shrank into himself. I was shocked at the venom with which she had yelled at him, even after all these years of hearing it. I asked, "What's this about the Mindanao Mother Lode?"

She said, "Aw, I invested a lousy hundred dollars in this oil drilling outfit in the Pacific a few years ago, and never heard a word about it. But from him I never *stop* hearing it! If he keeps rubbing it in, he's the one who's gonna suffer."

Much as I had wanted to protect him in the moment against her temper, after I left them I realized the passive-aggressive cunning of my father in employing just those words which would set her off. (It showed the same quiet ability to insert a dig as calling my previous girlfriend prettier than my current one. For all his solipsism, he was observant enough when

he wanted to be, and had a feel for other people's exposed
areas.)

A few months later the parental truce was irrevocably shattered. It seemed the toilet had overflowed while my father was
using it, and he didn't clean it up. He had phoned my sister
Molly to report the toilet had flooded, and she, not having any
time that day to stop by, gave him practical advice: Call the
maintenance man. He didn't; instead, he sat there for eight
hours "with his arms folded," as Molly put it. My mother came
home, saw his turds on the floor, the sight of which pushed her
over the limit for good.

It was the two women's interpretation that he was not "out
of it" at all but had contrived to punish his wife by his passivity, because only by provoking her fury could he get the attention he wanted from her. I suspected geriatric debility to be the
greater cause and was irked at my mother and sister for showing so little understanding of human frailty. On the other hand,
most of the burden for taking care of him had fallen on them,
not me. It was easy for me to play the compassionate relation
at a distance.

My father called me himself in Houston, a rare event, to
say that he would not be living at home anymore. My mother
was putting him in an adult home near Far Rockaway. I said
maybe it was for the best. He said, "Yes, well, in the sense that
we weren't getting along."

Desperate for some optimistic note, I added, "And it will be
near the beach. That's nice."

"Well, that part doesn't matter to me. I don't swim."

"Still, it's nice to see the ocean." He did not deign to reply
to this inanity. "And maybe you can make friends there," I
added.

"I didn't make any friends at the Senior Citizens Club. Although there, the people were walking in off the streets. Maybe here there'll be more people—of substance."

Around the time of the divorce, my family tended to split along gender lines. My brother Hal and I sympathized more with our father's eviction from his home, while the two girls shared my mother's point of view. Molly, a practicing Buddhist who usually preached compassion, surprised me by her adamance. "Why should I feel guilty for not visiting him regularly? He abandoned the family long ago." She had taken to calling him Mr. Ross, because, she explained, if you say "Albert Ross" quickly, it comes out "albatross."

After he was deposited in the home, my mother went around depressed for a while. Hal thought it was guilt; I thought it was being faced with a void. Whom would she blame now for her unhappy life? She had never admitted how dependent she might be on him, only the other way around.

My own impulse had been to sympathize more with my father, both because he seemed the weaker party and because my mother had cheated on him. As a young man, I had taken her infidelity very personally, as though she had somehow betrayed me. Objectively, I could appreciate that—being the young woman she was, lost in a miserable marriage—it was absolutely necessary for her to reach out to other men. Nowadays it isn't her affairs I hold against her, but the fact that, in justifying herself, she felt compelled to demean my father before his children's eyes. I know, I know, I am being unfair in blaming her for not "allowing" us to venerate him more, as though it were ever possible for her to lie about her most intense feelings—to situate him, by some *trompe l'oeil* of maternal tact, on the patriarchal throne.

THE STORY OF MY FATHER

I dropped in at my mother's before leaving New York. She was going on about how he'd got what he deserved. My mother, for all her psychological astuteness, is someone who speaks and acts out of a self-righteous wound. Her recognition that she may have hurt someone can proceed only from the perception that she was hurt first.

"Supposing there were two other people you were looking at whose marriage was this bad," I said, "wouldn't you be inclined to assume they were both a little at fault?"

"Yeah, I suppose," she said. "But he blew it."

"If he was so terrible, why did you stay with him so long then?"

"I wish I knew. That's the $64,000 question. He had so much promise! What happened to it? He just didn't have the drive. After he retired, I tried to get him to be interested in things, I took him with me to the community college. But he thought he was smarter than everyone else, and if they didn't appreciate that immediately . . . He dropped out, and I got my degree. To me, it was a challenge. To Al, a challenge was already a defeat."

My mother has so much life force it's hard to imagine what it must have been like to live with her opposite all those years. Vitality like hers, ever on tap, has been a constant delight for me but not a mystery. The mystery has been my father and his deep reserves of inanition.

5.

After my father was put in the nursing home, the next family crisis occurred when my mother announced she didn't want him at the Passover seder at her house. I was outraged. Then my friend Max, the soul of kindness, said he sympathized with her. She had suffered for years in an unhappy marriage, and now she was divorced. Why should she be hypocritical and welcome him? Why pretend we were an intact family when we weren't? Each of the children would have to learn how to adjust to this new arrangement; each would have to make a separate deal with our father.

I began going out to the Belle Harbor Adult Home in Far Rockaway. It took forever on the subway; you had to catch a spur train over Broad Channel the last couple of stops. Once off the train, you found a calm residential neighborhood, one- or two-family homes with hedges, an old-fashioned New York lower-middle-class feeling, with quite a few senior citizens residences and funeral homes in the vicinity. My father didn't like the area because the nearest newsstand was seven blocks away; he was used to a denser city life.

His half of the room contained a bed, a night table, some pictures of the family, and—I was both flattered and obscurely ashamed to see—my books. His roommate was deaf, a hundred years old, spoke only Yiddish, and was paranoid; when I tried to bring the empty chair near his side of the room over to my father's bed so that we could sit together, he barked at me. No words, just guttural attack-dog sounds.

My father, each visit, would fill me in on the deathwatch. "There's a guy here who dropped dead the other day from a coronary. Fell over into his soup. He seemed in okay health, too."

I wanted to make him feel better. So, one day I took it into my head to buy my father a pair of swimming shorts. Since he lived only a block away from the beach, surely there might come a time, even if he didn't swim, when he'd want to warm his legs in the sand. We walked the seven blocks to the retail street, taking over a half hour to do so. At the shop my father wouldn't let me get him swimming trunks but insisted on Bermuda shorts. He went into the dressing room to try them on.

"Do they fit, Pop?"

"Yeah, they fit." This was his highest accolade—the acme of enthusiasm—coming from my father.

On the way home I asked, "Do you think you'll wear them?"

"Not very often," he said, honest to a fault.

During this time I kept trying to buy my father gifts. First I bought a TV for his room (which he never watched, preferring the common room's), then a half-refrigerator for snacks, because he didn't like the food they served. I was doing this partly to lift his depression and partly to administer a lesson to my family on the right way to treat him—I did not like all their talk about his being an "albatross" or a "vegetable." The problem was, I kept coming up against my own upset at his lack of appreciation. The man had no talent for accepting gifts.

I needed to see my father as a poor, maligned Père Goriot abandoned in old age, who deserved our love as a matter of course and custom, and to dismiss the others' beefs against him as petty. I wanted to start with him on a clean, tender page. But to do so, I had to hide my own scars and keep my buried angers against him in check. And sometimes I could no longer overlook the meaner side of the man, which Molly insisted was holding together the works.

One weekend I checked him out of the adult home to

spend a few days at the loft I was subletting. In a sense, I was trying out my fantasy of what it would be like to have my father move in with me. I had bought us baseball tickets at Shea Stadium so that we could watch Doc Gooden go for his twentieth victory. The morning of our planned outing was drizzly, and Father moped that the game was going to be rained out. Luckily, the weather cleared up long enough for Doc to pitch—and win; but still my father seemed morose. All weekend I had cooked for him, taken him around, arranged dinner at a fancy restaurant, and nothing pleased him: the coffee was too weak, too strong. By the end of the weekend I was completely sympathetic with my mother. Every time he complained about something—say, wanting another radio station on the car radio—I could hear her voice in my thoughts: WHY DON'T YOU CHANGE IT YOURSELF? Though he didn't know how to drive, he was sure I was going the wrong way, and insisted we ask directions at the gas station. Moreover, he seemed completely uninterested in my life—every few hours asking, "When is Hal coming back from vacation?" Prolonged, continuous exposure to the man was eroding my idealized defense of him, making me see him exactly as the other family members did: infuriatingly passive, selfish, hurtful, uncouth.

Looking back at that weekend, I see now what it might have been like for him. He couldn't give himself over to the pleasures offered when they were so temporary, and when they came at the humiliating price of my expecting his gratitude. If this was indeed a test—a dry run for some possible future living arrangement—he could not afford to be on best behavior. My father would rather disappoint quickly and get the suspense over with.

The trek out to Far Rockaway was too long, the family members were visiting him less and less, and it was agreed that we should try to find a home for him closer to town. My brother was able to relocate him in an ultradesirable "adult residence" on the Upper West Side, near Lincoln Center. Once again he could walk to the corner and buy a newspaper. We could take him out to a variety of restaurants, all within a stone's throw of his building. He could look out the window and see Broadway, Citarella's fish store, Fairview's produce stand. He could get himself a haircut. He began perking up again, making observations. One of his repeated bon mots was "When it says 'hair salon' instead of barbershop, that means you're paying extra." Another: "When you see a cloth napkin, that means you're paying extra." This was his streetwise peasant side letting us know, You can't fool me, it's still the same baloney.

The new residence home seemed, at first, a paradise for seniors. There were classical music concerts, daily video screenings, poetry workshops (to which my father brought his half-century-old poems on onionskin about his wife's defection)—all in a building that felt more like an apartment house than a prison. Each resident had his own separate "apartment" (a room, really), while enjoying the social life of the common parlors. The pretense was that of dignified, autonomous seniors who just happened to need the additional services of a specialized hotel. The problem in such a place was that you could not falter. If you got too sick, too frail, too out of it, you were told you didn't belong in this establishment but in a nursing home, and were summarily kicked out.

After a while, there was no kidding ourselves: my father was on a slow, inexorable path downward. It was not just that he had cataracts (they could be corrected with surgery) or that he was a loner, acting, by the residence staff's standards, uncommunally. It was that he began to experience "incontinence problems"—in short, wet his pants, making him an undesirable presence in the dining room. The family took a crash course in adult Pampers, rubber diapers, prostate surgery, and behavioral modification training.

Incontinence was the precise metaphor to galvanize family arguments about my father's willpower. "He's doing it on purpose!" said Molly. "He can hold it in if he wants to."

"I don't think so," I said. Meanwhile, my father went around looking utterly hesitant to travel any distance farther than a half-block from the nearest bathroom.

I remember one particular night I had planned to take him to a screening at Lincoln Center. When I got there, he was so sloppily dressed that I decided to forgo the movie and just have dinner with him across the street, at a newly opened Italian restaurant.

We had the usual tepid time of it, neither hostile nor affectionate. The most interesting moment was when Father volunteered this short summary of his marriage: "I felt that I loved your mother more than she loved me." Undoubtedly true, and I realized I had probably contrived my whole romantic life until then so as not to be caught in the same situation.

He also said, "She always attracted dykes. She must have done something for that to happen."

I told my father that my mother's older brother, Uncle George, had died. There was a silence. He finally said, "I have mixed feelings about him."

"Why?"

"Well, I think he played around with her when she was a kid. And then she was madly in love with him, all during the time when we were first married. I couldn't prove anything, but . . ."

It seemed to me he was casting about wildly for rivals, to explain why my mother had come to dislike him.

When the meal ended, he tried to get up and couldn't seem to rise, so I gave him a hand and walked him to the men's room, one flight down. He had become very unsteady on his feet, especially managing stairs. "Why do they always put the men's room where you have to go up or down a flight?" he said. I waited outside the toilet door for ten minutes. After a while I thought maybe he had died in there. "Pop, you all right?" I called out. He grunted something in reply, so I knew he was still among the living. "Can I help?" I asked. "No," came his foggy voice uncertainly. Ten more minutes passed. "Pop, what's going on?" Finally I went inside to have a look. "I had an accident," he said. I noticed the tiled floor was smeared with shit. "I made in my pants. I couldn't get them off in time."

"Okay. Let's get outa here." I helped him up the stairs and we left quickly, before the waiters could see the bathroom floor. It's their problem, I thought. I'll never go back to that restaurant anyway.

"I'm sorry," he said as we crossed the street.

"It's not your fault, Pop. It's old age." I was already thinking ahead to what I would have to do. Get him undressed and into a shower. I was very calm, patient, the way I used to be when I was working with kids. We took the elevator upstairs to his room, and he immediately sat on the bed and took off his pants, smearing the bedspread in the process. I helped him off with his shirt and led him into the bathroom across the hall. Two minutes later I still hadn't heard the sound of running water.

"Pop, what's the matter?" He was standing outside the shower stall, dry and dirty.

"I can't get my socks off."

"Oh for crying out loud!" I said, sounding just like my mother. "The socks can get wet. Just go in the shower!"

I pushed him in.

"I can't get the hot water to work," he said. Now his total helplessness was getting on my nerves. He had turned on the hot water; it would just take a minute to warm up. Didn't he know that, after all these years on the planet? I gave him soap and told him to rinse well and left him there. Back in his room, I threw away his soiled underpants. I stripped the bedspread and bunched it on the floor, hoping his attendant would deal with it tomorrow. And I turned on the Mets game so that he would have something to watch when he returned.

He came back. One of his legs was still covered with shit. I cleaned it off as best I could with water and toilet paper. Wiping off my father's ass wasn't what I'd expected from the evening, but—all in the nature of reality. I tried to tell myself it was good for my spiritual development. As soon as he was lying down comfortably, however, I said good-bye. I could have stayed longer, but I didn't. He could have said thank you, but he didn't. He made his usual "okay" grunt. As I fled the building onto Amsterdam Avenue, a junkie was vomiting against the side of the car. What a night!

.   .   .

There was some hope that a prostate operation might improve the incontinence situation. In any event, he had to have one. After it was done, I received a call from the hospital to pick up my father. Molly was also there to help, but she seemed in a foul mood.

"How about if I go down to pay for his TV and phone," I said, "and meanwhile you can see that he gets ready."

"I've got to speak to you," said Molly. Taking me outside the room by the arm, she told me in a fierce whisper, "Look, I didn't get any sleep last night because I have a splitting headache and a cold, and I absolutely don't want to have to dress that old man and touch his body and see his old balls, I can't handle it today."

I was surprised to hear my sister sounding so squeamish, since she is a professional masseuse; but as usual I admired her bluntness. "Fine, I'll take care of it." I went back into the hospital room and found an elderly German-Jewish woman in a white hospital coat, who told me she was the social worker. I started to help my father on with his underwear when she told me, "Don't! He has to do it for himself." She then explained to me that the West Side Residence Home had told her they refused to accept responsibility for him unless he could dress himself and walk. The hospital, for their part, refused to keep him there any longer because "this is not a nursing home" and his operation was over and he'd had a few days' rest. So she would have to determine for herself whether he was capable of dressing himself. If not, the family would have to hire an attendant eight hours a day to take care of him in the residence home.

Molly lost her temper with the woman and yelled, "Why did they tell me yesterday that he could go? Which is it supposed to be, go or stay? Why don't you make up your frigging minds?!" She was carrying on like a street tough, and the social worker, who had probably seen it all (maybe even the camps), was undaunted.

I took Molly aside and told her, "She can't say which it is to be until she ascertains whether Father can take minimal care of himself."

"Oh fine! And he's going to play helpless because he wants to stay here, where they do everything for him."

The woman kept repeating what her responsibilities in the current situation were. Finally I said to her, as calmly as I could, "Look, we're all pretty bright here, we understand what you're saying."

She blinked her eyes and left the room.

I turned to Father and said under my breath, "Pop! Try very hard. Don't give up. It's important that you show her you can dress yourself. Otherwise they won't let you out. So give it your all."

"All right, I'll try," he said. And proceeded to do just that, dressing himself slowly, manfully, with dignity.

Not to be dissuaded by the evidence, Molly started hectoring him from the hallway. "What's the matter, you like it here, so you don't want to try to get out?"

"Sure. I'm crazy about the place," he answered sarcastically. "Show me someone who don't mind staying in a hospital and I'll show you a schmuck."

"You think if you just give up, everyone will wait on you hand and foot—right?" retorted Molly.

"Leave me alone! Stop giving me the business."

I caught my sister winking at me: this was her version of reverse psychology. I realized that the social worker, now nowhere in sight, might not believe he had dressed himself, so I hurried to fetch her. When I spotted her, I explained my errand, adding, "One thing you have to understand: my father has always been the kind of man who becomes more dependent when there are people around to do for him. But he was like that at thirty."

She nodded, with an appearance of understanding. I was trying to establish rapport with her. The stakes were high; we could never afford a full-time attendant. And where would he go if they kicked him out of his residence home?

The social worker returned just in time to see Molly buttoning my father's pants! Molly said, "That's the only thing he couldn't do for himself." But he still didn't have his shoes on. The three of us watched as Father, with agonizing slowness, tried to get his foot into the Velcro-strap sneakers that Hal had bought him. I tried to smooth the way by explaining, "He always has trouble putting his shoes on. Even before the operation."

"I wasn't told that," sniffed the social worker.

"The attendant at the home does it for him every morning," Molly said. Fortunately, he got his shoes on by himself, for once, and now the test was his walking ability. He started down the hallway past the nurses' station, the social worker walking alongside to monitor his progress.

"Maybe he needs a cane," she said. "Why does he take such small steps?"

"He always walks like that."

As he approached the nurses' desk, he quipped, "She's too old for me. Get me a younger one." The nurses cracked up. They all seemed to like him. (I'm fascinated by the fact that many people do take to my father right away.)

"Your dad has a great sense of humor," a nurse said.

"He's a riot," said the other.

"Good-bye, Mr. Lopat. You don't want to stay here with all these sick people, do you?"

He waved to his fan club. We bid adieu to the social worker, who reluctantly agreed that he was ambulatory.

An Academy Award performance. Molly and I got him quickly into a taxi, before he could collapse.

Shortly after that, the inevitable happened. He fell down one morning, and in consequence was kicked out of the West Side Residence (whose hoity-toity airs I had come to despise) and sent to his present nursing home. This is no doubt the Last Stop. There is nothing he can do here that will disqualify him from the right to sit in the common room with the TV on.

Recently, during a period when he had been feeling too despondent to eat, I visited him there and wheeled him out to nearby Fort Tryon Park. He noticed a magnificent elm overlooking the Hudson River. "That's a beautiful tree," he said.

"You see, Pop? It's not so bad being alive. Which would you prefer—tell me honestly: to be dead or alive?"

"Alive, of course." He was annoyed to be asked such a childish question.

For the next few minutes his senescent-poetic mind spliced the word "tree" into different sentences. "They don't brag so much about the trees. Especially since they had that . . . Holocaust."

. . .

Later I tell his social worker that, from my observation, my father likes to be placed in front of ongoing scenes of daily life. Especially activities involving youth: teenagers playing basketball, tots splashing through the fountain, pretty girls walking by.

She says skeptically, "You caught him at a good moment. We took him to the park, there were plenty of children around, and he dozed through it all, no interest whatsoever. You know what he wants? He wants you."

I hang my head guiltily.

"But in today's way of life . . ." she adds, that vague, exonerating statement.

I ask myself, Would it be possible to take him in? Where would we put him? The basement? The baby's room? A shed on the roof? We could manage, somehow, couldn't we? In the midst of this deliberation, I know that I will never do it. I take consolation from what a scientist friend tells me: "Societies choose differently what to do with old people. The Eskimos choose the ice floe, we choose the nursing home."

How much does my father understand? Has his mind become permanently loosed from its logical moorings—like that comment about trees and the Holocaust? At other times he seems to make perfect sense. During the staff meeting I had tried to explain the reasons for his depression, adding, "He's taken a lot of abuse from his family."

My father picked his head up and said, clearly, "I was also responsible for the discord."

A final word on failure. I once read an essay by Bill Holm, the gifted Midwestern writer, called "The Music of Failure," in which he tried both to argue against the hollow American obsession with success and to redeem failure, to find beauty in it. In effect, Holm was attempting to invert commonplace values and turn failure into a victory, or at least show how it could be better, more human than its opposite. Intriguing as the essay was, I finished it with a sigh, thinking, But there *is* such a thing as failure. There *are* failed lives, which no amount of rhetorical jiujitsu can reclaim as triumphs.

Maybe my father's insistence that he is a failure does not signal the obsessions of senility but grows out of a long, enforced, reluctant meditation at the end of his life, which has obliged him to take responsibility for some of his very real errors. In that sense, there is hope for all of us. I would like to give him the benefit of the doubt.

Postscript

Shortly after I had completed writing this, on June 26, 1995, my father passed away. He was a few months shy of his eighty-fifth birthday. The official cause of death was pneumonia and sepsis. As far as I could tell, he remained unconscious the whole time he was in the hospital; at least he did not die, as he had dreaded, in the nursing home itself. When I visited him during that last week, at the Allen Pavilion (his room overlooked Baker Field football stadium), the attending physician urged me to sign a "Do Not Resuscitate" form, and I did so.

About the time of his death, I was driving home and my car overheated and I had to pull over by the side of the road. I opened the hood and a plume of steam escaped. I like to think this was my father's spirit escaping from his body.

That night, after having been notified of his death, I called the hospital again and asked if I could see my father one last time. They said it would not be possible that evening, but I could come by in the morning and view him. The next morning they told me that, due to some bureaucratic mix-up, they had already sent his body off to be cremated.

THE INVISIBLE WOMAN

Do not understand me too quickly.
—ANDRÉ GIDE

I had just finished the day's work and had stretched out on the couch with a magazine when the phone rang. The voice on the end identified itself as belonging to one Lori Becker. Would I write an article about her? By way of background, she said, she was a conceptual artist whose recent show had consisted of getting various police artists to do sketches of her, based on her friends' descriptions. The new piece would involve writers writing magazine profiles about her, blowups of which would then be displayed on a gallery's walls, in the art-directed style of the intended magazine. Some might even end up being printed in those magazines, and there might also be a catalogue. It sounded like a scam, Tom Sawyer getting others to paint the fence, albeit well within present art practices. Ms. Becker added that she was a fan of my work and wanted very much to include me in the project. Susceptible as I am to flattery, I feared she might have gotten my name off a list, or said

the same to all prospective hymnists. I asked what other writers had agreed. She named a half-dozen working journalists. I
said I was not essentially a magazine writer but an essayist and
novelist. She said she knew that. By nature obliging, I also
liked being seen as hip enough for a downtown art show, and I
wanted to get back to my reading, so I agreed.

Offered the options to meet at a café or her place, I had
chosen the latter, as environment might provide clues to character. If she proved boring, I could at least describe the decor.
Besides, didn't August Sander always photograph subjects in
their milieux? I could see a new career blossoming for myself—
a literary Sander, a whole book of verbal portraits, of which this
could be the first. . . .

Her building, it turned out, was one I had always admired:
a blocklong cream-colored factory structure with geometric
colored tilework along the sides. Once part of Printers' Row, it
now held a mix of the commercial and the residential, upscale
enough to afford a lobby guard. I try to evade lobby guards, and
walked by his desk, looking purposeful. The elevator opened
on the tenth floor to a row of artists' lofts, the even placement
of whose doors suggested art-school lockers. Resigning myself
to seeing her studio, not her living quarters, I still felt some of
the excitement of a blind date, unsure what to expect, as I
knocked at the BECKER door. It was 3 P.M.: right on time.

A tall, slender, attractive woman with straight black hair
opened the door. She wore a green-and-black-striped jersey
and black pants, dark red lipstick—a classic Soho/TriBeCa outfit, somehow echoing a fifties beatnik look.

We shook hands. Her two-room studio, I saw at a glance,
was well plastered and had good light, with a spectacular Hudson River view. (My wife and I had been pricing a painting stu-

238   dio for her, and I knew we could not have afforded this one.) I
took off my coat and looked around for someplace to sit. Lori
Becker seemed shyly nervous suddenly, as though she had forgotten the purpose of the meeting and would have to invent
one. I chose a lumpy chair against the wall. She faced me on a
stool.

She remarked that she'd once seen me give a reading at St.
Mark's Church, had liked what she'd read of mine so far, and
"my boyfriend is a *really* big fan of yours." A complex moment.
I was pleased; I experienced a vestigial disappointment, as
when any pretty woman refers for the first time to her
boyfriend; and I wondered if she were trying to slough off some
responsibility for including me in the show onto him.

We began talking about her previous projects, surrounded
as we were by the *objets*. Police sketches of Lori faced me on
the wall opposite. There were clay statuettes of Lori on
pedestals in the middle of the room. Against a far wall were
blowups from her "Lori Coloring Book" project, written by her
but drawn by a professional illustrator and colored by schoolchildren. The coloring book self-mockingly depicted the fantasy ambitions of a Katy Keene–like young artist named Lori:
the successful opening, the chic party afterward, the glowing
Times review.

"I work in different genres, with myself as a control," she
said. "I'm interested in finding different ways of knowing and
talking about truth rather than necessarily talking about me."

"Couldn't you get at the truth as well by doing subjective
self-portraits?" I asked.

She was ready for my question. "Artists have been trying to
trick themselves out of their biases for a long time. If I were to
make art about myself, it would be limited by my taste, ability,

and capacity to see myself. Besides, what you don't know about yourself is the thing that's most haunting."

She was not stupid, that much was clear. I asked her to elaborate.

"For instance, the police-sketch project was a metaphor for being different things to different people. I learned a lot about myself from that."

"What did you learn?" I asked skeptically.

She paused. "Well, that there's not a single gestalt that's me. Is that something about the way I present myself to the world? Is there something that's hard to describe about me?"

"Offhand, I'd say you seem to project a very definite image of yourself. The variations might have more to do with the problem of distortions in second-hand information, like that old game 'Telephone.' "

She shrugged.

"How do you think your being a woman bears on this shifting gestalt?" I said, testing the feminist waters.

"It could have something to do with my sometimes being wishy-washy or accommodating," she said. Her frankness caught me by surprise; I had expected a more ideological response, and began liking her.

"I just meant the way women are oppressed in our society," I said, supplying the ideology myself, "and therefore have to be skilled at varying presentations of self. Sort of *As You Desire Me*."

"Mirroring the person you're talking to." She crossed her legs. We had scarcely met, and were already caught in a meta-conversation. "Well, it's true, women have to be very aware of their visual effect. . . . I don't try to deny that, I place it right up front."

She showed me some documentation of earlier work: court-room sketch artists depicting scenes from her daily life; life-study classes' drawings of her. The first part of our encounter was, willy-nilly, turning into a Studio Visit, that absurdly solemn ritual which has its own protocol. In this case, however, it was difficult to know what to say because the artist hadn't herself executed any of the visuals: if one murmured "That's lovely" about some rendering of her, it might be beside the point, given the artist's intentions to demonstrate only the var-ious projections involved in witnessing her. The nudes of her, done in academic style by art students, confirmed my impres-sion that she had an appealing body; but the piece, of course, did not have that intention—perish the thought.

The phone rang. I had a chance to look over the xeroxed sheaf of write-ups and reviews Lori had given me. My eyes glanced over (and glazed over) the artspeak about "questioning the nature of 'truth,' " "decontextualizing," "methodologies," "reinforce a wide range of female stereotypes," "the categories of representation," blahblahblah. Were such a document put in a time capsule, what would our descendants make of this mix-ture of flat assertion and theory; of the exaggerated taste for un-dercutting and subversions; of the way simple values like "work," "truth," and "fact" were punished for presuming to ex-ist by being placed in the stocks of quotation marks? I felt sorry for Lori, a nice girl like her, having to speak this language to get ahead.

My problem with her work so far was that the reflections it triggered were only mildly interesting, when not platitudinous (truth is subjective; images lie; different people see you differ-ently; women are viewed as sex objects), while, visually, the in-dividual pieces didn't register much. Even if they were never meant to, I couldn't help missing the sensuous jolt of the inevitable that I got from a satisfying composition by (to name another conceptualist) John Baldessari, not to mention an Agnes Martin or a Mark Rothko. But I felt crummy for having already decided her art was not worth taking all that seriously, while continuing to play the role of interested studio visitor. What made things worse was that I found Lori herself to be intelligent, likable, direct.

I wondered whether this "depiction by others" shtick was just her gimmick, her calling card to get in the door of the art world, or had a deeper, obsessional meaning. When she got off the phone, I asked, "How did you come to this approach?"

"I studied art at Barnard and the School of Visual Arts. After that, I did my own painting for years before deciding I needed a different direction, so I put that aside."

"Do you ever feel guilty for giving up handmade art after you'd been trained to do it?"

"No, not guilty. But sometimes I wonder whether viewers will feel that they're missing something."

"What about the 'exploitation' charge, that you might be ripping off other people's work and presenting it as your own?" I asked.

"I make explicit who does what. There's a lot of precedent recently for artists using fabricators. Robert Longo, Jeff Koons . . ."

"Mark Kostabi?"

She seemed distressed at the comparison. "People have compared him to me before. Probably just because he's been in the news." (Kostabi had sued several of his craftsmen for selling some of "his" mass-produced work without his knowledge.) "One distinction between what I do and what others do is that

I use people not just as craftsmen but for their own talents. And I recognize them by giving them credit as part of the piece."*

"How does what you do, then, differ from a curatorial function? You assemble all these other artists' work within a conceptual frame, like a curator."

"It has similarities. As a matter of fact, before I started doing this type of work, I curated a show at the New Museum called 'The Big Nothing.' " Lori began recounting how she got various artists to do "invisible" works at the museum. A part of me was too restless to hear the full explanation: I was pondering the now-thin line between curating and artmaking, while another corner of my brain turned over that Chandleresque title, *The Big Nothing.* . . .

"Why do you need a studio," I cut in impertinently, "if you don't fabricate the art?"

"To try out ideas. It also helps to show people I want to involve in my projects what my earlier pieces looked like. And I use the phone a lot here."

"Did you pay the police-sketch artists?" I asked.

"Yes," she replied with a faintly hurt look.

"Are you planning to pay the writers?" (Now we were getting to it.)

"I was thinking of it, yes," she said hesitantly. "There is some money for this project." She asked me what I thought a reasonable fee. We settled on a figure that was less than my usual slick magazine rate but enough to pay for a recent shopping spree at Bergdorf's.

---

*Up to a point, this may be true. But later I visited an installation of hers in a gallery and could find no evidence of the actual illustrators' names on the wall or on the price list.

"How many pages do you want it to be?"

"Oh—it doesn't have to be more than two pages. You know, the size of a magazine article," she said.

For two pages, I was being overpaid. As soon as I realized I was actually getting *money* for this job, I might add, my whole mood changed. I felt warmer, relaxed, no longer resentful at being taken advantage of.

Meanwhile, Lori seemed tense about how this new factor would affect the experiment. "If I pay you a fee," she rationalized aloud, "maybe you'll take the writing more seriously and work harder at it." That part hadn't occurred to me. I always work hard at a piece of writing, whether it's a freebie, a book review, or for a fat magazine fee. Lori began to specify deadlines: now *she* was afraid of being suckered; she had that slightly disenchanted air of an upper-middle-class woman buying a tradesman's loyalty or a tennis teacher's time, knowing that money talked.

Clearly she had her professional rap down pat. The point was to get past that well-worn cassette, to have her tell me her life story. "Where did you grow up?"

Miami, she answered. Their house was not far from Coconut Grove, an art colony that was then a hippy enclave, though her parents stayed as far away from it as possible. "I didn't get much exposure to art when I was young. But at school I always felt I was the best artist around," she said, foreshadowingly.

"What did your parents do?"

"My father is a lawyer, a real estate developer, and a banker. He's a respected businessman who has high moral standards and gets involved in idealistic projects. I'm not saying he works for Greenpeace, but ... my family's always been big on morality, compassion, community service. My parents helped raise money for Israel. They have tons of friends, and being there for people in times of trouble is of the utmost importance. Unlike me," she added, with just the faintest trace of irony.

"What does your mother do?"

"My mother doesn't work except for occasional charity functions. Yet she always seems busy, doing things for other people. She's had three children. I'm the oldest, then a sister and a brother. I remember my mother driving us around to all our activities when we were young. She also makes stationery for people as a sideline."

"What's your mom like?" I asked.

"Mom had a nervous breakdown when I was just past one year old, and she went away for six months. I always feel this is a significant factor in my development, though I'm not sure how."

"How do you think?"

"Maybe it left me with an innate insecurity."

"Was her nervous breakdown caused by postpartum depression?"

"It could have been that. Or a thyroid condition, which they discovered later. But probably it was just not being ready to deal with the responsibility of a family. She got married at twenty-five and had me at twenty-seven. Anyway, they both turned into these very outgoing, community-minded people. I'm not like that. I don't have so many friends, and I can be mean-spirited. Selfish."

"Give me an example of your 'meanness.' "

"I'll snap at people when no one is watching. Like cab-drivers."

Small potatoes. "Anything else?"

"My cousin just had his foot amputated. My mother wants me to call him up while he's convalescing. But he's fat, and he smokes a lot and—it's awful, but the idea of his amputated foot, I just refuse to call him."

Even that doesn't sound so mean. It seems to me she is rejecting not "morality" so much as a conventional, family code of manners; and in order to establish a separate identity as an artist, she may have to internalize some guilt for breaking away. Lori, however, sensing my inclination to let her off the hook, wants further to worry this problem of her selfishness.

"It's not just that. I detach myself from people easily. I often have disagreements with my parents because they say I'm without concern for other people's feelings."

"You mean spoiled? Do you see yourself as a JAP?" Suddenly this new defining category has clicked into place. Miami Beach, Israel bond drives, gold jewelry, a materialism mixed with ethicism—I can picture the upbringing. Oh, I understand the injustice of this acronym; but I am unable to give it up entirely as a valid social description, partly because I, coming from shtetl Judaism, still feel a romantic awe in the presence of young, glossy, well-bred Jewish women with elegant hairdos. I *want* there to be Jewish American Princesses.

Lori professes not to understand exactly how the term applies to her. "Can't a JAP be, like, white trash?" This confusion seems odd; it would be like an adult black not understanding what "nigger" means. (Perhaps it is her polite way of not getting into an argument with me while distancing herself from a term freighted with insult.)

"No, JAP usually refers to someone with money who's also a Daddy's Girl, both of which give her a sense of entitlement."

"If I do have that sense of entitlement," she says, "then I'm the only one in my family who does. I'm the only one who's spoiled like that. I can't even be around my family without making a scene, acting the epitome of self-centeredness."

"Could you give me an instance of such a scene?"

Lori hesitates. "This is probably not such a good example. It's never over anything important."

"Go on."

Lori says she went down to Miami to visit her family; her brother and sister-in-law had just had a baby, and Lori had bought the baby some clothes as a gift. Somehow, her sister-in-law had let slip the fact that their upstairs neighbor commented that *she* thought the colors of the baby clothes Lori brought were ugly. The fact is, she had also found the colors sort of ugly, "but ugly in an interesting way." After that remark, Lori says, she went into a total sulk. She refused even to play with the baby. Nor would she agree to see the new house that her brother and sister-in-law (who is an interior decorator) were building to replace the one that had been damaged in the hurricane. At the time, she saw no point in examining a place with just bare walls and no furniture. What Lori did do was occupy herself all weekend looking through a box of *her* old pictures and memorabilia, which her mother had dug out. This self-absorption she regards now as shameful. I suspect she also finds it intriguing, as a clue to her art projects, which are about finding traces of herself.

As she talked, I found myself sinking into the role of psychotherapist, already weighing several hypotheses and considering which ones, if any, to put forward. In the end I couldn't resist showing off.

"This was, first of all," I said, "a struggle over aesthetics—which is your professional domain. They were not granting you the respect you felt you deserved. You were frustrated because you couldn't explain to them that your artist eye had inverted the ugly into something interesting. And your sister-in-law, being an interior decorator, is a rival for the aesthetic crown and probably stands for a more conventional ideal of beauty, so you didn't want to honor that by seeing her new house."

"Actually, most of my arguments with my family *are* about aesthetics!" she said, sounding as impressed as if I were a fortune-teller who'd gotten something right. "And I do feel bad that they don't give me credit in my domain. I love my father, but he's a philistine. He's always telling me I should make work that's more 'saleable.' "

We laughed. Actually, I was laughing not in shared bohemianism but because I could see his point; someone must be footing the bill for all this artistic exploration, since Lori had no regular job.

"So you have a different aesthetic from them?"

"I feel I have a much more sophisticated sense of style than my family, though you wouldn't know it when I go down to visit. My mother's always criticizing the way I look."

"The second possibility," I went on, "involves your brother and sister-in-law's just having had a baby. Even if you're not jealous, even if you don't want a baby, you may still feel their pressure to have one, at this point in your life."

"So I was acting inordinately babyish, you're saying, to hold on to my status as the spoiled one, the baby."

I nod. *"Do* you want children, by the way?"

"I don't know that I ever want to have a baby. If I do have a baby, it will be like squeezing it in at the last moment. Maybe there's something wrong about that. But I just think it's hard for women to have full-scale careers as artists and raise children at the same time."

"That's true. Though there are examples: Elizabeth Murray, Joyce Kosloff, Sylvia Mangold, Yvonne Jacquette. . . ."

"But they were mostly established when they had kids," says Lori. The black necessity of "making it" once again darkens her brow, like the reminder of a chore she has forgotten to complete.

I have become more and more conscious of her Jewishness. It is something I had not noticed or even thought about at the offset, but now it seems to explain so much: the particular "Semitic" texture of her self-doubt, her analytical bent, her guilt, her earthy appeal (a tribal, sibling connection between us I had immediately felt, without understanding), and her materialism. Her Jewishness seems centered in her face, easily the most idiosyncratic part of her. It is a face that, in photographs, comes across as composed, static, pretty; but in person, the features are intensely mobile, divided, Jewishly worried, filled with interesting flaws—an imperfect complexion, a bumpy nose, an overbroad, determined chin, the close-set eyes, always casting about anxiously for answers, and the contradictory lips, the top thin and pursed, the bottom full, pouty, and sensual—all of which make her more touching.

When American Jewish men and women look at each other, they often register as flaws, as "coarse," those features most ethnically stamped. Whether the explanation is Jewish self-dislike or the drive to assimilate (the embarrassing presence of a fellow Jew accentuating one's provenance at the

moment one would like to "pass"), it is unarguable that many
Jews experience other Jews as vulgar. The obverse is
that unusual warmth a Jew often feels for another Jew encountered for the first time. The same too-rapidly-decoding, unil-
lusioned recognition, rooted in childhood ("I know that
type, I grew up with him, he can't fool me"), which makes it
difficult for Jewish men and women to find each other altogether sexually desirable, also locks them into an imme-
diate sympathy. It is the recognition of the same fate, the same
scar.

She has descended into a pensive state. "Maybe not wanting to have a child now has something to do with the relationship I'm in. I don't know how to say this without getting
myself into trouble."

"Go on."

Lori tells me she lives with her boyfriend Michael in his
TriBeCa apartment. She describes him as smart, cultured,
Christian, and well-read. They get along well, have a cozy life
together, but she is worried they have settled into a "passion-
less rut." She sees it as the dilemma of deciding between the
person who is "right" for her, which Michael seems in many
ways to be, versus some wild, inappropriate type who is wrong
for her but might trigger more desire.

"I'm also concerned that Michael may be mildly depressed," she says in a carefully thought-out way.

"What is he depressed about?"

"Well—he just doesn't see the possibility of joy in a lot of
things. He comes from a family with a lot of alcoholism. He
does love movies, but he says he would like to quit his nine-to-
five banking job and just watch movies. That sounds depressed,
doesn't it?"

I, being a film addict, am at least halfway on his side in this. Plus he seems to have good literary taste. I am for this guy. In any case, doesn't she know (or is she too young to) that most stable relationships wear out their passionate element?

Though Lori clearly feels hesitant—disloyal—talking about her boyfriend, she is too preoccupied by the subject not to. For each negative statement she makes, she balances it scrupulously with a positive, and vice versa. For instance, he is very supportive of her art and "thinks a lot about my ideas. In every relationship, there tends to be one person whose work occupies the more important space. For once, it's mine. On the other hand, I can't help wondering about his own unexplored desire for creativity."

"Not everybody has to be an artist," I say.

"I know."

I ask her about her earlier relationships with men.

Her previous boyfriend had been an up-and-coming artist who dropped her when he started getting successful.

After that, she had been without a boyfriend for three or four years, and during that time she had developed a life as a single person. It was a relief for her to settle down with Michael, but she still goes out by herself on Saturday nights to gallery openings, not just because of her boyfriend's limited interest in art-world functions but because, frankly, she doesn't feel comfortable with him being there. (I can picture Lori as a huntress at openings, using her solo attractiveness to network; perhaps secretly hoping to stumble upon a new love.)

"Sometimes I think that maybe I should find someone who is more—brilliant, more of a successful intellectual. Not necessarily an artist. I'm just anxious that I would be too threatened by such a person, and that he would expect things to revolve around him. I like things to revolve around me," she says with a disarming smile.

"Were you always that way?"

"No, I was quiet. I had this 'look' from puberty on," she recalls, "but I didn't have the personality to go with it. So I kept quiet. The less said, the more they could project onto me. I was trying to be 'mysterious.' It surprised me to learn I had a reputation—undeserved!—for being easy. I was just trying to seem accommodating."

It's the second time she's used that word, and I sense she is speaking obliquely again about the underpinnings of her art (misperceptions of her, etc.). I wonder how consciously she is laying out these clues for me to find.

"I used to have a lot of crushes. I remember in the ninth grade I had this awful crush on a senior who was sort of wild. I had a crush on Neil Young. I used to listen to music all the time—I loved Dylan and the Stones. Now I don't have crushes. And I don't even listen to music."

"Why not?"

"Oh, because music represents a kind of desire that there's no outlet for in my life right now."

That sounds sad. Perhaps picking up a look of concern on my face, she adds, "But maybe not having it allows me to focus better on my work."

One of the temptations of an interview is to pose questions you would have no idea how to answer yourself. "What do you think crushes are about?" I ask.

She reflects a moment.

"Crushes are about the excitement of thinking you're attractive to some very desirable person."

Hm. For her, it's *not* the dream of possessing a fantasy lover,

252   but rather, more passively, appearing attractive to him. Is this a
male-female difference? The man thinking, "I love her"; the
woman, "He loves me"? Or is it something more specific to
Lori—the same force that causes her to make art pieces out of
others' images of her?

"How do you perceive yourself physically?"

"I'm attractive, I guess, but not beautiful. I think I'm overweight. I don't work out hard enough. I just don't think I'm
getting the most out of my appearance."

Again, this nagging sense of not maximizing some aspect of
herself: career, love life, looks. She has an almost consumerist
relationship to herself as a package. Is this also a female issue?
Is it a function of her materialistic middle-class background?
Or are we all like that now, discontented consumers of ourselves?

"Do you worry about aging?"

"I'm starting to see age on my face. That bothers me a little. The comforting part about staying with my boyfriend is being able to think, This is the person I'm going to spend the rest
of my life with. I don't have to get myself into perfect shape
and be supersexy to try to attract somebody new. And maybe
by that time my career will be stable enough that it's no longer
an issue."

"How old are you, by the way?"

"I usually don't tell people my age," she says. "I lie."

"Tell me first how old you really are, and then the lie."

"I'm—thirty-four. But that sounds a little old to be where I
am. I should be having a mid-career show at this point. There
are artists my age whose success I fetishize."

"Like whom?" I ask. I want some benchmark. She refuses to
answer.

"Why not?" I tease. She shakes her head no.

Too humiliating, I suppose, or it would give them too much satisfaction to know of her envy. But how desperate it seems, this anxiety over making it young and having "mid-career" shows! Surely art is more forgiving; Cézanne started late.

I begin to see Lori as the representative of her thirtysomething age group—a generation that, fresh out of college, with pocket money, took Manhattan in the eighties, set the tone for the yuppie boom, flooded the new loud restaurants, holding on to their student camaraderie as long as possible in the face of the cold metropolis, went dancing at the clubs, read about themselves in Brat Pack novels, and were convinced they would always remain in the stylistic vanguard. Now they were in their mid-thirties, worrying about their first gray hairs, their slowing careers.

The phone rings again. While Lori takes the call, I have time to scrutinize, in front of me, a large leather address book filled with names and phone numbers of magazine editors, TV news producers, writers. This address book merits a special display case in her next show. The fundamental tool of today's artist may not be the paintbrush but the Rolodex, the Filofax. How is it that Claes Oldenburg hasn't gotten around yet to a Rolodex sculpture?

In the fifties movie *It Should Happen to You*, Judy Holliday's character, an aspiring actress, rents billboards with her name and image all over Manhattan so that she can become an instant celebrity. She was ahead of her time, in wanting the fame without having first done the work. It seems understandable, in a society where celebrity most surely validates identity, that those who have done nothing to warrant it should nevertheless feel unfairly victimized by their anonymity and mediocrity.

Perhaps Lori Becker's work is a witty commentary on that petulant demand. One would like to think so. That is, one would like to think that it is not itself a shrill demand for art star status, but a gloss on celebrity mania. She must know how, well, ordinary she is—which is why, rather than magnifying claims to specialness, she delivers information about herself with an apologetic shrug, as though acknowledging its banality.

During the awkward first stage of our interview, I had asked Lori if she was nervous, and she had replied, "Just because I make myself the subject of my work doesn't mean that I'm extroverted, or have a particularly smooth self-presentation." And indeed, she does not seem a narcissist in the megalomaniacal, diva sense. There is a modest, attentive, hesitant, "accommodating" side to her. Yet she is, clearly, self-absorbed; her hesitancy *is* her narcissism, it is the self-absorption that springs from defining her personality as essentially problematic—askew, missing something. As though she were always asking, "What do *you* see that I'm doing wrong? Do I seem incomplete?"

I fantasize myself as a private detective, hired to find a missing person: the real Lori Becker. Maybe she sees her identity—all identity—as a shell game, and fears that there's no real person inside her, that she herself is a "Big Nothing."

For the last hour she has been confiding to me from that dreamy, confiding place of the analysand; and I have been framing questions in an open-ended, therapeutic manner, asking about her emotions, her family, her fantasies, or lobbing back interpretations, or simply being silent, to let her fill in the gaps with speech. A dangerous by-product of psychotherapy is that one learns how to mimic the analyst's control elsewhere, in social situations. Consciously or not, I had been opting for a slightly formal, reserved, dignified manner, like a doctor gathering a patient's history. Yet I'd also felt empathy because, beneath the ordinariness of the tale, she was suffering. That may sound like a grandiose term for her uneasiness; but, to me, suffering was the clearest thing about Lori. She was engaged in a forlorn, desperate struggle to make something of herself.

Perhaps it is a typically male response to focus on a woman's forlornness or pain and find it so evocative—the better to play the sensitive rescuer. So my wife tells me.

Every so often, however, I had been conscious of rupturing the empathetic flow of conversation, to see what she would do or, what is worse, to give vent to that sadistic (also typically male), cat-and-mouse side of my character. Like when I pushed her to tell me which of her contemporaries she envied. I don't like myself for doing it; but I suspect I was trying to warn her I was not entirely the gentle mensch she seemed to take me for.

When she got off the phone, I asked her if she had ever been in therapy and she said, yes, off and on, from the time she was a senior in college. It hit me that "analysand" was her purest identity—the role that expressed her character most completely. For the last four years she has been seeing a Lacanian analyst.

"We focus more on the present than on the past or my family. Often I'll ask his advice about how to handle a professional matter, like whether to phone back a dealer. Sometimes I don't trust my own instincts. One of the issues I've been working on in this analysis is channeling a free-floating talent into getting acknowledged for it."

Always that damned careerism! Even in therapy hour.

As I listened to Lori, I found myself superimposing over her my friend Ella, a photographer who was also raised in a

Southern city with a balmy, slow, genteel tempo. Both rejected the suburban ease they were brought up with for the more stimulating, uncomfortable metropolis; but both are still "provincial" (i.e., hopeful) enough to be distressed by their distress and to take it as a neurotic condition that needs correcting. A native New Yorker would assume that unhappiness is incurable.

I saw Lori as one of that army of artistic young people who come to New York to make their mark and quickly learn they can't put a dent on it. Meanwhile, the move to the city disconnects them from family and community. So they strive to have their identity validated by other means: an analyst, a lover, or, best of all, the media. They had first gotten to know the city, as adolescents back home, from magazines hyping what was hot, what was not; and they continued to believe in the power and glamour of the print media. To be written about was to have a self.

Lori says, "Another writer asked me, 'Why do you want to be famous so much?' I said, 'I'm not sure that I do. It's more important for me to be written about than to be famous.' "

We've talked for two hours; we are winding down now. A glorious sunset is sitting over the Hudson. I look at my watch, time to go, and I say, "So—how do we arrange this? You give me the check when I'm done, and I hand you the manuscript, like, under a lamppost?"

"Are you laughing at me?" she says.

It is a strange comment. I had actually been trying to defuse the awkwardness of payment by alluding to spy movies. But of course I'm also laughing at her. I'm laughing at both of us. The whole setup is inherently comic. We're like two con artists swindling each other: she's buying my pen to promote herself in the art world; and I'm using her dough to write what I feel like.

I went home. Crazy as the project still seemed to me, I told myself that patrons have commissioned artists to paint their portraits for centuries; why not writers? But the art patron's desire is usually to be flattered. (Kees van Dongen: "I make the women thinner and the jewels fatter.") What were Lori Becker's expectations of me? Did she want the unvarnished truth as I saw it? I was already planning to write such an article, because—why not? That's the way I write best. But I thought guiltily of Joan Didion's line "Writers are always selling somebody out." Be honest, I told myself. If she is commissioning people to write articles about her, she probably wants the equivalent of a celebrity profile. Even a satiric celebrity profile. (Celebrity profiles are generally puff pieces, which is why I refuse to do any.) But she *asked* me to write about her and she said she knows my work: she must realize what she's letting herself in for. . . .

Underneath her intriguing bluster, I could smell the futility. One knows that special pathos of art world hustling, a pathos which cuts across styles and generations: appearing in a group show, one or two works in a cheesy gallery or co-op space; acting as if the opening really mattered, though it's all relatives and wannabe artists even lower down on the scale; the thought that maybe a *real* gallery owner will come by and pluck you out of the chorus; the decades of showing little and selling less, of chasing down teaching jobs all over the map, of throwing dinner parties to woo buyers, dealers, and critics.

Afterward, nosing around, I discovered that Lori's Lacanian

analyst had quite a clientele among artists. Perhaps just being treated by him was seen as a good career move. The art world is very selective in its intellectual appropriations. It takes only those ideas it needs to reinforce its self-involved preoccupations: Baudrillard in philosophy, Beckett in literature, Philip Glass in music, David Lynch in film. Why then Lacan in clinical psychology?

New York's art world has always been inclined to import its ideas from Paris. I knew that Lacan had traveled in bohemian circles, befriended Giacometti and Picasso, and was something of an artist temperamentally, a Zen master type who cut short his sessions at whim; and that mischievous, theatrical side of Lacan would appeal to artists. But was he a real genius or a charlatan?

I decided to amend my ignorance of Lacan by reading Stuart Schneiderman's book about him, *Jacques Lacan: The Death of an Intellectual Hero*, and his Lacanian anthology, *Returning to Freud*. Schneiderman proved to be an excellent guide to this terrain.

As it turned out, a number of Lacanian motifs could be easily applied to Lori Becker. The "mirror phase," for instance, is Lacan's notion that the child first acquires a sense of ego by seeing himself in a mirror. As Schneiderman paraphrases Lacan: "We must add that when the child first recognizes his image in a mirror, he greets the discovery with jubilation. . . . In a sense the child will invest his image narcissistically because it responds or appears to respond unfailingly to his cues."

Lacan also emphasized "desire as the basis for action. This is the only path to the overcoming of narcissism, because desire is always the desire of the Other, as he put it, and because desire always seeks recognition by the Other's desire." With Lori, the career itself, I thought, was invested with eros. She seemed convinced that she must sacrifice her longing for more sexual desire, at least for now, so as to concentrate on her art-work, which was, interestingly, all about commissioning images of herself. Did the artists and writers rendering Lori's portrait constitute various flawed mirrors? Were these projects a step forward to maturity—an attempt to surmount the imperious ego by trapping its reflection—or a step back to narcissism? What would Lacan have said? I had no idea. But I wondered to what extent Lori's speaking about her desires had been shaped by Lacanian analysis.

According to Lacan/Schneiderman, the analyst knows only one thing, and that is eros. The neurotic is someone who is out of touch with his desire, "who does not know what he wants." And "the analysand sees in his analyst his own desire, which is obviously something to which he has been attached and which he wants to recover or retrieve, often at any price." In Lori's case, I thought, she is treating the whole world as her analyst; she has misplaced her desire, or some essential part of herself, and she is asking the world to witness her, to image her, as a way of getting her self back. According to Lacan, "what I de-sire is always something that I lack, that is other than me." Can it be that Lori is reacting to her acute sense of lack by multi-plying and fragmenting images of herself, so as to make herself into an Other? Like Cindy Sherman's work, Lori Becker's mul-tiple reproductions of herself seem an ironic commentary on an absence, rather than mythomania. But what differentiates her from a visual self-portraitist—or a personal essayist, for that matter—is that Lori wants others to make her images so that she can disclaim responsibility for them, point out how false they are, and preserve her sense of being misunderstood; a mys-tery.

Finally, Lacan devised something called "the pass" for

training analyses, by which the trainees' progress would be judged by peer reports rather than by self-accounts. "How others see you is as important as how you see yourself," Lori told me. She may not yet be a fully formed artist, but she is already a Lacanian fabricator par excellence.

In getting writers to write about her, she is also asking to be judged, to receive a pass or fail. I speculate that she has a need to be judged. Or am I merely rationalizing in advance my writing about her in a way that may cause her pain? According to Lacan, "all demands are ultimately demands for love." If so, then she is not asking to be judged; she is asking to be loved. This portrait will not make her happy.

No one likes to be held up as an epitome, a prototype of the times. However, what struck me most in my encounter with Lori was how typical all her concerns seemed. Every word she spoke about career struggles, uncertainties over boyfriend and therapist, every self-deprecation, doubt, fear of being overweight, guilt toward her parents, desire for public attention, worry about missing out on passion, even the very texture of her honesty and insight—seemed characteristic of the way people express themselves now. The spirit of the age was in her. As a writer handed all this hauntingly *current* material on a silver platter, I was excited by the discovery; for once, I was not tempted to seek shelter in the congenial past. Yet as soon as I tried to put that excitement on the page, I began to doubt myself, to suspect that it was fool's gold. Had I really "gotten" Lori, or was I only seeing her through a set of rapidly inserted, convenient lenses (hustling artist, thirtysomething, Jewish American Princess, Southern provincial in the big city, Lacanian analysand), which accentuated her emblematic quality? Had she, for instance, played the perfect analysand because I'd led her to do so or because that was her true character? To ask these questions was to tip my hat to Lori and admit that there was more validity to her schema than I had first imagined. Her strategy was working. I was caught in the hall of mirrors.

Postscript

The final loop in this confusing business occurred when I turned in the above (give or take some small changes). My patroness was upset by the piece, which she felt could have damaging repercussions. No one wants to be mocked. But what hurt most, she said on the phone, was that I hadn't taken her more seriously as an artist. I had not treated her as a peer; I had condescended to her. Perhaps her "authors' profiles" piece wasn't entirely perfected, but hadn't I ever been in a muddle while working on a piece?

There is something wrong here, I thought. I may have condescended to her, but we were not peers just because she declared herself an artist, and me one too. This I could not bring myself to say; but I did manage to defend my author's right to judge the subject I was writing on.

But I had not judged fairly, she said; I had been "prejudiced" against her kind of art (conceptual), and should have announced that prejudice in advance.

To this I replied that I did not dislike all conceptual art by any means—though she was certainly right to note that I was moved more by painting and sculpture than by conceptual pieces.

She said I had not given her enough credit for irony and intent. Didn't I realize that almost all the insights and meanings I had extracted from our conversation, she had *meant* to be part of the artwork? She had told me those things herself.

I answered: That may be, but I cannot give you full credit

for the authorship of a work whose every piece has been written by others. It goes against the grain of my whole life as a writer.

Now we came to the damage-control part of the phone call: she hoped I would not find it necessary to publish my portrait. I thought this ironic, since she had just gotten finished saying she was responsible for the piece's insights, and since she had commissioned it in the spirit that anything a writer said was fine by her, as it would only show the more the distorted projections of witnessing. Did she not understand the terms of her own art project? What did she expect when she asked writers to describe her?

I got some answer when she sent me an article about herself in an art magazine; it was another of her commissioned jobs, and the author, with that effortlessly Warholian democratic stance toward poseurs ("super-stars") and genuine talents alike, such as one finds in underground fashion publications, asked her questions on the order of: What is your favorite color and sex fantasy? In this way, a wannabe is embraced for a moment by the celebrity machine and no harm is done.

She had asked that I change her name if the piece was ever published anywhere; and I have honored that request. "Lori Becker" is a fictitious moniker. This rest is pretty much true—or "true," as one now says.

MEMORIES OF GREENWICH VILLAGE:

A Meander

1

I began going to Greenwich Village when I was a teenager, around 1959: I would take the train from Brooklyn into Sheridan Square, often with a pal or two, seeking Kerouackian adventures. Since we had almost no money, we would consult the *Village Voice* listings for free entertainment, usually winding up in some abysmal semiamateur church theater performance of *Medea* or *The House of Bernarda Alba*, watching a non-"scale" tragedienne chewing up the minimalist scenery. Then we would wander over to the bookstores on Sheridan Square (all gone now, don't bother to look for them), with their glowering posters of Lawrence, Freud, Kafka, Joyce: these patriarchal window gods seemed unfair competition for the young women we hoped to meet within. My own pickup technique was to browse through every book in the store, looking up and whirling around at intervals to stare at the nearest girl, who probably never guessed my intent. We ended up at Riker's, a Sheridan

Square diner that attracted junkies and other romantically downbeat types (on the site now stands a vitamin center!), before grabbing a subway home.

This was the "White Negro" period, late fifties, early sixties, when the cutest girls seemed always to be walking with an ebullient mulatto-skinned boy carrying a guitar case. The Village had turned folknik. I was a serious jazz fan who detested folk music (except for country blues). I would stay up all night to hear Monk and Coltrane at the Jazz Gallery, then walk west on Eighth Street to catch the IRT subway back to my Columbia dorm. Eighth Street was particularly deserted one February night, in the early A.M. peace of a winter snow, except for a laughing, staggering couple ahead of me: a graybearded, targlecoated, bespectacled type who must have been a writer or at least a professor, reeling a bit with the bulky Sunday *Times* in one arm and his mate in the other, nibbling his ear. They had a way of walking that made you sense they were on home turf, would turn into a doorway any moment and go upstairs, to make love amid the *Times* sections and croissants from Sutter's. I envied these authentic Villagers; I wanted to grow up fast and have settled ideas and a potbelly; but another part of me felt a young man's pity for their middle-aged carnality, with its compensatory air. Live and learn.

By late adolescence I had burned out on the Village. I associated it with endless tease and no delivery. In my twenties I gave it a wide berth. During the high sixties all the action had moved east anyway, to the area, once Polish-Ukrainian, that was being sold by realtors as the East Village, though I never accepted it as part of the real Village. The real Greenwich Village, the West Village, seemed a played-out tourist trap for overpriced earrings, leather thongs, and T-shirts.

True, parts of that gingerbread-house Village looked very fetching, I couldn't help noticing, whenever an errand or rendezvous took me there. But it seemed unimaginative to love the Village; it was like falling in love with San Francisco—its blatant picturesqueness aroused my disdain.

The problem with perverse judgments is that they have a way of turning on you, and demanding ever more contrarian reversals. By the mid-eighties my long-held resistance to Greenwich Village bored even me. Just at that moment my interest in urban form peaked: I had come to value the rarity (for American cities) of the area's historical texture, human scale, and labyrinthine layout, which gave the walker a holiday from the puritanical grid.

In 1986, having just returned to my native city from eight years of teaching in Texas, I was determined to live in the Village and nowhere else. I took a place on Bank Street. Though the monthly rental was steep for my wallet, the space felt so echt Greenwich Village, so My Sister Eileen, that I signed immediately. The main room had a working fireplace, white-trimmed molding, a large built-in bookcase waiting to receive the bulk of my collection, knotholed walls, oak-planked floors, and metempsychotic fantasies of Edmund Wilson and Edna St. Vincent Millay disporting—which perhaps said less about my reincarnative karma than about the tinglings of upward mobility.

Located on the second floor, rear, of a three-story 1840 Federal-style brick townhouse that had once been a single family's dwelling, this apartment essentially consisted of the one large, all-purpose studio room (formerly the family parlor), to which had been added a small, doored bedchamber like a captain's cabin on one side and a kitchenette and bathroom on the other. The glory of the place, however, was beyond the Dutch doors: my own private balcony, large enough to double the living space in good weather. Nestled between buildings, this outdoor porch, facing a cherry tree that blossomed in April and greenly shaded in summer, gave me the feeling of being in a treehouse. I could peer like James Stewart in *Rear Window* into neighbors' apartments, or sway in a hammock reading a book, or invite friends for a barbecue. I had stumbled on the best of both worlds: a little nature (yard cats, squirrels, bluejays) and the city's stimulation close by.

Perhaps the most unique feature of the apartment was its quiet. Except for an occasional ambulance siren from nearby St. Vincent's Hospital, you would not know you were in Manhattan. The city's sounds arrived muffled as a waterfall. I attributed this quiet partly to being in the back and partly to Bank Street's isolation from through traffic, held as it was in cul-de-sac parentheses by Abingdon Square at one end and St. Vincent's at the other.

Bank Street is one of the prettiest blocks in New York. Shade trees oversee old New York brownstones and older Federal brick townhouses, some recently and rubicundly repointed, others wearing a mottled, flaking appearance as studied patina, contained by peeling iron railings, like something out of New Orleans, and front gardens overgrown with black-eyed Susans. At the street corners, where mass is meant to accumulate, solid six-story apartment buildings complete the picture that realty ads summarize as "charm." So unsecret is this "charm" that movie crews descend periodically with their officious ADs, off-limits Danish spreads, and Winnebagos hogging the parking, threatening the tree limbs. But eventually the crews depart, and Bank Street returns to its privileged existence. Not that all Bank Streeters are rich—far from it; but all are favored in having found a sanctuary from the city's harsher incursions.

After I moved into Bank Street, I could never get enough of walking to the corner, where it intersected with West Fourth Street, and turning either way. This stretch of West Fourth, between Seventh and Eighth avenues, with its mediocre tourist restaurants and antique shops, never failed to please me, but why? Was it the proportion between narrow, two-lane roadway, slender sidewalk, low building height and sky? Or the variegated facades of brick, brownstone, wood slatting? Or the ornamental gargoyles, porch lights, lampposts? Why do certain streets comfort us—what topographical harmonies bring a smile to our lips as we stroll open-jacketed down one part of town—while ten blocks away, we shudder and pull our coats tighter, against an imagined flu or mugger's knife? We would need a psychoanalyst of streets to provide the answers.

I hastened to get to know the newsdealer, the Korean deli owner, the locksmith. These establishments, more than landmarks or monuments, are the heart of a neighborhood. Around the corner from me was a prime example: Chez Brigitte, a hole-in-the-wall French diner that accommodated eleven customers, maximum. Six stools, attached to a yellow Formica counter, bleached by countless washings, faced the stove, pie case, coffeepots, and cook; five stray chairs hugged a thinner counter. The two rows of customers sat with backs to each other, and the aisle in between them was so tight that the robust blond waitress delivering food to the outer group could

268 not help brushing your behind as she maneuvered through. Often she simply passed the dishes over the front customers' shoulders to the outer group, with a *"Pardon—bon appétit!"* Reading a newspaper at either counter required contortions of finesse.

Chez Brigitte served a menu of simple entrées that never varied: filet of sole meunière, boeuf bourguignon, veal cutlet, roast chicken, with string beans and a choice of rice or potato, and a selection of sandwiches on French bread that included veal and peppers, meatballs, and flounder. To drink, there was 7-Up, Coke, or Perrier water; the place had no liquor license. The pleasure in eating at Chez Brigitte was that there were no surprises; the mystery was that the meal always tasted good. You would see them preparing it before your eyes, heating up the oil in a pan, breading the veal, nothing oversauced, everything tasting nourishing, homemade, but a "homemade" I was incapable of duplicating at home, as often as I watched the trick performed.

Another plus in Chez Brigitte's favor: its prices were moderate. The regular customers included interns at nearby St. Vincent's, who did not have the time for a leisurely tablecloth dinner; recluses who came every night and stared straight ahead; and bachelors like me. The servers, polite but formal in the French roadhouse manner, never intruded on your solitude, which prompted you to fantasize about them all the more: this middle-aged blond woman, with the air of a hardworking Parisienne exiled to the colonies, Simone Signoret in a Jean Gabin film, she spoke French and Portuguese equally well—what was her story? Was she Brigitte, or was that the drawn, skinny woman with curly brunette hair who never smiled? And the stocky, mustachioed Provençal cook on night duty—was he the husband of either, neither, or both? Even the wistfulness you caught in their eyes, which suggested they had more pressing worries than the order they were filling—perhaps a wholly different life they had intended to lead—made the atmosphere like that of a family dinner.

I also loved strolling up West Fourth Street to Garber's, where I tested the patience of the jaded, omniscient hardware men; I loved taking my shirts to the Chinese laundryman with the kind, birth-marked face, who wore the same blue-black checkered flannel shirt every day; I loved directing a taxi late at night in the rain to Bank Street, and running those last few steps from the cab door up the brownstone stairs to the entrance of my building; I loved reading the newspaper at Patisserie Lanciani, nursing a cappuccino while eavesdropping on two women friends catching up with each other at the next table. I loved knowing that, just down the block from me, at 5 Bank Street, one of my favorite writers, Willa Cather, had written her greatest novels. (True, the actual house she lived in had been torn down to build the Seventh Avenue subway; but a plaque on the apartment house that had replaced it marked her tenancy.) And it tickled me to learn that my old professor, Lionel Trilling, had lived on this very block in 1929. "I signalized my solidarity with the intellectual life by taking an apartment in Greenwich Village," he wrote. "What is more, my address was Bank Street, which, of all the famous streets in the Village, seemed to me at the time to have had the most distinguished literary past. . . ."

Finally, when I discovered that Meyer Schapiro, the great art historian, another of my former profs, lived just around the corner from me on West Fourth, near the Patisserie Lanciani, I no longer wondered why these streets felt so civilized. I would see him occasionally, ascending from his basement apartment to take out the garbage. We were safe, for the moment, from barbarism.

Bank Street seemed part of the memory pool of New Yorkers. When I mentioned my address to older people, their voices would thicken and they would recall an *inamorata* they had visited on my street thirty years before, or a summer they had spent in my very house—or was it three doors down?

One time Anatole Broyard, the critic at the *New York Times*, came by Bank Street to pick me up before going out to dinner with me. Anatole sniffed the familiar air of my Bank Street digs, admired the balcony, and looked at home yet puzzled, as though something was missing. While we walked to the restaurant, I must have let on that I was high on the neighborhood and New York in general, because he started a long discourse, the gist of which was "Ah, if you'd only known the Village after the war—then it was alive!" Our differing views of Greenwich Village in particular and New York City in general became a recurring conversational motif: I would obstinately insist that New York was still full of life, still fascinating, and Anatole would say, in effect, "You think this is life? You think this is Greenwich Village? You poor fool, this is nothing but a necropolis—a Potemkin Village!" As I found the area around Bank Street still so amiable, I wondered what blight, what shroud he was referring to in the streetscape that he could see and I couldn't. To him it was as though a neutron bomb had been dropped, leaving the buildings intact but killing off all the spirit and people of interest.

It seemed important to try to bring him around a little,

because then there would be common ground in our experience of the Village, and a better chance for our budding
friendship. I wanted to say, "Look, Anatole, not all the interesting people have died or left. How vapid can the Village be,
if *I* live in it?"

Testimonials about the banquet years of any celebrated
place, be it Montparnasse, Bloomsbury, or Greenwich Village,
tend to have a depressing effect on me. Can every creative type
really have known every other and partied together nightly—
something unthinkable in today's megalopolis? Discounting
memoirists' tendencies to promote their own set as the only
important historical group, or to confuse their energies' decline
with the world's, I wondered whether I should feel cheated or
skeptical.

2.

Greenwich Village is like Rome, a pile of old buildings and
sites on which one generation after another projects its yearnings. The twisting web of cobblestoned streets, town houses,
tenements, half-hidden mews, coffeehouses, and boutiques carries the burden of an idea: call it freedom, tolerance, naughti-
ness, avant-gardism, culture.

When we speak of a neighborhood, we mean an idea. And
it is usually an idea that cannot sustain itself, that is bound to
disenchant. In our day, few words are as pious as "neighborhood"—spoken, like "mother," with a catch in the throat.
Neighborhood is that fragile ideal that historical forces begin
to erode almost from the moment it is declared.

In the early twentieth century the patrician values of Henry James's Washington Square united with the déclassé bohemianism of Sheridan Square to conjure the illusion that the Village was a bulwark against the vulgarity of middle-class American materialism. (Actually, Bohemia's relations with Capital have always been more parasitic than antagonistic.) Almost from the start, however, commentators were declaring this idyllic cultural preserve moribund. In 1916 Djuna Barnes wrote a sketch, "Greenwich Village As It Is," in which she said, "And so people are standing before Greenwich Village murmuring in pitying tones, 'It is not permanent, the colors will fade.' . . . What can we do? Nothing. The damage has been done, we find, and the wing of the butterfly is already crumbling into dust."

But the twenties revived Greenwich Village as a cultural haven. "The 'Village' was the center of the American Renaissance or of artiness, of political progress or of long-haired radical men and short-haired radical women, of sexual freedom or of sexual license—dependent upon the point of view," reported *The WPA Guide to New York City*. Every major writer of the period who was not in Paris seemed to take up Village residence. And for each accomplished, productive artist, there were five pretenders, street hucksters peddling their flower paintings and verse. Eighth Street was the Wall Street of poetry, noted Maxwell Bodenheim in *My Life and Loves in Greenwich Village*; culture taverns held poetry readings and staged fistfights for the benefit of "gaping out of towners" brought in by tourist buses. The Village has always been susceptible to playacting and sham. Bodenheim, himself part charlatan, describes the Villagers as mostly poor, subsisting on donuts, coffee, and the pity of landlords; girl bohemians subsisted on the gullibility of "Elks." ("For the benefit of the uninitiated, an 'Elk' is a man who lives in Flatbush or the Bronx but who is attracted to the Village by its reputation as 'the Devil's Playground.' ")

By the late thirties the Village found itself again in a low cycle. "If in 1939 there were more serious artists and writers . . . than in other American centers," observed the WPA Guide, "the number each year was lessening."

Anatole Broyard's memoir, Kafka Was the Rage, asserts that the forties were actually the great Village period. "Nineteen forty-six was a good time—perhaps the best time—in the twentieth century. The war was over, the Depression had ended, and everyone was rediscovering the simple pleasures. . . . The Village was as close in 1946 as it would ever come to Paris in the Twenties. Rents were cheap, restaurants were cheap, and it seemed to me that happiness itself might be cheaply had." Jan Morris, in Manhattan '45, seconds this notion that the city's postwar years were its "culminating moment. . . . Never again, perhaps, would it possess that particular mixture of innocence and sophistication, romance and formality, generosity and self-amazement. . . ."

(In that annus mirabilis, 1946, I was three years old, a chubby baby slow for my age, living in Queens, not yet self-amazed and not particularly struck by the era's sublimity.)

Bodenheim predicted in the early fifties that "the Village was fated to go bourgeois and bow to the God of Real Estate. . . ." He was right but premature. By the time I had moved to the Village, Bodenheim's prediction had come true in spades. The neighborhood was pleasant, congenial, but of no particular importance as an artistic community.

What destroyed the bohemian Village? Some would argue

that the old Bohemia had not vanished so much as dispersed, to Soho, TriBeCa, Tompkins Square, Hoboken, and Williamsburg. Yes, but a fractionated, decentralized "art crowd" is no longer a true Bohemia. Maybe the art market had grown too sophisticated for the fake-Gypsy costume balls of yesteryear. Imbibing patterns also changed: what held the Village together in its Golden Age, kept its denizens glued to their stools night after night, all the memoirists agree, was huge amounts of alcohol. "Derangement of the senses" is no longer, thankfully, part of one's required artistic dues.

An older friend tells me that people also used to hang out more in bars and cafeterias because it was the only way to get in touch with them. Many didn't have telephones: sometimes you had to wait over six months, or pretend you were pregnant, to obtain a private line. Lionel Abel, in his Village memoir, *The Intellectual Follies*, recalls: "Those were the days when people would drop in on one another without telephoning first. Happy days!" The changes wrought by media— phone, television, fax—have kept people in their homes more at night, as has fear of crime. Bohemia's passing needs to be seen in the larger context of the decline of the urban public realm.

On the plus side, cultural consumption in the last forty years has been democratized (formerly, artists used to have museums to themselves, now everyone goes), which makes it harder to keep the line clear between "us" and "them." The bohemian ideal requires a strong, confidently monolithic middle class to oppose. The white middle class, now on the defensive, can no longer set itself up as representing America. It is consigned, like its nemesis, Bohemia, to one more fuzzy, competing lifestyle. Home from the office, corporate America slips into jeans, goes to a cappuccino bar, and becomes bohemian in the few hours of freedom remaining.

Then maybe Anatole was right about the Village. It was precisely because he no longer lived in the Village (he had commuted to his job on the *Times* for years, sometimes "staying in town" a few nights) that I regarded him secretly as the true Villager and myself as the impostor. He saw Greenwich Village as a state of mind rather than a geography; and once that mentality had died, it was his duty—the duty of all true Villagers—to take themselves off, sorrowfully, philosophically, to other parts: for it would be the ultimate betrayal of those memories to continue living in the shell of the past when the substance had vacated.

Okay, he was right, the Village *was* dead; but somehow I didn't care. One reason I didn't is that I suspected I could not have fit well into Greenwich Village in its heyday. I have no talent for hanging out, and the Village's pretensions to artistic monopoly and its hostility to working stiffs would have put me off. During the sixties, when Max's Kansas City was "the place," and downtown chauvinists bragged that they never went above Fourteenth Street, I somehow found a way to rent in Inwood, two hundred blocks north. One night, sampling the coming revolution at the Dom on St. Mark's Place, listening to Lou Reed's Velvet Underground with Nico on vocals, in front of a film of Gerard Malanga whipping various Warhol Superstars, with poet Ted Berrigan at my side telling me how lucky I was to be there on that particular night, I found myself wondering what the place had been like as a Polish catering hall. I am like a worm that prefers to enter a dying organism; I savor the perishable echoes of a place, the worn typefaces of merchant logos imprinted above the entrance. It excites my imagination more to take an archival angle on the past than to go where it is "happening." So when Anatole suggested I had missed out on the whole party, it did not bother me. I thought of parties I had not missed out on—loud, dislocating, dissonant scenes where envy was the ever-popular hors d'oeuvre—and rejoiced that at this moment I had the Village all to myself, from my favorite vantage point: retrospective.

3.

Anatole Broyard and I had only recently struck up a friendly acquaintance when he came to visit me on Bank Street. Several years earlier he had written a very favorable review of my essay collection *Bachelorhood* in the daily *Times,* I had sent him a thank-you note, and he had used me a time or two as a reviewer for the *Book Review,* so that, when I moved back to New York, I called him and we made the first of many dates for lunch or dinner.

Anatole had had a peculiar career. He had evolved from a promising experimental writer (with a story included in *The Beat Generation* anthology) to the book review desk at the *New York Times,* as Establishment a post as one could imagine, from which he turned out hundreds of newspaper essays and reviews. His weekly column of book chat for the *Book Review* usually consisted of three mini-essays, each about 350 words long (Anatole was a master of concision): generally some fanciful speculation about a classical character or author, some boulevardier's anecdote about running into a writer-friend, and some response to a literary fad. The tone was ironic, urbane, thorny, in self-conscious descent from the nineteenth-century belletrists, such as Hazlitt and Lamb. One reason, perhaps, that he had responded positively to *Bachelorhood* was that we were both fans of the classical essay manner, in love with the contrarian, the epigrammatic, the lightly learned, and the skeptical.

I knew writers who hated Anatole Broyard, cursed and spat every time his name was mentioned. This was partly because when he wrote a negative review, it was negative all the way. He had a critic's capacity for outraged indignation, which occasional reviewer/writer types like myself, weakened by collegial sympathy, rarely muster. Wanting to meet the man behind the by-line, I had been warned by a fellow *Times* writer that he had a malicious side to him—a sting in his tail. But I pressed forward.

As it happened, I liked Anatole from the start. He was a superb conversationalist: attentive, playful, very smart. He rolled on his feet with athletic cockiness (the boxer signature of his literary generation), had thick curly hair and a youthful, handsome face. It was hard to believe he was close to seventy. I had just rounded forty, and the difference in generations presented a tantalizing challenge for me. I should explain that I have always been attracted to older people; with my elders I make it a point to pretend I am their age, invoking references from their youth, not mine. Our elders' memories are sacrosanct, History; our own are trivial in comparison.

I would meet Anatole for lunch at the Times Building on West Forty-third Street, and we would stroll to some traditional Italian restaurant nearby. He was a hearty eater, and it improved his appetite to "dish." During these leisurely lunches, few reputations escaped intact. He would start on his coworkers and supervisors at the *Times*, viewing that empire with a politburo survivor's jaded incredulity. Then he would make mincemeat of some of the middlebrow popular writers of his generation, and finally move on to the literary flavor-of-the-month. He relished running down minority authors whose reputations struck him as inflated—partly from mischief and partly from sincere belief that a writer should not get extra points for ethnicity.

(There was also that "Creole" mystery surrounding Anatole, the rumors that he, originally from New Orleans, was part black; that he had used this identity when he first came to the Village, then dropped it years later. I never worked up the nerve to ask him. But I wondered if his umbrage at the hyping of some African-American writers may have derived from personal sensitivity on that score.)

Anatole would deliver scampishly un-PC comments in my presence, perhaps to smoke out my liberal-humanist side. In politics he seemed not so much a conservative as a pessimist aesthete allergic to ideology of any kind. Taste alone mattered. For all my attempts to reassure him that I liked good reactionary writers too, he mistrusted me, I believe, for being younger and "pinker" than himself. Also, my thinking had been shaped by feminism, the most significant movement of thought in my time. Anatole was not only phobic about feminist discourse, he succeeded in making me blush with certain remarks I would never have had the audacity to think, much less say. And yet (perhaps it is no paradox), I noted what consideration he showed toward women in social settings; his manners were far more gallant than my own.

Broyard excelled at travel writing, bringing a wit and cultivated palate to that potentially dullest of genres. He would dramatize his appetites, clothing a worldly, finicky sensibility in sparkling prose whose "desserts" were the epigrams that ap-

proached general laws. Broyard wrote especially feelingly about
France. I admired the discipline of his epicureanism. A true literary sensualist, he had no trouble appreciating even an anti-
hedonistic posture like mine; for him, negativity had its own
savor, its delightfully sour bouquet. In short, it seemed to me,
Anatole had enthusiasm, he knew how to live.

Thus, it came as a jolt, calmly reading the paper one Sunday morning, to stumble across this mention of me in his book
column:

> While having dinner one night with Phillip
> Lopate, the novelist and essayist, I wondered what it
> would be like to be friends with him because I like his
> work. But, notwithstanding the title of his most recent
> book—"Against Joie de Vivre"—he was so positive
> about life, about people, writing and movies, even
> about the dinner we ate, that he made me feel grumpy
> and opinionated. It's easier to be friends with people
> who are dissatisfied, because sharing dissatisfaction is a
> deep bond, like having loved and been rejected by the
> same woman. I suspect that complaint is the true capi-
> tal of literary friendships.

I was struck by the irony of our negative/positive dance.
Anatole was the one with savoir vivre, I had thought. How
had I come to be the bubbly optimist? Clearly my curmudgeon
persona on the page had not fooled him: he'd sniffed out my
hopefulness on our Village walk. Perhaps what he could not
forgive was the greater stock of life I had still available. If I saw
myself as perpetually in training for middle age, he saw me as
still filled with the sap of promise, a whole new life, perhaps—
love, marriage, family. My prolonged bachelorhood had re-

tarded the aging process and kept me unnaturally boyish. Anatole, facing retirement, had made his bed and was getting ready to lie in it, while I still seemed to be casting about for a mattress.

I won't deny it was a bit of a shock to read in the morning paper that someone you respect has implied a friendship between you is unlikely. On the other hand, I was flattered to turn up in his weekly column; at least he was thinking of me. I decided I would go on treating him as if he were my friend, despite what he had said in print.

Not long after that paragraph appeared, Anatole invited me out to his summer house on Martha's Vineyard, and we spent a wonderful day and evening together, which fitted my definition of friendship, if not his, in every particular. The sad part of the visit was that I learned for the first time that he was ill. We were on the tennis court, and Anatole told me he had been diagnosed with prostate cancer—though I was not to worry, he insisted, he felt fine, he was in remission. As if to prove it, he beat me soundly, all the while offering gracious encouragement for the more tolerable parts of my game.

Afterward, we rejoined his lovely wife, Alexandra, a psychotherapist, at a dinner party they threw for their Vineyard friends and me. Anatole was at his most conversationally entertaining, carrying the ball all evening. Before I left, he gave me the manuscript of a memoir he'd been writing about Greenwich Village in his salad days. It was not quite finished, he said: he had planned to end the book with the death of his father, but seemed dissatisfied with this plan, fearing it might come off as a sentimental gimmick offsetting the hard-nosed material that preceded it. What did I think, honestly?

I am drawn to memoirs in general, and Broyard's, which I

read the next day, was a particularly savory, self-aware example
of the form. I urged him to finish it.

Soon after their Martha's Vineyard summer, Anatole and his
wife moved from Connecticut to Cambridge, Massachusetts. I
think he relocated partly because it brought him closer to the
cancer treatment center, but this was little stressed. He told me
excitedly on the phone that Cambridge was like the Greenwich
Village of the old days—lively, intelligent conversation, lots of
socializing, dinner parties every night. I listened skeptically,
knowing the Cambridge potential for stodginess, and also
doubting that the postwar Village had been marked by nightly
dinner parties; perhaps the older, settled Broyard was confusing
the comforts of middle age with the revelries of youth. His insistence that Cambridge was the reincarnation of the Village suggested a need to close the circle and link his bohemian past with
his retirement years. It was also part of his attempt to get me to
share his disenchantment with present-day New York.

In one of our phone calls after he retired, Anatole told me
that he was putting aside the Village memoir to do a book of
personal essays about illness. My first reaction was that this was
a bad idea: if it was true that he had only a limited amount of
time left, then he should not fragment his energies with a new
manuscript but try to finish the nearly completed one. My
guiding principle, that the responsible action is always to finish what one has started, turned out to be wrong here; Anatole
sensibly ignored my advice. He had a passion for this new
"turf," disease, as he once had had for Greenwich Village; it
was pointless to try to return to a manuscript grown cold when
he could think of nothing but his cancer. The wisest thing an

author can do is to mine his obsession. He went ahead and wrote the frank, scalpel-sharp meditation *Intoxicated by My Illness*, which is among his best work and makes an enduring contribution to the literature of infirmity.

"I would advise every sick person to evolve a style or develop a voice for his or her illness. In my own case I make fun of my illness. I disparage it," wrote Broyard. While he asserted that "I'm not interested in the irony of my position. Cancer cures you of irony. Perhaps my irony was all in my prostate," it was still important for Anatole to uphold the "skeptical, ironic" side of himself while dying, and to keep a sense of style ("I really think you have to have a style in which you finish your life"). Since he viewed style as "the instrument of your vanity," he recommended that cancer patients "buy a whole new wardrobe, mostly elegant, casual clothes." He mocked his friends' responses to his illness (whenever Broyard invoked "my friends" in his writing, he conjured up a gallery of Job's consolers): "I can't help thinking there's something comical about my friends' behavior—all these witty men suddenly saying pious, inspirational things. . . . Since I refuse to, they've taken on the responsibility of being serious. . . . It's as if they had all gone bald overnight."

On the phone, I sensed that I also was failing to meet some standard of playfulness; my questions were too prosaically concerned with his prognosis. He was much more grateful when I offered some barbed criticism or gossip about a writer on the scene. "I cling to my belief in criticism, which is the chief discipline of my own life. I secretly believe that criticism can wither cancer," he stated in *Intoxicated by My Illness*. As it happened, cancer spoke the final word of criticism. I lost a friend whose delightful company I had too briefly enjoyed.

In the Prefatory Remarks to *Kafka Was the Rage*, Broyard's Greenwich Village memoir (published, alas, in posthumous, unfinished form), he wrote: "My story is not only a memoir, a history—it's a valentine to that time and place. It's also a plea, a cry, an appeal for the survival of city life." The valentine to one's past is the narcissistic, expected part: the plea for the survival of city life is surprising and touching—especially coming from a longtime suburban commuter.

Broyard's memoir paints an engaging portrait of his younger self, fresh out of the army at World War II's end, moving to the Village and living *la vie de bohème*; studying at the New School, with its stellar refugee professors, on the GI Bill; going briefly into analysis ("it wasn't respectable not to"); and opening a used bookstore as an excuse to read all day. "Education was chic and sexy in those days. It was not yet open to the public," he cheekily remarks.

Of the allure of reading in general, he says:

> I realize that people still read books now and some people actually love them, but in 1946 in the Village our feelings about books—I'm talking about my friends and myself—went beyond love. It was as if we didn't know where we ended and books began. Books were our weather, our environment, our clothing. We didn't simply read books; we became them. . . . Books were to us what drugs were to young men in the sixties. They showed us what was possible.

If culture was eroticized, sex in turn became a difficult modern text. "She made love the way she talked—by breaking down the grammar and the rhythms of sex." Much of the first two thirds of Broyard's Village memoir concerns the narrator's affair with one Sheri Donati, a prototypically "wild" bohemian girl of the Village, a protégée of Anaïs Nin, and an aspiring painter. She is attractive—Broyard has to fend off his friends—and a little nutty. She lies a lot: for instance, inventing a heart condition just so that he will carry her up the stairs. In retrospect, he is grateful: "she had to find a way to break the monotony. Young men are so monotonous." Back then, however, they fought: "Each of us hated and feared what the other stood for. In my heart I thought of her as weird and in her heart she saw me as ordinary." One night, he awakes to find she has turned the gas jets on. He decides to leave her; but not long after doing so, he visits his parents' home in Brooklyn and finds Sheri sitting on his mother's lap—a grotesque, "Kafkaesque" image—looking over some family photo albums. "I didn't want Sheri to see them. . . . If she saw me, me as a child, she would molest that child."

In the second part of the memoir, after his breakup with Sheri, he portrays various New York intellectuals he knew—Delmore Schwartz, Dwight Macdonald, Clement Greenberg, Milton Klonsky, and Saul Silverman. These (mostly Jewish) brains stirred the Catholic-raised Broyard with admiration: "They were bred to it—their minds had the quickness of racehorses." He feels dumber by comparison, yet superior, thinking them "strangled by their smartness."

He writes compellingly about the role of sex back then:

> A naked human body was such a rare and striking
> thing that the sight of it was more than enough to start
> our juices flowing. People were still visually hungry. . . .
> Undressing was a drama in itself. A girl standing with

her arms behind her back, at the clasp of her bra, had some of the beauty of a crucifixion. She also looked as if she was hiding something behind her, a gift. Pausing, gazing past me into the middle distance, her arms still back, handcuffed by hesitation and desire, she was trying to see the future or the end of love. And when her breasts sprang loose, she looked down at them with as much amazement as I did. . . . Perhaps, when she undressed, a girl would apologize for her body, say it was thin or fat, that her breasts were too small. . . . She might end her undressing with a little shrug, as if to say, This is all I have.

Broyard's sympathetic wonderment at the girls' disrobing captures the absolute strangeness that men and women can have for each other. The memoir is finally about the narrator's maturing awareness of difference. Women and Jews are the mysterious Other. As with women, so with his dying friend, Saul, who holds Anatole's sympathy at bay: "He was disappearing into the difference between us, into his history. He was saying, You can't understand how I feel, what I am. My tragedy is older and darker than your tragedy. You can't come into my ghetto."

Broyard's moving account of Saul's death comes in the last third of the book; and I now see that it provides a sort of climax for the memoir that would have made a second death, that of Broyard's father, redundant. Perhaps that it is why Anatole resisted "finishing" the manuscript: he understood that its emotional arc was already complete.

4.

As dogs and their masters are said to come to resemble each other in time, the Bank Street apartment and I grew together, so that I felt most uncannily myself inside it. I liked the "given" of the forthright cube that served as all-purpose living/dining/study/guest room. I was fond of my shrewd landlady, Nancy, who lived below in the garden apartment. She had grown up in that very house—had, in fact, inhabited my unit as a "start-up" apartment after graduation. She kept stacks of the *New York Times Book Review*s around, to catch up with books she would never have time to read; and, in this way, she occasionally came across a review I had written. Proximity with celebrity of even the mildest kind pleased her. She would tell me about the other creative folk who had rented her rooms. I saw what I was meant to, assured her that I was happy there, and tried to prove it by keeping the place clean and inviting over anyone I was eager to impress.

One such friend who visited me on Bank Street was Leonard Michaels, the brilliant short story writer (*Going Places, I Would Have Saved Them If I Could*) and novelist (*The Men's Club*). Michaels is a gaunt, handsome, compact man, about the same medium height as Anatole and with a similar priapic strut, but moodier and more obsessed. I have always associated his sardonic hipster, street-smart way of talking with another Lenny, Lenny Bruce. Michaels is impressively well educated, but downplays that side. He always seems to be under a feverish idée fixe—a crush on Tuesday Weld, a high cholesterol count—and if he likes you, will signal his trust by sharing that day's obsession the moment he is in your presence. Alongside, and in contrast to, this nervous, self-preoccupied manner are a generosity, kindness, and willingness to help others that one rarely meets in the literary life. It was Lenny, for instance, who championed and published my essay "Against Joie de Vivre" in a journal he guest-edited. Lenny, too, with his characteristic antipathy to cruelty, counseled me to tone down some possibly too-candid passages in my Donald Barthelme piece that might give pain to the widow. (These were the passages, ironically, that Anatole Broyard had most appreciated. In the end I took Broyard's advice.)

When Lenny walked with me through the Village, his old neighborhood as well, his nostalgia was tinged with remembered dread. It was here on Macdougal Street that he had lived in misery with his first wife, Sylvia; here where he underwent his humbling literary apprenticeship; over there, the back alley they ducked through to avoid the landlord; and next door, the bar where he hid during one of Sylvia's tirades. For Michaels these narrow lanes and mews, innocent as they might be to my eyes, were as haunted as a horror movie set. He had fled to the opposite coast to escape the air of these defeats; yet he still returned from California about once a year to visit his aged mother in the ILGWU projects and conduct business, and each time he seemed walloped by bitter memories of New York.

If Broyard saw Greenwich Village through the lens of the free-and-easy postwar era, Michaels bore witness to a different, sinister Village, dating from the sixties. As he wrote in *Sylvia*, his own Village memoir: "Weird delirium was in the air and in the sluggish, sensual crowds . . . along Macdougal Street, as in a lunatic carnival, screaming, breaking glass, wanting to hit, needing meanness."

Safe in my Bank Street backwater, I wondered how much Michaels's eye for apocalyptic menace had edited out the area's daytime charm. Yet he was right in asserting that parts of the Village, particularly around Sixth Avenue and Bleecker Street eastward, had turned clangorous and hard at that time—and so they have remained. Nowhere is this truer than on Eighth Street, the Village's main artery, once the home of classical record shops and art-movie theaters, Joe Gould and the priceless Eighth Street Bookstore. But fast-food outlets, chain clothing stores, and head shops replaced them, and now it is an urban mall for teenage kids, mostly boys—down-scaling retail turns demographics male—who bring a little dangerous swagger to their window shopping.

Michaels's "Sylvia" captures the Village on the cusp of that shift. A memoir (or "autobiographical fiction," as the author calls it) with the claustrophobic, restricted focus of a novella, it tells the story of Michaels's return to New York as a defrocked graduate student; his meeting the beautiful, hysterical, insecure, possessive Sylvia Bloch and instantly becoming her lover (she hangs the bathing suit of her previous lover on the doorknob to signal that his reign is over); their living together in constant fighting and remorse, he trying to turn himself into a writer, she, into a classics major at NYU; their disastrous marriage; his breaking away from her; and, most shocking of all, her retaliation by committing suicide in his presence. (Actually, she excused herself to down the barbiturates in the bathroom, and by the time she told him what she had done, it was too late to reverse their effects.)

The first time I read "Sylvia," in *Esquire*, it struck me as a powerful, anguished, courageous narrative, beautifully written, in a spare, Handke-like way, yet not quite resolved emotionally. The author seemed still to be blaming his ex-wife for their tragedy; too often he presented himself as innocent, put-upon

schlemiel and she as punishing shrew. It was a raw record of the
most traumatic experience in the author's life, torn, as it were,
unwillingly from his still-flinching vitals.

I hasten to point out that the problems of the memoir, as it
originally appeared in *Esquire* and in Michaels's prose collection *Shuffle*, were later corrected in an expanded, book-length
Sylvia, through greater perspective, self-criticism, balance, and
psychological insight. The revised memoir's focus also opens up
to include more material about the couple's social background,
parents, mutual friends, and cultural life. Finally, Michaels
complicates his grief-numbed protagonist by admitting a
deeper sense of attachment and loss at the conclusion. Originally it ends:

> The nurse waited outside the phone booth. She
> told me to go now to Sylvia's room, collect her things.
> My feet walked to her room. I didn't remember what
> things I was supposed to collect. I saw a clean, white,
> empty bed. I saw emptiness. I left the hospital with
> nothing, nothing at all.

Which is fine, in its way, but too heavy on the blank, Hem-
ingwayesque *nada*. Now it concludes:

> I didn't know what I felt for myself. I believed I was
> doing all right, attending classes, studying for exams. It
> didn't seem strange to me that I'd wake up in the mid-
> dle of the night feeling certain she had called my name,
> but I began to dread going to sleep. I was afraid I might
> dream. I stayed up late, reading until my eyes burned
> and I could no longer follow the sense of the pages.
> Then I'd go to sleep, and hope to fall quickly below the

level of dreams into oblivion. Once I fell into the morgue, Sylvia lying there, a white sheet up to her chin. It was like the old days, the two of us in a small room, Sylvia asleep, me miserable. I started crying, pleading with her, making no concessions to reality. My need was the only reality, more real than death. Sylvia had to stop this. She had to open her eyes and sit up. She did. I hugged her and asked if she would like to go to the movies. She said yes, but could we get something to eat first? I said we could do anything she wanted, anything at all, and we went out to look for a restaurant, desperately happy.

The original "Sylvia" was the cornerstone of Michaels's third collection, *Shuffle*. As its title implies, *Shuffle* is a miscellany—daringly, riskily so: some of the pieces are highly polished personal essays; others are mosaics composed of fragments that at times read like Kafka's diaries and at others seem like merely a writer's emptying out his notebooks. At the time, I found it an uneven but engrossing performance overall: a field report from the teeming, embattled mind of Leonard Michaels.

As *Shuffle*'s publication date approached, Lenny began calling me with predictions that he was going to get the shaft. He had "heard" they were cooking up something, the Eastern literary honchos, they were out to get him this time, he was going to get *slaughtered*. "Oh Lenny," I said, impatient with the whiny, paranoid sound of this, "who's 'they'? There is no Eastern literary establishment. What do you think, the power brokers have time to get together at a midtown restaurant and decide your fate? Relax. It's a good book, the reviews will be fine."

Lenny remained worried, particularly about what the *New York Times Book Review* would do. Impossible to overstate the importance of the *NYTBR*: those who get a negative review in it sometimes never recover, they are injured deep in the soul, while those whose books are not reviewed there must roam the earth like shades that can never be laid to rest.

Finally the *Times Book Review* came out with a devastating hatchet job of *Shuffle* by my friend Anatole Broyard. What made the review so flamboyantly unfair (to the point of being talked about for months) was that Broyard was not content to voice his displeasure with the book at hand: he went back over the author's whole career with a machete. Indeed, he spent most of the article whittling down Michaels's prior reputation, before dismantling *Shuffle* in three short paragraphs. It was an unusual strategy, to say the least, based on a logical fallacy: Now that we see where this author has headed, we can dismiss the promise of his earlier work and rewrite our earlier praise.

The review began with a witty, contextualizing setup, of the essayistic sort Broyard did so well:

> Contrary to public opinion, a literary reputation is one of the hardest things in the world to lose. People are loyal to their mistakes. An author can write a first novel that shows promise and then follow it with six more that plainly fail to keep that promise—yet the public, ever slow to change, clings to its first assessment. J. P. Donleavy's "Ginger Man" is one of the many examples.

He went on to analyze the appeal of Leonard Michaels's early writing: "flair," trendiness, urban sophistication, "danceable" if sometimes "cute" sentences. The analysis was a classic case of taking away with one hand what one gives with the other. "He had discovered that, if you intensify a fault, it may turn into a style." Broyard then zeroed in on what he saw as the real flaws in Michaels's work: gratuitous violence, sex, and self-absorption. "Mr. Michaels seems to write about sex almost exclusively. And there's something disreputable about characters— or authors—who are no longer in their first youth investing so much energy in the pursuit of sex." Worse, "sex doesn't often make Mr. Michaels's characters happy. Instead, it's like a depressed sport. . . . So many disconsolate couples, obscurely angry young men and exasperating women."

Having read Anatole's own memoir, which was filled with melancholy musings about sex ("sex belongs to depression as much as to joy") and exasperating women, it seemed to me that Broyard was indicting Michaels partly for being a younger version of himself. Broyard had had a more Don Juanish reputation in his earlier days than Michaels; but now Michaels had held up an unflattering mirror to the Village Lothario, at a time when Anatole needed desperately to believe he had ascended to a higher wisdom.

More criticism followed, until Broyard reached his conclusion, turning almost absentmindedly to the work being reviewed: " 'Shuffle,' Mr. Michaels's new collection—one doesn't know what to call it—is a shockingly bad book for a man of Mr. Michaels's stature. All the wryness has dried up and left him with a bad taste in his mouth. The book is like a man combing his hair in a bathroom mirror, and then inspecting the comb, counting the hairs."

Anatole's review was, as always, well written, eloquent, and persuasive. I found *myself* almost being persuaded by it—and I knew better, having already read the collection with enjoyment. What Broyard had failed to acknowledge was that, even on his off-days, Michaels is one of the best sentence-writers in America, and there was some terrific, passionately engaged writing here, especially in "My Father" and "Sylvia." Interestingly, Broyard's review barely mentions "Sylvia." One sentence: "There's even a wife, and she, of course, is insane."

There are few situations more loaded than seeing one friend excoriate another in print. Above all, I felt sorry for Lenny; I also felt childishly proud of knowing both these public antagonists; and I felt, I admit, a trace of *Schadenfreude* at the skewering of a talented contemporary, as well as relief that it wasn't I. Lenny almost cackled when I phoned long distance to commiserate. "I told you!" he exclaimed. "Look, even paranoids have enemies," I gamely repeated the old joke. Then he said, with a bitterness I'll never forget, "They gave my book to a guy who's dying and who spewed me with his deathbed bile and poison." I wanted to defend Anatole to Lenny, explain that he was really a nice guy, but it seemed the wrong moment.

"I secretly believe that criticism can wither cancer," Anatole had written. Maybe, I wondered in retrospect, this was Anatole's last attempt to make criticism heal him. Shortly after the review appeared, he died—so soon after, that I keep connecting the two shocks in my mind.

5.

Recently I reread Broyard's *When Kafka Was the Rage* and Michaels's revised *Sylvia*. I was struck not only by what an invaluable contribution each makes to the literature of urban memoir but by how much they each have in common.

Some of the similarities are superficial, if curious: both

writes employ a streetwise, aphoristic style with tough-guy overtones; both narrators are aficionados of jazz and Latino music; both invoke similar descriptions of Greenwich Village, friendships, intellectual culture. On a much deeper level, each memoir revolves around the author's experiences with a Crazy Woman he finds in the Village, who is self-indulgent, difficult, demanding, sexy, theatrical, and self-destructive. Indeed, it is impossible to read the account of Broyard's waking up to the smell of gas and finding Sheri Donati sitting naked, eerily calm, and not shiver at its tonal similarity to the suicide of Sylvia. Could this be why Broyard was so repelled by Michaels's book? Did their territory, and their guilt, overlap too much? Anatole was more fortunate than Lenny in managing to save his Crazy Woman from killing herself, just as he was luckier, or more prudent, in never marrying her in the first place. But in other respects they could be talking about the same woman.

Here is Broyard: "There was no peace with her. She was like a recurrent temptation to commit a crime . . . she liked to make difficulties. For her, difficulties were art, an art form. . . ." And Michaels: "I was the object of terrific fury, but what had I done? What had I said? Sometimes I would have the impression that the anger wasn't directed at me. I'd merely stepped into the line of fire, the real target being long dead." And Broyard: "Now, looking straight at me, she pushed the button and she and my mother fell back into a horizontal position. Sheri's bare legs flew up . . . to show my mother and father that the woman I lived with wore no underpants." And Michaels: "Another time she pulled all my shirts out of the dresser and threw them on the floor and jumped up and down on them and spit on them." And Broyard: "She talked like a bird pecking at things on the ground and then arching its neck to swallow them. She went in for metaphors and reckless generalization. . . . Everything she said sounded both true and false." And Michaels: "Sylvia was going on and on, both of us overwhelmed by her luminous ravings."

Are they describing the same woman? No. They are describing, and very accurately, the same relationship, or the same way a young man who doesn't understand much about women goes about weaving a relationship with Woman-as-Hysteric. Each woman is a bad nurturer, the seeming opposite of the young men's doting moms: Sylvia insists that the fevered, shivering Lenny stand in the cold while she makes the bed; Sheri never cooks. Actually, in the Crazy Woman's demanding dependency, which includes a willingness to kill herself if left, the young man finds, unconsciously, an echo of a totalistic Mother Love. Each man has picked (he thinks) a woman as far removed from his nurturing mother as possible; and this girlish, nonmaternal quality liberates his genital aggression and erotic fascination. Yet the sex, wild, exhaustive, and exhausting as it is, does not climax. Michaels: "I had sex only with Sylvia, me coming without much pleasure, she without coming." Broyard: "Most people agree on some kind of rhythm in sex, but Sheri refused all my attempts at coordination. She never had orgasms—she said she didn't want them." The insecurity of each young man, in not being able to bring his female lover successfully to orgasm, leads him the more readily to that defensive explanation: She must be crazy.

What is the allure of the Crazy Woman? Both Michaels's and Broyard's accounts suggest that the Crazy Woman represents a dangerous rite of passage that they must undertake to achieve full manhood. She is partly a sexual instructress, partly a seer, full of garbled, gnostic wisdom, which they simultaneously crave and mistrust. "You'll never be a man . . . until you can live without explanations," Sheri tells Broyard. These well-brought-up, cautious young explainers, self-described Mama's boys, must break the curse of niceness by taking up with a woman who wears no panties (Broyard), who lives like "a pig" (Michaels), who has no compunction about making scenes (both). Unsure of their own capacity to feel, they move in with a Crazy Woman, who is always close to operatic hysteria and who forces them into the arena of emotion.

Most important, the Crazy Woman judges the young man. She has a bottomless supply of behavioral standards, often improvised on the spot, which the aspiring young writer unknowingly violates until she points them out to him. The Crazy Woman offers insight into what is wrong with the aspiring young writer, who has been sensing all along that there is something rotten beneath his pleasant demeanor. If he is to be complex, he must be rotten. The would-be writer suspects himself rotten as an advance payment of professional guilt for his intended detachment and exploitation of human suffering. The woman's judgmental insight is also manna for the young man's narcissism: the harsher, the better. At least someone is taking a good hard look at him. Writes Michaels:

> Sylvia discovered an incapacitating, sentimental disease in me. Together, we nourished it. I wasn't a good enough person, I'd think, whereas she was a precious mechanism in which exceedingly fine springs and wheels had been brutally mangled by grief. Grief gave her access to the truth. If Sylvia said I was bad, she was

right. I couldn't see why, but that's because I was bad.
Blinded by badness.

Not to be overlooked is that the Crazy Woman promises to
be good fictional material: while he can only brood, she acts—
violently, colorfully. And finally, by being unhinged and un-
trustworthy, she confirms whatever frightened contempt he
may feel for the female sex.

I know something about this phenomenon because I was
myself involved with a "Crazy Woman" for seven years: longer
than I would like to admit. While we were together, Kay
jumped out of cars, threw tantrums, picked apart my flaws in
marathon sessions, threatened suicide, took hourlong showers
to escape from me, slept twelve hours a day in her periods of
depression. Curiously, she has since settled down and is con-
tentedly married. Which raises the question: To what degree is
the Crazy Woman truly crazy, and to what degree is her exasperating behavior a situational response to the ultrarationalist,
guilty, emotionally detached, ambitious, "superior" figure of the
Young Male Writer?

The Young Male Writer's condescension: he picks a Crazy
Woman who is brilliant, at times—how else could she appreciate *his* brilliance?—but in an unsustained way, and who has
artistic talent while lacking the discipline to make a successful
career in the arts. A full-fledged woman artist would be too
much of a threat. Sheri Donati, protégée of Anaïs Nin, exhib-
ited some of Nin's self-indulgent mythomania. Broyard admits
that he could not fathom Sheri's paintings. And the implica-
tion is that she was not very good, which readers are ready to
accept, since she has zero artistic reputation. Sylvia, of course,
died too early to make a mark in any field, nor did she wish to

be an artist; but Michaels includes several of her drawings in the book-length *Sylvia*, and they seem like the work of a sensitive child: poignant, stunted, morose cartoons.

By raising these issues, I do not mean to minimize the degree to which Sheri and Sylvia were full-fledged neurotics (there *are* crazy women, after all), but only to ask what responsibility the men involved with them must bear for the resultant emotional mess. I know that, in my case, part of what drove Kay crazy was my refusal to make a commitment to her—because, as I told myself circularly, she was too crazy to commit to. Broyard held Sheri at a distance, in part to protect his literary vocation. Michaels did go all the way, as he puts it in a memorable passage: "Then one night in bed, Sylvia said, 'Call me whore, slut, cunt . . .' I was eventually to call her my wife." But marriage seems to have been less a heartfelt commitment for him at the time than an exercise in Dostoevskian debasement and self-pity.

A feminist critic might say, with reason, about these portraits of Crazy Women that their authors have missed the boat. These descriptions are not of real women but of male projections. The original women were never wholly real to them, which explains their obliqueness on the page, as well as the authors' use of complex, strained metaphors to pinion them.

Fair enough. But I believe there is literary validity in drawing an incomplete portrait from life, and in at least trying, as these two writers have, to render the truth of their bewildering experience of encountering the wall of the other person. Since self-absorption may not be so much the aberrant as the common condition of mankind, for writers as well as everyone else, perhaps the critics should be less quick to dismiss as narcissistic those who succeed in understanding "only" themselves.

Which leads us to the final irony in this tale. Just as Anatole Broyard had faulted Leonard Michaels for self-absorption, so Morris Dickstein, the reviewer of *Kafka Was the Rage*, castigated Broyard for the same crime when it came time for the posthumous author to receive *his* grade from the *New York Times Book Review*:

> Nearly everyone in this book comes off as a grotesque, a monster of eccentricity, a type. The issue is finally a failure of human sympathy, a narcissistic self-absorption that gave Broyard style, bravado, even gaiety during his final illness but doomed his hope of being a novelist. It turns "Kafka Was the Rage," for all the chiseled brilliance of its prose, into a monologue about the past, a rumination in which all but one of its characters, along with the Village itself, remain muffled, remote, indistinct presences.

Dickstein, usually more intelligent in his textual reponses, seems tone-deaf here to the first-person provocateur tradition Broyard was trying to operate within. Moreover, he expresses, intentionally or otherwise, a questionable literary hierarchy that places fiction above autobiographical nonfiction. The issue of Broyard's not writing novels ("doomed his hope of being a novelist") seems to me a complete red herring, since he ended his life in a blaze of literary glory with two nonfiction books that deserve to endure. Perhaps I am being defensive myself, as a largely autobiographical writer; but finally, what else is a memoir except "a monologue about the past"? Personal essays and memoirs traditionally tolerate large dollops of self-preoccupation; nor do they necessarily require the sort of rounded portrayals of secondary characters featured in realistic novels. Their subject matter is, classically, the awakening, developing consciousness of the teller, and it is this adventure which Broyard and Michaels choose to emphasize in *Kafka Was the Rage* and *Sylvia*.

Broyard and Michaels both came to a Greenwich Village as young men hoping to forge a literary identity in the crucible of bohemianism. Both men—sooner rather than later—left the bohemian Village and settled into a more bourgeois model of the writer's life: steady job, family, and children.

We know what propelled Michaels out of Greenwich Village: it was hell on earth for him. Of course, at that self-excoriating stage of his life, he might have found Hell in any neighborhood; but the excess of potentialities and disorders that the Village boasted added to his stress. In Broyard's case, we have the fond record of his bohemian years, but no clear statement of what dissatisfactions pushed him out of that nook. Even if he had lived long enough to complete his manuscript, the explanation might never have arisen: from what I could see, the memories of these formative years held such sweetness and power for him that they became a compartmentalized retreat, providing solace from the wearier aspects of his responsible, *Times*-serving life.

In the final analysis, Broyard and Michaels—for all their attraction to that life—tilted at the windmill of bohemianism and gave up. Perhaps you have to be a depressive to stay the course. The stamina of the bohemian is depression.

. . .

My case was different: I came to the Village in my early forties, with a vocation already in place. The Greenwich Village I found was easy, gracious, tolerant of difference, but no longer a crucible or rite of passage—no longer a Crazy Woman, so to speak. Quite the contrary: today's Village represents a model of the gentrifying of a historic district, in all its benign and petrifying aspects. The more chocolate-colored historic markers and old-fashioned bishop's-crook lampposts are installed to commemorate its rollicking past, the more keenly aware one is that the spirit of adventure has fled. All those cold-water flats have been fixed up and are now heated, cozy, and costly.

The truth is, this Village suited me better. In middle age, I wanted comfort, I wanted coziness, I didn't want to stumble over the artistic pretensions and energies of youth every time I left the house.

If anything, what I have found distressing about the Greenwich Village of today is the never-ending tension between its residential and recreational functions. It has one meaning for its local residents and another one (a playground) for the city at large. On a warm summer night, you will see every jerk from the surrounding boroughs and New Jersey, plus tourists from every part of the planet, all bent on having a wild time. (That I may glimpse myself, or the adolescent fun-seeker I once was, in these hordes does not make them any more bearable.)

Accentuating this awareness was the fact that I no longer lived in my Bank Street sanctuary, but closer to the noisy crowds. I had been forced to give up Bank Street for the best of reasons, love. When I was getting married, my soon-to-be-wife pointed out that while my cozy studio made excellent bachelor's quarters, it was not big enough for two people. Besides, she argued sensibly, we ought to start our marriage in a new home, instead of one of us trying to adapt to the other's space. So we moved to a larger one-bedroom on West Tenth Street in Greenwich Village (it had to be the Village, that was my only demand), attractively old-fashioned, with good light, and with a roof garden that almost compensated for my Bank Street porch, but noisier. I experienced the maelstrom, the big parade of Christopher Street a block away.

And now it was borne in on me as never before that I lived in a gay neighborhood. This made me, over a long period of time, a little uncomfortable. Not that I am homophobic, I'm not, but a certain adjustment was required of me, as a minority member—the kind, admittedly, that homosexuals must continually make in the larger society. Different mores, different emphases, a more exhibitionistic libertine edge, challenged my reserved nature. And of course this was not an entirely representative gay community—overrepresenting, as it did, the street hustlers, the extroverted queens, the muscle beach leather set. Sometimes I would be awakened in the middle of the night by fights over money or sex or drug deals gone bad; knives would be pulled, garbage cans overturned.

Our West Tenth Street home was on the fifth floor of a walkup, and the noise from the street carried all too well. Still, we loved the apartment and our neighbors in the building, and figured to stay put. Then Cheryl got pregnant, and we decided that five flights of stairs might not be too good an idea with a stroller and a baby. So we looked all over the Village for an apartment that could accommodate the three of us, and my need for a writing room and Cheryl's for a work space; and of course Greenwich Village is notorious for its small apartments, unless you have a million dollars and can buy a town house. Then we looked around all of Manhattan, in every neighborhood, for an apartment large enough to address our living and working needs and still fit within our budget. In the end it occurred to us that such a place did not exist. So we said goodbye to the West Village and to Manhattan, and bought a house in Brooklyn. After eight more or less contented years, my Greenwich Village days were over. With regret if not surprise: deep down, I think, I had never really expected to end my life in the Village. But now, every time I wander into covelike Bank Street, I feel a pang of distressing perplexity. It is the vestigial Villager inside me, calling to his nest.

DELIVERING LILY

Ever since expectant fathers were admitted into delivery rooms, a few decades ago, they have come armed with video cameras and awe. Before I became a father, I often heard men describe seeing the birth of their baby as "transcendental," the greatest experience in their lives. They would recall how choked up they got, even boast about their tears . . . it sounded kitschy, like the ultimate sunrise. Being a nontranscendentalist, with suspicions, moreover, about my affective capacities, I was unsure how I would react. One had seen birthing scenes often enough in movies: how much more surprising could the reality be? I wondered, as someone who used to pass out at the sight of my own blood filling syringes, would I prove useless and faint? Or would I rise to the occasion, and be so moved into the bargain that at last I could retire those definitions of myself as a detached skeptic and accept the mensch allegedly underneath?

Whatever reactions would befall me, I prepared myself for a minor role. The star of any birth is the mother; her costar, Baby; her supporting leads, the medics. At nativity, every father feels himself a Joseph.

September 16, 1994, around four in the afternoon, I came across my wife Cheryl lying on the couch. She said she had "spotted" earlier, and wondered if this teaspoon's worth of sanguinous discharge could be what the books referred to, more scarletly, as "the bloody show."

I had already made a date with a friend—poet and fellow Brooklynite Harvey Shapiro—to attend the end of Yom Kippur services at the local temple, after which I was to bring Harvey back to our house to break the fast together. Harvey would supply the traditional challah bread and herring, and Cheryl the rest of the meal. I promised her I would return with Harvey no later than seven.

At the Kane Street Synagogue, the rabbi was taking her own sweet time, and I knew Cheryl would be annoyed if her dinner got cold, so I prevailed on Harvey to leave the service early. Just as well. We were sitting around the table, getting ready to enjoy Cheryl's lamb and baked potatoes, when she pointed mysteriously to her belly.

"What's up?" I asked.

"I think it's starting."

She smiled. If it was indeed starting, she could skip her appointment the following week for an artificial induction. The fetus was at a good weight, and the doctors hadn't wanted to take the chance of the placenta breaking down, as happened often with overdue deliveries. Cheryl had felt sad at the thought of being artificially induced—missing the suspense of those first contractions—but now the baby seemed to be arriving on her due date, which meant we were in for the whole "natural" experience after all.

First-time parents, alienated from the natural, we had wondered whether we would *really* be able to tell when it was time. Would we embarrass ourselves by rushing off to the hospital days early, at the first false quiver? How to be sure whether the sensations Cheryl reported were *the* contractions? As instructed, we began timing them. Meanwhile, our downstairs neighbor Beth popped in, and stayed to witness potential history.

Harvey, a man in his late sixties and a grizzled veteran of parenthood, distracted us with stories of his boys' infancies, while I kept my eye on the second hand. The contractions seemed to be spaced between seven and five minutes apart. We phoned our obstetricians (plural, because the team consisted of a group of physicians who took turns delivering, depending on who was on call). The office was closed for the Jewish holiday, but the answering service relayed the message to Dr. Arita, who was on call that night. Arita told Cheryl not to come into the hospital until contractions began occurring regularly, at five minutes apart, and lasted a full minute.

As soon as we had clocked two one-minute contractions in a row, I was impatient to start for the hospital. I had no wish to deliver a baby on the kitchen floor. Cheryl seemed calmer, as she described her condition to Dr. Arita. It was now 10 P.M., and he told her she would probably be coming into the hospital "sometime that night." This phraseology sounded too vague to me. I marveled at my wife's self-possessed demeanor. Cheryl was manifesting her modest, cheerfully plucky side—the side she presented to my friends and to outsiders; it was not a lie, but it gave no hint of her other self, that anxious, morose perfectionist she often produced when we were alone.

At ten-thirty the contractions began to arrive five minutes apart, and with more sharpness. Arita, beeped, said to come in, I pulled together a few last items (rubber ball, ice pack) on the checklist of what to take to the delivery room, and, saying good-bye to our guests, had gotten halfway to the door when I noticed Cheryl was, as usual, not quite ready to leave the house. She decided she had to water the mums.

For months we had debated which neighborhood car service to call for the hourlong trip from Carroll Gardens to Mount Sinai Hospital, on the Upper East Side of Manhattan. Cheryl, a superb driver, with no faith in my own lesser automotive skills, had even considered taking the wheel herself when the time came. Now suddenly she turned to me and said, "You drive. Just don't speed."

I maneuvered the car with caution over the Brooklyn Bridge, then up the FDR Drive, while Cheryl spoke happily of feeling empowered and in control. The contractions, she said, were not that painful. "I like these intense experiences that put you in contact with life and death." Premature bravado, I thought, but kept this to myself, glad to have her chatting confidently away; it meant she wouldn't have as much chance to find fault with my driving.

We parked the car in the hospital's indoor lot. Cheryl began walking very slowly up the ramp, holding her back. "I can't walk any faster," she snapped (the first sign of a change in mood?), as if responding to an unspoken criticism she sensed me making about her pace, when in fact I was stumbling all over myself to support her.

It was close to midnight as we entered the eerily quiet Klingenstein Pavilion. I approached the security guard, busy flirting with a nurse's aide, for directions. We had preregistered weeks before to avoid red tape at zero hour. After signing in, we were directed down a long creepy corridor into Birthing Room C. Mount Sinai Hospital has one of the largest maternity wards in the country, which is one reason we chose it; but suddenly its very magnitude made us uneasy. We no longer felt dramatic or special, but merely one more on an assembly line that was popping babies up and down the hall.

The expectant couple was deposited in Room C and left alone. It would be difficult to describe Room C except in regard to absences: it was not cozy, it was not charming, it was not tiny, it was not big, it was not even decrepit, it had nothing for the eye to fasten on. It was what you expected, more or less, of an anonymous hospital room with a quick turnover; but Cheryl, I sensed, had hoped for more—more ambience, amenities, *something* for the money. A visual designer by trade, she could, I knew, be preternaturally sensitive to new environments. Like a bride who finds herself in a nondescript wedding chapel, Cheryl may have long nurtured a fantasy of the ideal first-time birthing chamber, and something told me this was not it.

Often I allow myself to be made captive of my wife's moods, registering in an instant her first signs of discontent, and trying (usually without success) to gentle her out of it. I suspect that this catering to her anxiety—if only by playing the optimist to her pessimist—is really laziness on my part: it saves me the trouble of having to initiate emotions on my own.

Cheryl was given a hospital gown to wear. The moment she put it on, her confidence evaporated. She became an object, a thing to cut open. I cast about for ways to regain our light mood in the car, but it was no use. "Let's get out of this room. It gives me the willies," she said.

We went for a walk around the ward, opening doors like naughty children and peering inside. Our best discovery was a conference room, dark and coffee-machined and air-conditioned—freezing, in fact—which suited her just fine. We hid out for fifteen minutes in this nonmedical haven. But her contractions eventually drove us back to Room C.

Cheryl lay down. She took an instant dislike to her berth, saying "I don't like this bed!" and fiddling with the dials to raise and lower it. (An aversion, I thought, to proneness itself, which brought with it the surrender of her last sense of control.) I turned on the TV to distract her. The second half of *Working Girl,* with Melanie Griffith, was on; Cheryl said she didn't want to hear the dialogue, I was just to keep the sound loud enough to provide a background of "white noise." This was certainly a temperamental difference between us: if *I* had been giving birth, whatever the ordeal, I think I would have wanted the dialogue as well as the visuals of the movie on television. But I obliged; besides, we had already seen it.

For some reason, I had imagined our being swamped by medical personnel the moment we entered the hospital. We had not anticipated these quarter hours of waiting alone, without instructions. We sat about like useless tourists who arrive in an economy hotel after a long trip, too tired to attempt the streets of a foreign city, yet too hemmed-in by the unlovely room to enjoy a siesta.

How glad we were to see Dr. Arita walk in! A silver-mustached, suavely Latin, aristocratic type, he was one of Cheryl's favorites on the team. (She had been instructed to "establish a rapport" with all four obstetricians, since you never knew who was going to be on call during the actual delivery.) Cheryl had once admitted to me she thought Arita handsome, which made me a little jealous of him. He wore the standard teal-green cotton scrubs with PROPERTY OF MT. SINAI HOSPITAL printed on the material (still wrinkled, pulled straight from the dryer, no doubt: in former times they would have been crisply ironed, to maintain authority and morale) and, improbably, had on a shower cap, which suggested he had come straight from surgery; this fashion accessory, I was happy to see, reduced somewhat his matinee-idol appeal.

It was Dr. Arita who had, months before, performed the amniocentesis, which ascertained among other things that our baby was to be a girl. Arita had a clinical terseness, never taking five words to say what four could accomplish. He asked the patient if she wanted Demerol to help her sleep and cut the pain.

Cheryl had her speech all ready. "No, I don't want Demerol. Demerol will make me groggy. It'll turn my brain to mush, and I hate that sensation."

"All right. If you change your mind, let me know." With those succinct words, he exited.

From time to time a nurse would see how the patient was getting by. Or the resident on the floor would pop in and say, "You're doing great, you're doing great!" Increasingly, Cheryl wasn't. Her contractions had become much more intense, and she began making a gesture with her hands of climbing the wall of pain, reaching her arms toward the ceiling. Finally she cried out, "Painkiller. Painkiller! DEMEROL!"

I ran to fetch the resident.

"I'd give it to my wife," he said, which seemed to soothe Cheryl somewhat. Exhausted by her pain, she had entered a cone of self-absorption, and only a doctor's or nurse's words seemed able to reach her. She had tuned me out, I thought, except as a potential irritant—a lowly servant who was not doing his job. "More ice," she said, rattling the cup as though scornful of the lousy service in this joint.

During prenatal Lamaze pep talks, the husband was always being built up as an essential partner in the birthing process. This propaganda about the husband's importance, the misapplied fallout of equal sharing of domestic responsibilities in modern marriage, struck me as bunk, since the husband's parturient chores appeared menial at best. One of my spousal duties was to replenish the ice that Cheryl sucked on or rubbed across her forehead. Throughout the night I made a dozen of these ice runs, dashing into the kitchenette and filling the cup with chips. Back in the room, Cheryl would cry out "Ice," then "Ice, *ice!*" with mounting urgency, as though the seconds between her request and my compliance were an eternity marking my bottomless clumsiness. I was rushing as fast as I could (though I must confess that when someone yells at me to fetch something or perform any manual action, it releases a slight physical hesitation on my part, perhaps no longer than 1.5 seconds, but this 1.5-second delay was enough to drive Cheryl wild. It is, you might say, the 1.5-second factor that makes conjugal life so continuously absorbing). Also, if I gave her a piece she deemed too small or too large, she would berate me in tones of "How could you be so stupid?" This irritableness went on for hours.

Her underlying reproach seemed to be that I was not hooked into her brain—was not able to anticipate her needs through ESP or heightened sensitivity—and she would have to waste precious breath articulating them. I would occasionally try to ease the tension by giving her a neck rub or caressing her hand, all recommended consolations by the Lamaze instructor. She shook me off as if I were a cockroach. We husbands had been instructed as well to make "eye contact" with our wives: but whenever I tried this, Cheryl acquired the look of a runaway horse made acutely distressed by an unwanted obstacle in her path.

Sadly, I was not sufficiently generous to rise above feelings of being unfairly attacked. Days later, it surprised me to hear Cheryl telling people I had been wonderful during labor: "like a rock." Why, if this was so, I asked her, had she been so mean to me at the time? She explained rather reasonably that she was just taking her pain and putting it on me as fast as possible.

Sometimes, during contractions, she would literally transfer her pain to me by gouging my leg. Mistakenly thinking she was attached to my foot, I offered it to her, only to have it pushed away. "No, not the foot, I don't want the foot, I want the hand!" she screamed. (Being abnormally sensitive to smells all during pregnancy, she had picked up an unpleasant odor from my socks.)

What she liked best, it turned out, was to grip my trousers belt and yank hard. Eventually we worked out a routine: as soon as she started climbing a contraction, I would jump out of my chair, which was on her left side, run over to her right side, and stand beside her as she pulled and thrashed at my belt for the duration of the spasm. All the while I would be counting off every five seconds during the contraction. I was not entirely sure what purpose I served by counting aloud in this fashion; they had told us husbands to do so in Lamaze class, in connection with certain breathing exercises, but since we had thrown those exercises out the window soon after coming to the hospital, why, I wondered, was it necessary to keep up a count?

I should explain that we had never been ideal Lamaze students. Too preoccupied with our lives to practice the breathing regularly at home, or perhaps unable to overcome the feeling that it was a bit silly, when the actual labor came, it was so unremitting that we could not be bothered trying to execute these elegant respiratory tempi. It would be like asking a drowning woman to waltz. Cheryl continued to breathe, willy-nilly; that seemed enough for both of us. (I can hear the Lamaze people saying, "Yes, but if only you had followed our instructions, it would have gone so much easier. . . .") In any event, I would call out bogus numbers to please Cheryl, sensing that the real point of this exercise was for her to have the reassurance of my voice, measuring points on the arc of her pain, as proof that I was equally focused with her on the same experience.

In spite of, or because of, this excruciating workout, we were both getting very sleepy. The wee hours of the morning, from 2 to 6 A.M., saw the surreal merging of agony with drowsiness. Cheryl would be contorted with pain, and I could barely stop from yawning in her face. She, too, would doze off, between contractions; waking suddenly as though finding herself on a steeply ascending roller coaster, she would yowl "Ooowwwww!" I'd snap awake, stare at my watch, call out a number, rush to the other side of the bed, and present my belt for yanking. When it was over, I would go back to my chair and nod off again, to the sound of some ancient TV rerun. I recall Erik Estrada hopping on a motorcycle in *Chips*, and *Hawaii*

Five-O's lead-in music; and early morning catnap dreams punctuated by a long spate of CNN, discussing the imminent invasion of Haiti; then the repeat of a CBS news show featuring Dan Rather's interview with the imperturbable dictator, Raoul Cedras, and "Ice, *ice!*"

During this long night Cheryl put her head against my shoulder and I stroked her hair for a long while. This tenderness was as much a part of the experience as the irritation, though I seem to recall it less. It went without saying that we loved each other, were tied together; and perhaps the true meaning of intimacy is not to have to put on a mask of courtesy in situations like these.

Demerol had failed to kill the pain: Cheryl began screaming "PAINKILLER, PAINKILLER, HELP!" in that telegraphic style dictated by her contractions. I tracked down the resident and got him to give her a second dose of Demerol. But less than an hour after, her pain had reached a knuckle-biting pitch beyond Demerol's ministrations. At six in the morning I begged the doctors to administer an epidural, which would numb Cheryl from the waist down. An epidural—the open sesame we had committed to memory in the unlikely event of unbearable pain—was guaranteed to be effective; but the doctors tried to defer this remedy as long as possible, because the numbness in her legs would make it harder to push the baby out during the active phase. (My mind was too fatigued to grasp ironies; but it perked up at this word "active," which implied that all the harsh turmoil Cheryl and I had undergone for what seemed like forever was merely the latent, "passive" phase of labor.)

The problem, the reason the labor was taking so long, was that while Cheryl had entered the hospital with a membrane 80 percent "effaced," her cervix was still very tight, dilated only one centimeter. From midnight to about five in the morning, the area had expanded from one to only two centimeters; she needed to get to ten centimeters before delivery could occur. To speed the process, she was now given an inducement drug, Proactin—a very small amount, since this medication is powerful enough to cause seizures. The anesthesiologist also hooked Cheryl up to an IV for her anesthetic, which was to be administered by drops, not all at once, so that it would last longer.

Blessedly, it did its job.

Around seven in the morning Cheryl was much calmer, thanks to the epidural. She sent me out to get some breakfast. I never would have forgiven myself if I had missed the baby's birth while dallying over coffee, but Cheryl's small dilation encouraged me to take the chance. Around the corner from the hospital was a Greek coffee shop, Peter's, where I repaired and ate a cheese omelette and read the morning *Times*. I can't remember if I did the crossword puzzle: knowing me, I probably did, relishing these quiet forty minutes away from the hospital, and counting on them to refresh me for whatever exertions lay ahead.

Back on the floor, I ran into Dr. Raymond Sandler, Cheryl's favorite obstetrician on the team. Youthfully gray-haired, with a melodious South African accent and kind brown eyes, he said the same things the other doctors did, but they came out sounding warmer. Now, munching on some food, he said, "She looks good!" Sandler thought the baby would come out by noon. If so, delivery would occur during his shift. I rushed off to tell Cheryl the good news.

Momentarily not in pain, she could still not eat or drink anything. I held her hand and she smiled weakly. Our attention drifted to the morning talk shows. (Cheryl had long ago permitted me to turn up the volume.) Redheaded Marilu Henner was asking three gorgeous soap opera actresses how they kept the zip in their marriage. What were their secret ways of turning on their husbands? One had the honesty to admit that ever since the arrival of their baby, sex had taken a backseat to exhaustion and nursing. I liked her for saying that, wondering at the same time what sacrifices were in store for Cheryl and me. Marilu (I had never watched her show before, but now I felt like a regular) moved on to the question, what first attracted each woman to her husband. "His tight buns." The audience loved it. I glanced over at Cheryl to see how she was taking this: she was leaning to one side with a concentrated expression of oncoming nausea, her normally beautiful face looking drawn, hatchet-thin. She seemed to defy the laws of perspective: a Giacometti face floating above a Botero stomach.

We were less like lovers at that moment than like two soldiers who had marched all night and fallen out, panting, by the side of the road. The titillations of the TV show could have come from another planet, so far removed did it feel from us; that eros had gotten us here in the first place seemed a rumor at best.

Stubbornly, in this antiseptic, torture-witnessing cubicle, I tried to recover the memory of sexual feeling. I thought about how often we'd made love in order to conceive this baby— every other night, just to be on the safe side, during the key weeks of the month. At first we were frisky, reveling in it like newlyweds. Later it became another chore to perform, like moving the car for alternate-side-of-the-street parking, but with the added fear that all our efforts might be in vain. Cheryl was thirty-eight, I was fifty. We knew many other couples around our age who were trying, often futilely, to conceive—a whole generation, it sometimes seemed, of careerists who had put off childbearing for years, now wanted more than anything a child of their own, and were deep into sperm motility tests, in vitro fertilizations, and the lot. After seven months of using the traditional method, and suffering one miscarriage in the process, we were just about to turn ourselves over like lab rats to the fertility experts when Cheryl got pregnant. This time it took. Whatever torment labor brought, we could never forget for a moment how privileged we were to be here.

"You've got to decide about her middle name!" Cheryl said with groggy insistence, breaking the silence.

"Okay. Just relax, we will."

"Elena? Francesca? Come on, Phillip, we've got to get this taken care of or we'll be screwed."

"We won't be 'screwed.' If worse comes to worse, I'll put both names down."

"But we have to make up our minds. We can't just—"

"Well, which name do you prefer?"

"I can't think straight now."

A new nurse came on the day shift: a strong, skillful West Indian woman named Jackie, who looked only about forty but who told us later that she was a grandmother. As it turned out, she would stay with us to the end, and we would become abjectly dependent on her—this stranger who had meant nothing to us a day before and whom we would never see again.

At nine centimeters' dilation, and with Jackie's help, the first pushes started. "Pretend you are going to the toilet," Jackie told Cheryl, who obeyed, evacuating a foul-smelling liquid.

"She made a bowel movement, that's good," Sandler commented in his reassuring way. Jackie wiped it up with a towelette, and we waited for the next contraction. Jackie would say with her island accent, "Push, push in the bottom," calling to my mind that disco song "Push Push in the Bush." Cheryl would make a supreme effort. But now a new worry arose: the fetal monitor was reporting a slower heartbeat after each contraction, which suggested a decrease in the baby's oxygen. You could hear the baby's heartbeat amplified in the room, like rain on a tin roof, and every time the sound slowed down, you panicked.

Dr. Sandler ordered a blood sample taken from the infant's scalp, to see if she was properly aerated (i.e., getting enough oxygen). In addition, a second fetal monitor was attached to the fetus's scalp (don't ask me how). My poor baby, for whom it was not enough to undergo the birth trauma, was having to endure the further insult of getting bled while still in the womb.

The results of the blood test were positive: "Not to worry," Dr. Sandler said. But just in case, he ordered Cheryl to wear an oxygen mask for the remainder of the labor. This oxygen mask frightened us, with its bomb shelter associations.

"How will the baby be delivered?" Cheryl asked as the apparatus was placed over her face. "Will they have to use forceps?"

"That will depend on your pushing," answered Dr. Sandler, and left. I did not like the self-righteous sound of this answer, which implied that it was ours to screw up or get right. We had entrusted ourselves to the medical profession precisely so that they could take care of everything for us!

Often, after a push, the towelette underneath Cheryl was

spattered with blood. Jackie would swoop it up, throw it on the floor, kick it out of the way, raise Cheryl's lower half from the bed, and place a fresh towelette underneath. The floor began to smell like a battleground, with blood and shit underfoot.

"Push harder, push harder, harder, harder, harder," Jackie chanted in her Barbados accent. Then: "Keep going, keep going, keep going!" Cheryl's legs were floppy from the epidural; she reported a feeling of detachment from her body. In order for her to have a counterpressure to push against, I was instructed to lift her left leg and double it against the crook of my arm. This maneuver, more difficult than it sounds, had to be sustained for several hours; a few times I felt that my arm was going to snap and I might end up hospitalized as well. It was probably the hardest physical work I've ever done—though nothing compared, of course, to what Cheryl was going through. I feared she would burst a blood vessel.

Around eleven Jackie went on her lunch break, replaced by a nurse who seemed much less willing to get involved with our case. A tense conversation ensued between Sandler and the new nurse:

"This patient is fully effaced," he said.

"My other patient is fully, too."

He sighed, she shrugged, and the next minute they were both out the door. Left alone with a wife buckling in pain, I felt terrified and enraged: How dare Jackie take a food break now? Couldn't we page her in the cafeteria and tell her to get her ass back here? It was no use, I had to guide Cheryl through her contractions as if I knew what I was doing. This meant watching the fetal monitor printout for the start of each contraction (signaled by an elevating line), then lodging her leg against my arm and chanting her through the three requisite pushes per

contraction, without any firm idea exactly when each was supposed to occur. The first time I did this I got so engrossed pressing her leg hard against me that I forgot the cheerleading. I
have a tendency to fall silent during crises, conserving energy
for stocktaking and observation. This time I was brought up
short by Cheryl yelling at me: "How am I supposed to know
how long to push?" I wanted to answer: I'm not a trained
medic, I have no idea myself. The next time, however, I
bluffed, "Push, push in the bottom!" doing my best Jackie imi-
tation until the real Jackie came back.

Sometime near noontime Dr. Sandler made an appearance
with his colleague Dr. Schiller and began explaining the case
to her. Cheryl had never felt as confident about Laura Schiller
as she had about Sandler and Arita, either because Schiller was
the only woman on the team (not that Cheryl would have
agreed with this explanation) or because the two women had
simply not had the opportunity to "develop a rapport." With a
sinking sensation, we began to perceive that Sandler was aban-
doning us. Actually, he probably would have been happy to deliver Lily, if only she had arrived when he had predicted, before
noon. Now he had to be somewhere else, so he turned the job
over to his capable colleague.

Dr. Schiller brought in a younger woman—a resident or in-
tern—and they discussed whether the baby was presenting OA
or OR (whatever that meant: probably something to do with
the baby's head position). Now they turned to the expectant
mother and got serious. Dr. Schiller proved to be a much
tougher coach than Jackie. "Come on, Cheryl, you can try
harder than *that*," she would say. Cheryl's face clouded over
with intense effort, her veins stood out, and half the time her
push was judged effective, the other half, not. I could never

fathom the criteria used to separate the successes from the failures; all I knew was that my wife is no shirker, and I resented anyone implying she was. If some of Cheryl's pushes lacked vigor, it was because the epidural had robbed her of sensation below and because the long night of pain, wasted on a scarcely increased dilation, had sapped her strength.

Over the next hour, doctor's and patient's rhythms synchronized, until something like complete trust developed between them. Schiller cajoled; Cheryl responded. We were down to basics; the procedure of birth had never seemed so primitive. I couldn't believe that here we were in the postindustrial era and the mother still had to push the fetus, by monstrously demanding effort, fractions of an inch down the vaginal canal. It was amazing that the human race survived, given such a ponderous childbearing method. With all of science's advances, delivering a baby still came down to one of three timeworn approaches: push, forceps, or Caesarian.

This particular baby, it seemed, did not want to cross the perineum. "If the baby's no closer after three more pushes," Dr. Schiller declared, "we're going to have to go to forceps."

Forceps would necessitate an episiotomy—a straight surgical cut of the pubic region, to keep it from fraying and tearing further. An episiotomy would also leave Cheryl sore and unable to sit for weeks. Knowing that I would probably be accused of male insensitivity, and sensing my vote counted marginally at best, I nevertheless expressed a word in favor of forceps. Anything to shorten the ordeal and get the damn baby out. Cheryl had suffered painful contractions for eighteen hours, she was exhausted, I was spent—and I was dying with curiosity to see my little one! I couldn't take the suspense any longer. Obviously not a legitimate reason. Cheryl worried that the forceps might dent or misshape the baby's skull. Dr. Schiller explained that the chances of that occurring were very slight, given the improved design of modern instruments.

Cheryl pushed as hard as she could, three times, with a most desperate look in her eyes. No use.

"I always try to give a woman two hours at best to push the baby out. But if it doesn't work—then I go to forceps," Dr. Schiller said authoritatively. Cheryl looked defeated. "Okay, we'll try one more time. But now you really have to push. Give me the push of the day."

The "push of the day" must have felt like a tsunami to Lily, but she clung to the side of her underwater cave.

They readied the scalpel for an episiotomy. I turned away: some things you can't bear to watch done to a loved one. Dr. Schiller, kneeling down, looked inside Cheryl and cried out, "She's got tons of black hair!" Standing over Cheryl, I could make out nothing inside; the fact that someone else had already peeked into the entranceway and seen my baby's locks made me restless to glimpse this fabled dark-haired creature.

The last stage was surprisingly brief and anticlimactic. The doctors manipulated the forceps inside Cheryl, who pushed with all her might. Then I saw the black head come out, followed by a ruddy squirming body. Baby howled, angry and shocked to find herself airborne in such a place. It was such a relief I began to cry. Then I shook with laughter. All that anguish and grief and triumph just to extract a writhing jumbo shrimp—it was comic.

The doctor passed the newborn to her mother for inspection. She was (I may say objectively) very pretty: looked like a little Eskimo or Mexican babe, with her mop of black hair and squinting eyes. Something definitely Third World about her.

An overgrown head on a scrawny trunk, she reversed her mother's disproportions. A kiss from Cheryl, then she was taken off to the side of the room and laid on a weighing table (seven pounds, four ounces) and given an Apgar inspection by Jackie under a heat lamp. Lily Elena Francesca Lopate had all her fingers and toes, all her limbs, and obviously sound vocal cords. She whirred like a whippoorwill, then brayed in and out like an affronted donkey.

Abandoned. For while Cheryl was being stitched up by Dr. Schiller (who suddenly seemed to us the best doctor in the world), Lily, the jewel, the prize, the cause of all this tumult, lay on the table, crying alone. I was too intimidated by hospital procedure to go over there and comfort her, and Cheryl obviously couldn't move, and Jackie had momentarily left the room. So Lily learned right away how fickle is the world's attention.

Dr. Schiller told Cheryl she would probably have hemorrhoids for a while, as a result of the episiotomy. Cheryl seemed glad enough that she had not died on the table. She had done her job, delivered up safely the nugget inside her. I admired her courage beyond anything I had ever seen.

Happy, relieved, physically wrung out: these were the initial reactions. For hours (I realized after the fact) I had been completely caught up in the struggle of labor, with no space left over for distancing. But that may have had more to do with the physically demanding nature of assisting a birth than with any "transcendental" wonderment about it.

That night, home from the hospital, I noted in my diary all I could recall. Consulting that entry for this account, I see how blurred my understanding was—remains—by the minutiae of medical narrative. What does it all "mean," exactly? An experience, on the one hand, so shocking and strange; on the other hand, so typical, so stupefyingly ordinary.

When people say that mothers don't "remember" the pain of labor, I think they mean that of course they remember, but the fact of the pain recedes next to the blessing of the child's presence on earth.

Odd: what I remember most clearly from that long night and day is the agitated pas de deux between Cheryl and me, holding ourselves up like marathon dancers, she cross at me for not getting her ice fast enough, me vexed at her for not appreciating that I was doing my best. Do I hold on to that memory because I can't take in the enormity of seeing a newborn burst onto the plane of existence, and so cut it down to the more mundane pattern of a couple's argument? Or is it because the tension between Cheryl and me that night pointed to a larger truth: that a woman giving birth finds herself inconsolably isolated? Close as we normally were, she had entered an experience into which I could not follow her; the promise of marriage—that we would both remain psychically connected—was broken.

I remember Cheryl sitting up, half an hour after Lily was born, still trembling and shaking.

"That's natural, for the trembling to last awhile," said Dr. Schiller.

Weeks afterward, smiling and accepting congratulations, I continued to tremble from the violence of the baby's birth. In a way, I am still trembling from it. The only comparison that comes to mind, strangely enough, is when I was mugged in the street, and I felt a tremor, looking over my shoulder, for months afterward. That time my back was violated by a knife; this time I watched Cheryl's body ripped apart by natural forces, and it was almost as if it were happening to me. I am inclined to say I envied her and wanted it to be happening to me—to feel that intense an agony, for once—but that would be a lie, because at the time, not for one second did I wish I were in Cheryl's place. Orthodox Jews are taken to task for their daily prayer "Thank God I am not a woman." And they should be criticized, since it is a crude, chauvinistic thought; but it is also an understandable one in certain situations, and I found myself viscerally "praying" something like that while trying to assist Cheryl in her pushes.

Thank God I am not someone else. Thank God I am only who I am. These are the thoughts that simultaneously create and imprison the self. If ego is a poisonous disease (and it is), it is one I unfortunately trust more than its cure.

I began as a detached skeptic and was shoved by the long night into an unwilling empathy, which saw Cheryl as a part of me, or me of her, for maybe a hundred seconds in all, before returning to a more self-protective distance. Detachment stands midway between two poles: at one end, solipsism; at the other end, wisdom. Those of us who are only halfway to wisdom know how close we still lean toward the chillness of solipsism.

It is too early to speak of Lily. This charming young lady, willful, passionate, and insisting on engagement on her terms, who has already taught me more about unguarded love and the dread meaning of responsibility than I ever hoped to learn, may finally convince me there are other human beings as real as myself.

Phillip Lopate was born in New York City in 1943. The author of eight books, including *Bachelorhood, Against Joie de Vivre, The Rug Merchant* and *Confessions of Summer,* and the editor of *The Art of the Personal Essay,* his works have appeared in *Best American Essays, The Paris Review, Esquire, Vogue,* and many other publications. He also edits an annual of notable essays which will begin appearing in 1997. He worked with schoolchildren in creative subjects for many years, an experience detailed in his account, *Being With Children,* taught at Columbia and the University of Houston, and currently is Adams Professor of English at Hofstra University. A recipient of Guggenheim and National Endowment for the Arts Fellowships, he has judged the Pulitzer Prize and National Book Awards, and served on the selection committee of the New York Film Festival. He lives in Brooklyn, New York with his wife, Cheryl, and their daughter Lily.